R. Paul Maiden, PhD
Rich Paul, MSW
Christina Thompson, MSW
Editors

Workplace Disaster Preparedness, Response, and Management

Workplace Disaster Preparedness, Response, and Management has been co-published simultaneously as *Journal of Workplace Behavioral Health*, Volume 21, Numbers 3/4, 2006.

Pre-publication REVIEWS, COMMENTARIES, EVALUATIONS . . .

"These chapters provide insight into how EAPs are helping people return to work and productivity by better managing their mental health. They also shed light on how EAPs can help an organization prepare for any type of disaster or workplace change while staying focused on supporting its workforce. In addition, the chapters stress the importance of teaching EAP professionals how to take care of themselves during a time of crisis."

Mandie Hajek, LCSW, CEAP
Consultant, Towers Perrin

More pre-publication
REVIEWS, COMMENTARIES, EVALUATIONS . . .

"**A**N IMPORTANT BOOK FOR EVERY EAP PROFESSIONAL. This experienced and distinguished group of authors guides us through a number of important lessons learned from recent traumatic events, both national and local in scope. They also provide helpful ideas for preparing for future disasters, for responding in effective ways, and for reminding us to take care of ourselves in the process. When I put the book down, I was reminded how essential EAPs have become in helping employers deal with these types of events that seem to have jeopardized the news in the last few years. One of the most critical lessons and reminders the book provided for me was the importance of understanding and knowing a work organization before deciding on intervention plans and responses. Every model of intervention and prevention has an appropriate application. The organizational culture and relationship with the EAP become guiding factors in deciding what works best.

The book also instructs us that no matter how carefully we plan for a trauma, we may not be prepared for all the possibilities and we may take on roles we never anticipated. As one of the authors reflects–sometimes we just listen, sometimes we help with medical problems, sometimes we find clothes and food, sometimes we do clinical interventions, and sometime we end up being the communicators. This book is A TESTAMENT TO HUMAN RESILIENCY AND THE IMPORTANCE OF STRONG EAP PROFESSIONALS. We need to continue learning about preparing and responding to workplace traumas and this book makes an incredible contribution in our education."

Lisa Teems, DMin, LCSW, CEAP, CAC
Director, EAP
U.S. Department of Health and Human Services

"**A**N EXCELLENT COMPENDIUM of articles regarding Employee Assistance responses to workplace disasters, whether man-made or natural. Starting from the shared premise that effective response to disasters impacting the workplace is beneficial to both the impacted organizations and their individual employees, the authors show a variety of ways that EA programs and professionals have prepared for and responded to multiple disasters in diverse organizational settings. Articles cover a broad range of thoughts and ideas from the conceptual to the practical, including: utilizing a public health approach in response to the September 11 attacks; first-person accounts providing excellent "hands-on" tips from the experience of an "embedded EAP" in response to Hurricane Katrina; identifying how EA professionals can help to foster organizational and individual resiliency; presenting research on the impact on EA professionals of providing crisis response services. All EA practitioners, whether small and local or large and national, will find ideas of use to them in this book. I HIGHLY RECOMMEND IT."

Steven M. Haught, LCPC, CEAP, CSADC
Executive Director,
Personal Support Program, AFSCME IL

"**T**he reader is brought into the micro level of EAP trauma service delivery with the moving and poignant experiences of dedicated EAP counselors. . . . By taking us back and forth from specific examples of crisis work to research, policy, organizational, and crisis intervention model recommendations this book presents a comprehensive look at how the EAP field can be the most effective in this important role of disaster preparedness. This book is A MUST READ FOR EAP PRACTITIONERS, VENDORS, AND EMPLOYERS of any size as we look forward to prepare for what the next decade will bring."

Dale Masi, PhD
President and CEO of Masi Research Consultants, Inc., Professor Emerita, University of Maryland School of Social Work

More pre-publication
REVIEWS, COMMENTARIES, EVALUATIONS . . .

"Workplace Disaster Preparedness, Response, and Management is A 'MUST HAVE' FOR EVERY EA PROFESSIONAL AND ORGANIZATIONAL LEADER DEALING WITH CRISIS INTERVENTION AND RESPONSE. Written by seasoned EA and mental health professionals, the book's articles serve as both guide and leader for our important work in assisting work organizations prepare for, respond to and address the emotional and mental health needs of our customer organizations and their employees in response to large-scale natural or person-made disasters.

The balanced use of case studies, interview, research, personal accounts and the developing literature is AN EXCELLENT AND TIMELY APPROACH TO THE TRAINING AND EDUCATIONAL NEEDS OF TODAY'S EA PROFESSIONAL who is being tasked with and expected to provide efficient and effective post-trauma management services. A lot is at stake and these articles definitely give us A WEALTH OF IMPORTANT INFORMATION."

Dorothy K. Blum, PhD, CEAP
President, Employee Assistance Professionals Association

The Haworth Press, Inc.

New York • London • Victoria (AU)
www.HaworthPress.com

Workplace Disaster Preparedness, Response, and Management

Workplace Disaster Preparedness, Response, and Management has been co-published simultaneously as *Journal of Workplace Behavioral Health*, Volume 21, Numbers 3/4, 2006.

Monographic Separates from the *Journal of Workplace Behavioral Health*™

For additional information on these and other Haworth Press titles, including descriptions, tables of contents, reviews, and prices, use the QuickSearch catalog at http://www.HaworthPress.com.

The *Journal of Workplace Behavioral Health*™ is the successor title to *Employee Assistance Quarterly*™, * which changed title after Vol. 19, No. 4, 2004. The *Journal of Workplace Behavioral Health*™, under its new title, begins with Vol. 20, No. 1/2/3/4, 2005.

Workplace Disaster Preparedness, Response, and Management, edited by R. Paul Maiden, PhD, Rich Paul, MSW, and Christina Thompson, MSW (Vol. 21, No. 3/4, 2006). *Examination on strategies to provide crisis response services for professionals and employers responsible for planning and coordinating organizational responses to disasters.*

The Integration of Employee Assistance, Work/Life, and Wellness Services, edited by Mark Attridge, PhD, Patricia A. Herlihy, PhD, RN, and R. Paul Maiden, PhD, LCSW (Vol. 20, No. 1/2/3/4, 2005). *"A must read for anyone who is providing or purchasing employee assistance, work-life, or wellness programs." (Paul A. Courtois, MSW, Senior Auditor, Corporate Audit Services)*

Accreditation of Employee Assistance Programs, * edited by R. Paul Maiden, PhD (Vol. 19, No. 1, 2003). *Accreditation ensures private or public sector organizations that an employee assistance program (EAP) has acceptable level of experience, advisement, and expertise.* Accreditation of Employee Assistance Programs *gives you the information you need to get an employee assistance program accredited. Thorough and focused chapters by respected authorities discuss the value of EAP accreditation to future customers, the development of accreditation standards for employee assistance programs, and the smoothest road to travel to your destination of EAP accreditation.*

Global Perspectives of Occupational Social Work, * edited by R. Paul Maiden, PhD (Vol. 17, No. 1/2, 2001). *A broad survey of the development and current practices of occupational social work as practiced in seven countries around the world.*

Emerging Trends for EAPs in the 21st Century, * edited by Nan Van Den Bergh, PhD, LCSW (Vol. 16, No. 1/2, 2000). *"An excellent book. . . . Relevant with respect to contemporary practice and current state of the art for EAPs. A sound disciplinary input for both program development and service delivery." (William L. Mermis, PhD, Professor of Human Health, Arizona State University)*

Employee Assistance Services in the New South Africa, * edited by R. Paul Maiden, PhD (Vol. 14, No. 3, 1999). *Addresses the many issues affecting the development of EAP programs in the new South Africa.*

Women in the Workplace and Employee Assistance Programs: Perspectives, Innovations, and Techniques for Helping Professionals, * edited by Marta Lundy, PhD, LCSW, and Beverly Younger, MSW, ACSW (Vol. 9, No. 3/4, 1994). *"A valuable resource and training guide to EAP practitioners and managers alike. Most importantly, it increases the sensitivity of women's issues as they relate to the workplace." (R. Paul Maiden, PhD, Chair, Occupational Social Work, Jane Addams College of Social Work, University of Illinois at Chicago)*

Employee Assistance Programs in South Africa, * edited by R. Paul Maiden, MSW (Vol. 7, No. 3, 1992). *"The first comprehensive collection of perspectives on EAPs in an industrializing third-world country." (Brian McKendrick, PhD, Professor and Head, School of Social Work, University of the Witwaterstrand, Johannesburg)*

Occupational Social Work Today, * edited by Shulamith Lala Ashenberg Straussner, DSW, CEAP (Vol. 5, No. 1, 1990). *"A well-organized overview of social work practice in business . . . interesting and timely." (Journal of Clinical Psychiatry)*

Evaluation of Employee Assistance Programs, * edited by Marvin D. Feit, PhD, and Michael J. Holosko, PhD (Vol. 3, No. 3/4, 1989). *"The definitive work in the field of program evaluations of EAPs. . . . A must for anyone considering planning, implementing, and most importantly, evaluating employee assistance programs." (Dr. Gerald Erickson, Professor and Director, School of Social Work, University of Windsor)*

Alcohol in Employment Settings: The Results of the WHO/ILO International Review, edited by
D. Wayne Corneil, ScD (cand.) (Vol. 3, No. 2, 1988). *Valuable insights into attitudes about alcohol and the effects of its use with courses of action for educating and treating employees who need help with alcohol problems.*

EAPs and the Information Revolution: The Dark Side of Megatrends, edited by Keith McClellan and Richard E. Miller, PhD (Vol. 2, No. 2, 1987). *A serious examination of treatment methods that can be used to help working people cope with a rapidly changing economic society.*

Workplace Disaster Preparedness, Response, and Management

R. Paul Maiden, PhD
Rich Paul, MSW
Christina Thompson, MSW
Editors

Workplace Disaster Preparedness, Response, and Management has been co-published simultaneously as *Journal of Workplace Behavioral Health*, Volume 21, Numbers 3/4, 2006.

The Haworth Press, Inc.

New York • London • Victoria (AU)
www.HaworthPress.com

Workplace Disaster Preparedness, Response, and Management has been co-published simultaneously as *Journal of Workplace Behavioral Health*, Volume 21, Numbers 3/4, 2006.

The development, preparation, and publication of this work has been undertaken with great care. However, the publisher, employees, editors, and agents of The Haworth Press and all imprints of The Haworth Press, Inc., including The Haworth Medical Press® and Pharmaceutical Products Press®, are not responsible for any errors contained herein or for consequences that may ensue from use of materials or information contained in this work. With regard to case studies, identities and circumstances of individuals discussed herein have been changed to protect confidentiality. Any resemblance to actual persons, living or dead, is entirely coincidental.

The Haworth Press is committed to the dissemination of ideas and information according to the highest standards of intellectual freedom and the free exchange of ideas. Statements made and opinions expressed in this publication do not necessarily reflect the views of the Publisher, Directors, management, or staff of The Haworth Press, Inc., or an endorsement by them.

Cover design by Kerry E. Mack

Library of Congress Cataloging-in-Publication Data

Workplace disaster preparedness, response, and management / R. Paul Maiden, Rich Paul, Christina Thompson, editors.
     p. cm.
    "Co-published simultaneously as Journal of Workplace Behavioral Health, volume 21, numbers 3/4, 2006."
    Includes bibliographical references and index.
    ISBN-13: 978-0-7890-3450-2 (hard cover : alk. paper)
    ISBN-10: 0-7890-3450-6 (hard cover : alk. paper)
    ISBN-13: 978-0-7890-3451-9 (soft cover : alk. paper)
    ISBN-10: 0-7890-3451-4 (soft cover : alk. paper)
    1. Employee assistance programs. 2. Crisis management. 3. Employees–Counseling of.
I. Maiden, R. Paul. II. Paul, Rich. III. Thompson, Christina. IV. Journal of workplace behavioral health.
  HF5549.5.E42W676 2006
  658.4′77–dc22

                                    2006013953

Indexing, Abstracting & Website/Internet Coverage

This section provides you with a list of major indexing & abstracting services and other tools for bibliographic access. That is to say, each service began covering this periodical during the year noted in the right column. Most Websites which are listed below have indicated that they will either post, disseminate, compile, archive, cite or alert their own Website users with research-based content from this work. (This list is as current as the copyright date of this publication.)

Abstracting, Website/Indexing Coverage . . . . Year When Coverage Began

- *British Library Inside (The British Library)*
  <http://www.bl.uk/services/current/inside.html>. **2006**
- *Cabell's Directory of Publishing Opportunities in Management >*
  (Bibliographic Access) <http://www.cabells.com> **2006**
- *Cambridge Scientific Abstracts (a leading publisher of*
  scientific information in print journals, online databases,
  CD-ROM and via the Internet) <http://www.csa.com> **2006**
- *EAP Abstracts Plus <http://www.eaptechnology.com>* **1994**
- *EBSCOhost Electronic Journals Service (EJS)*
  <http://ejournals.ebsco.com>. **2001**
- *Elsevier Eflow-D <http://www.elsevier.com>*. **2006**
- *Elsevier Scopus <http://www.info.scopus.com>* **2005**
- *Entrepreneurship Research Engine*
  <http://research.kauffman.org> **2004**
- *Family & Society Studies Worldwide (NISC USA)*
  <http://www.nisc.com>. **1996**
- *Family Index Database <http://www.familyscholar.com>* **2004**
- *Google <http://www.google.com>*. **2004**
- *Google Scholar <http://scholar.google.com>* **2004**

(continued)

(continued)

*Special Bibliographic Notes related to special journal issues
(separates) and indexing/abstracting:*

- indexing/abstracting services in this list will also cover material in any "separate" that is co-published simultaneously with Haworth's special thematic journal issue or DocuSerial. Indexing/abstracting usually covers material at the article/chapter level.
- monographic co-editions are intended for either non-subscribers or libraries which intend to purchase a second copy for their circulating collections.
- monographic co-editions are reported to all jobbers/wholesalers/approval plans. The source journal is listed as the "series" to assist the prevention of duplicate purchasing in the same manner utilized for books-in-series.
- to facilitate user/access services all indexing/abstracting services are encouraged to utilize the co-indexing entry note indicated at the bottom of the first page of each article/chapter/contribution.
- this is intended to assist a library user of any reference tool (whether print, electronic, online, or CD-ROM) to locate the monographic version if the library has purchased this version but not a subscription to the source journal.
- individual articles/chapters in any Haworth publication are also available through the Haworth Document Delivery Service (HDDS).

In Memoriam

To the 2948 Individuals Who Lost and Gave Their Lives
on September 11, 2001

This Book Is Dedicated to the Law Enforcement Officers, Firefighters,
Emergency Rescue Personnel, and Health Care Professionals Who Worked
Tirelessly to Search for and Rescue the Victims and to the Employee
Assistance and Other Mental Health Professionals Who Aided So Many
in This Hour of Need

Workplace Disaster Preparedness, Response, and Management

CONTENTS

ABOUT THE EDITORS

R. Paul Maiden, PhD, is the editor of the *Journal of Workplace Behavioral Health.* He is also Associate Professor of social work at the University of Central Florida in Orlando. He is a recipient of two Senior Fulbright Scholar awards to Russia and South Africa. He has been in the EAP field for 25 years and has an extensive portfolio of domestic and international publications, presentations and consultations on a wide range of workplace human service issues. He is editor and contributing author of *Employee Assistance Programs in South Africa, Total Quality Management in EAPs, Global Perspectives of Occupational Social Work, Employee Assistance Services in the New South Africa, Accreditation of Employee Assistance Programs,* and *The Integration of Employee Assistance, Work/Life, and Wellness Services* (with Attridge and Herlihy).

Rich Paul, MSW, is Vice President of Health and Performance Solutions within ValueOptions' Employer Solutions Division. He is responsible for national operations and product development and best practices supporting all workplace-based services and products. Mr. Paul has 15 years of EAP and behavioral health experience and is a frequent speaker and author on issues impacting the workplace. He currently serves as president of the Employee Assistance Society of North America (EASNA), an association focused on advancing knowledge, research and best practices toward achieving healthy and productive workplaces.

Christina Thompson, MSW, is Vice President of Employee Assistance Programs and Addictions Services for Magellan Health Services in their Employer Solutions Division Strategic Business Unit. Ms. Thompson has over 26 years experience in the EAP/Behavioral health field and has been with Magellan for 15 years and is responsible for the leadership and coordination of the EAP/Addictions products/services including clinical/operational oversight, the development and maintenance of policy, program enhancements, product development, support of sales and marketing, COA EAP accreditation and better practices for multiple accounts nationally and internationally. Over the years Tina has been involved in many boards and committees whose focus is with the advancement of EAP, Behavioral Health care and related issues. She is an active speaker and has published on a variety of EAP and Workplace topics.

About the Contributors

Daniel J. Barnett, MD, MPH, is an Instructor in the Department of Environmental Health Sciences at the Johns Hopkins Bloomberg School of Public Health. He is on the staff of the Johns Hopkins Center for Public Health Preparedness in Baltimore, Maryland, where he conducts trainings and research on public health emergency preparedness and response (E-mail: dbarnett@jhsph.edu).

David M. Benedek, MD, is Associate Professor of Psychiatry and Assistant Chairman for Education at the Uniformed Services University School of Medicine. He is also a Senior Scientist at the Uniformed Services University's Center for the Study of Traumatic Stress. His studies include first responders to the December 2004 tsunami, and U.S. military members deployed in peacekeeping operations. He has written extensively on military and disaster psychiatry, traumatic death and grief recovery. He was a major contributor to the development of Rapid Knowledge Dissemination Program for Hurricane Katrina national and local responders. In addition to his operational experience in Bosnia and Croatia Dr. Benedek has deployed to Cuba, Iraq and Kuwait in conjunction with the Global War on Terrorism. In 2004 he was appointed Consultant to the U.S. Army Surgeon General for Forensic Psychiatry (E-mail: dbenedek@usuhs.mil).

Mark Braverman, PhD, is a principal of The Braverman Group LLC, located in the Washington, DC, area. He has developed protocols for disaster recovery in community and organizational settings and on the psychological aspects of occupational injury and disability. He has consulted to private corporations, government agencies, nongovernmental organizations and public entities in the prevention, response, mitigation and recovery from disasters, violence and business crises–providing training, policy development, and acute crisis intervention. His publications include "The Challenge to Corporate Leadership: Managing the Human Impact of Terrorism on Business Recovery," in Kamien, ed., *The Mcgraw-Hill Handbook of Homeland Security*, Spring, 2005, *Preventing Workplace Violence, a Guide for Employers and Practitioners*, Sage Publications, 1999, and "Post-traumatic Stress Disorder and Its Relationship to Occupational Health and Injury Prevention" in *Encyclopaedia of Occupa-*

tional Health and Safety, ed. Hurrell, Murphy, Sauter, Levi, ILO Press, Geneva, 1998 (E-mail: mbraverman@bravermangroup.com).

Bernard E. Beidel, MEd, is Director of the Office of Employee Assistance at the U.S. House of Representatives in Washington, DC. He is responsible for the planning, development, management, evaluation, and continued enhancement and integration of the House's employee assistance service into the organization and its continuity of operations planning and execution. Prior to joining the House of Representatives in 1991, he developed and directed the EAP for the New Jersey State Police throughout the 1980s–a position that provided him a foundational framework and extensive experience in critical incident stress management (CISM) and trauma response services. His initial EAP experience came as an external provider managing an employee assistance consortium in rural Virginia (E-mail: bern.beidel@mail.house.gov).

Sally Bishop, MA, is a Senior Account Executive with Magellan Behavioral Health managing EAP, Managed Behavioral Health and Disease Management Specialty Products. Sally has more than 18 years of direct and consultative experience in disasters and other traumatic issues for the workplace. Her work with employers following Hurricane Andrew was a feature story in *USA Today*. She has also worked with corporations whose personnel are exposed to repeated or recurrent critical incident stress related to criminal and terrorist acts. Sally also has expertise in aviation disaster response and considerations for aviation personnel. Sally has experience with business partnership development and enhancement, employer/employee training, executive reporting and briefings and collaborative best practices for optimal workplace outcomes (E-mail: sabishop@magellanhealth.com).

George S. Everly, Jr., PhD, is Associate Professor, The Johns Hopkins University School of Medicine, a faculty member in The Johns Hopkins University Bloomberg School of Public Health Center for Public Health Preparedness, and is Professor of Psychology, Loyola College in Maryland. Dr. Everly served as Senior Research Advisor to the Social Development Office, Office of His Highness the Amir of Kuwait subsequent to the 1991 Gulf War and has responded to major disasters including the Oklahoma City bombing, and the World Trade Center bombing of 2001. He is the editor of the textbook *Mental Health Aspects of Disasters: Public Health Preparedness and Response*, and author of the recent texts *A Clinical Guide to the Treatment of the Human Stress Response, Personality-based Therapy of Posttraumatic Stress Disorder*, and *Psychological Counterterrorism and World War IV* (E-mail: geverly@jhsph.edu).

Carol S. Fullerton, PhD, is Research Professor in the Department of Psychiatry at the Uniformed Services University of the Health Sciences School of Medicine (USUHS), Bethesda, Maryland. She is the Scientific Director of the Center for the Study of Traumatic Stress (CSTS). Dr. Fullerton is widely published in the areas of post-traumatic stress disorder and the behavioral and psychological effects of terrorism, bioterrorism, traumatic events and disasters, and combat. Dr. Fullerton has conducted empirical investigations and provided consultation to the following numerous disasters and traumatic events including: Ramstein Air Force Base air show crash; Norton Air Force Base cargo plane crash; USS Iowa gun turret explosion; United Flight 232 DC-10 crash, Sioux City, Iowa; Armenian earthquake; Operation Desert Storm; the USNS Comfort Desert Storm deployments; Typhoon Ohmar; Hurricane Andrew; dentists following Waco disaster; 9/11 Pentagon personnel; USNS Comfort 9/11 deployment; effect of terrorism on State Department Officers and families; the effects of the 2004 Florida hurricanes on the FL Department of Health; and the 2004 South East Asia Tsunami (E-mail: cfullerton@usuhs.mil).

Robert K. Gifford, PhD, is a senior scientist in the Center for the Study of Traumatic Stress at the Uniformed Services University of the Health Sciences. Dr. Gifford served in the United States Army for thirty years, retiring as a colonel. While in the Army, he conducted psychological research in the field in the Persian Gulf War (Operation Desert Shield/Storm), in Somalia, and in Bosnia as well as at field sites in Germany and the United States. He served as Research Psychology Consultant to The Army Surgeon General and later as the Army Medical Service Corps' Assistant Chief for Medical Allied Sciences. He has extensive experience with both interview research at multiple levels within organizations, and survey questionnaires for larger populations. He has also been active in education about traumatic stress and developing resiliency in organizations and individuals, having lectured on the topic both in the United States and in Europe. His publications include the entry on "War and Conflict: Effects on Military Personnel" for the *Encyclopedia of Psychology*, published by the American Psychological Association and Oxford University Press (E-mail: rgifford@usuhs.mil).

Richard Gist, PhD, is Principal Assistant to the Director of the Kansas City, Missouri (USA) Fire Department and Associate Professor of Psychology at the University of Missouri-Kansas City. He has played active roles in major disasters from the Hyatt hotel collapse and Exxon Valdez oil spill to the recent Gulf Coast hurricanes, helping to craft responses and evaluate performance in public, corporate, and NGO domains (E-mail: richard-gist@kemo.org).

Kristina L. Greenwood, PhD, is Vice President, Outcomes Research at ValueOptions, and is responsible for the leadership and strategic direction of behavioral health research and integrated care initiatives. With 20 years of experience in health care operations, clinical outcomes research, and quality management, she has held senior management positions within managed care and health care research organizations (E-mail: kris.greenwood@valueoptions.com).

Girish S. Hiremath, MD, MPH, trained as a physician in India. He has a master of philosophy in hospital and health systems management, and he earned his MPH from the Johns Hopkins Bloomberg School of Public Health. He has worked for the Indian Navy for five years and the World Health Organization for three years. Currently, he is working as a post doctoral fellow in the Department of International Health at Hopkins. His areas of interest include: prevention and control of infectious diseases, child survival, and public health preparedness (E-mail: ghiremat@jhsph.edu).

Jodi M. Jacobson, PhD, is Assistant Professor at Towson University, Family Studies Department. As a licensed clinical social worker, she maintains a small private practice and is a Senior Researcher with MASI Research Consultants, Inc. Currently Dr. Jacobson co-chairs the EAPA Workplace Disaster Preparedness Subcommittee (E-mail: jjacobson@towson.edu).

Gosia Kubiak, MSc, is a Biostatistician/Epidemiologist at the Naval Environmental Health Center. Ms. Kubiak has experience in analysis of clinical trials, longitudinal studies, and healthcare data, as well in survey design and research methodology. Before joining NEHC, she was employed at ValueOptions as a Statistician in the Department of Quality Management; as well as at the University of California, San Diego as a Statistician in the Biostatistics Core in the Department of Psychiatry. Ms. Kubiak received a BS in Applied Mathematics from the University of California, San Diego, and a MSc in Statistics from the University of Manchester (UK) in 2003 (E-mail: kubiakg@nehc.med.navy.mil).

Lyle Labardee, MS, is the founder and CEO of Crisis Care Network and has been featured as an expert in crisis management on news broadcasts and has appeared in national publications such as the *Wall Street Journal*, *Trauma Response*, and *Security* magazine (E-mail: lyle.labardee@crisiscare.com).

Jonathan M. Links, PhD, is Professor of Environmental Health Sciences in the Johns Hopkins Bloomberg School of Public Health, with joint appointments in Radiology and Emergency Medicine in the School of Medicine. He directs the Johns Hopkins Center for Public Health Preparedness, a CDC-funded training center for frontline public health workers. Dr. Links is Baltimore City's on-call radiation terror expert (E-mail: jlinks@jhsph.edu).

R. Paul Maiden, PhD, is the editor of the *Journal of Workplace Behavioral Health*. He is also Associate Professor of social work at the University of Central Florida in Orlando. He is a recipient of two Senior Fulbright Scholar awards to Russia and South Africa. He has been in the EAP field for 25 years and has an extensive portfolio of domestic and international publications, presentations and consultations on a wide range of workplace human service issues. He is editor and contributing author of Employee Assistance Programs in South Africa, *Total Quality Management in EAPs, Global Perspectives of Occupational Social Work, Employee Assistance Services in the New South Africa, Accreditation of Employee Assistance Programs*, and *The Integration of Employee Assistance, Work/Life, and Wellness Services* (with Attridge and Herlihy) (E-mail: pmaiden@mail.ucf.edu).

Bob McCullough, MSW, has 15 years in the EAP/behavioral health industry and is Clinical Supervisor for Magellan's Critical Incident Stress Management Unit. During his 5 years with Magellan, the CISM unit has responded to more than 20,000 requests for onsite interventions including air disasters, school shootings, terrorists attacks, workplace violence, natural disasters and industrial accidents. The unit is responsible for product development and implementing best practices in the area of critical incident response. He has written and conducted several trainings on crisis response in the workplace to support client requests (E-mail: rmmccullough@magellanhealth.com).

Rich Paul, MSW, is Vice President of Health and Performance Solutions within ValueOptions' Employer Solutions Division. He is responsible for national operations and product development and best practices supporting all workplace-based services and products. Mr. Paul has 15 years of EAP and behavioral health experience and is a frequent speaker and author on issues impacting the workplace. He currently serves as president of the Employee Assistance Society of North America (EASNA), an association focused on advancing knowledge, research and best practices toward achieving healthy and productive workplaces (E-mail: richard.paul@valueoptions.com).

Nolan Phipps, MBA, is Director of Outcomes Research for the Health Plan and Employer Solutions Divisions of ValueOptions. Mr. Phipps has 18 years experience in managed care, including extensive experience in analysis and reporting, and five years of experience in outcomes management. Before joining ValueOptions in 1998, he was employed by Sentara Health System, where he was the Director of Data Analysis for Optima Health Plan (E-mail: sonny.phipps@valueoptions.com).

Dorothea U. Schneider, MA, is a National EAP Consultant for Federal Occupational Health, Program Support Center, U.S. Department of Health and Human Services. Dorothea has worked in the EAP field since 1980 and has experience in providing direct service, program development, program management, and consultation. She has a particular interest in working with joint management-union programs as well as developing critical response paradigms (E-mail: DSchneider@psc.gov).

Martin F. Sherman, PhD, is Professor of Psychology and Director of Master's Education: Thesis Track at Loyola College in Maryland. He teaches SPSS in the doctoral program along with Social and Cultural Bases of Behavior. He recently completed data analysis of 6,000 New York City health care workers' ability and willingness to report to duty during catastrophic disasters. Currently he is analyzing the data from a large sample of evacuees of the World Trade Center disaster of 9/11 (E-mail: msherman@loyola.edu).

Amy Stapleton, PsyD, graduated from Loyola College in Maryland with a doctoral degree in clinical psychology. She is currently the Outreach Coordinator at Mississippi State University's Student Counseling and Testing Services. Dr. Stapleton's clinical and research interests include trauma, crisis intervention, and sport performance enhancement. She has also consulted with local and state law enforcement agencies, social service agencies, and academic institutions (E-mail: drstapleton@nctv.com).

Diane Stephenson, PhD, is Associate Director with Federal Occupational Health, Program Support Center, U.S. Department of Health and Human Services. She has over 20 years of healthcare experience in the management and direction of behavioral health and employee assistance programs, organizational and efficiency analysis, quality review, and direct clinical practice. A clinical psychologist, she has authored a number of professional articles and served on the boards of social service agencies (E-mail: DStephenson@psc.gov).

Lourens Terblanche, PhD, is Associate Professor and Chair of the EAP sequence in the Department of Social Work and Criminal Justice at the University of Pretoria, South Africa. He also has experience in the South African mining industry and has consulted with a number of firms on the development and effectiveness of EAPs (E-mail: lourie.terblanche@up.ac.za).

Christina Thompson, MSW, is Vice President of Employee Assistance Programs and Addictions Services for Magellan Health Services in their Employer Solutions Division Strategic Business Unit. Ms. Thompson has over 26 years experience in the EAP/Behavioral health field and has been with Magellan for 15 years and is responsible for the leadership and coordination of the EAP/Addictions products/services including clinical/operational oversight, the development and maintenance of policy, program enhancements, product development, support of sales and marketing, COA EAP accreditation and better practices for multiple accounts nationally and internationally. Over the years Tina has been involved in many boards and committees whose focus is with the advancement of EAP, Behavioral Health care and related issues. She is an active speaker and has published on a variety of EAP and Workplace topics (E-mail: tthompson@magellanhealth.com).

Robert J. Ursano, MD, is Professor of Psychiatry and Neuroscience and Chairman of the Department of Psychiatry at the Uniformed Services University of the Health Sciences, Bethesda, Maryland. He is Director of the Center for the Study of Traumatic Stress which has over six million dollars in research funding. In addition, Dr. Ursano is Editor of *Psychiatry*, the distinguished journal of interpersonal and biological processes, founded by Harry Stack Sullivan. Dr. Ursano was the first Chairman of the American Psychiatric Association's Committee on Psychiatric Dimensions of Disaster. Dr. Ursano is a member of the Advisory Board of the National Partnership for Workplace Mental Health (American Psychiatric Association); the White Paper Panel on Bioterrorism and Health Care, Joint Commission on Accreditation of Health Care Organizations; the Scientific Advisory Board on Bioterrorism of SAMSHA (HHS), Center for Mental Health Services; the Advisory Board of the Center on Terrorism of the University of Oklahoma School of Medicine; the National Academies of Science, Institute of Medicine, Committee on Psychological Responses to Terrorism; and the National Institute of Mental Health Task Force on Mental Health Surveillance. Following the September 11th terrorist attacks, he provided consultation to New York State Governor's Office, New York City Mayor's Office, Department of HHS, National Capital response teams, and the Department of Defense Pentagon response groups (E-mail: rursano@usuhs.mil).

Bob VandePol, MSW, serves as President of Crisis Care Network, the provider of Critical Incident Response Services to business and industry. He consults with corporations, insurers, EAPs, and behavioral health professionals regarding how to manage the behavioral risks inherent in workplace tragedies. Active as a speaker and trainer, Mr. VandePol has published and been featured in numerous business and clinical journals (E-mail: bob.vandepol@crisiscare.com).

Laurie Van der Heide, PhD, is a licensed Clinical Psychologist and Registered Nurse employed as the Corporate Director of Quality Improvement for ValueOptions. She has worked in managed behavioral healthcare for nearly 20 years, with a focus on accreditation, indicator development, client reporting, and HEDIS measurement. Dr. Van der Heide received her doctorate in Clinical Psychology from Fordham University, New York and her Diploma in Nursing from Mount Sinai Hospital School of Nursing, New York (E-mail: laurie.vanderheide@valueoptions.com).

Nakiya Vasi, MSW, graduated from the University of Maryland, School of Social Work in the MACO-Clinical/EAP Specialization Track. Nakiya had the opportunity to be an Employee Assistance Program intern at Magellan Health Services and worked on various EAP projects such as policy review, COA re-accreditation, product development, and network credentialing (E-mail: nakiyavasi@gmail.com).

Nancy T. Vineburgh, MA, is Assistant Professor in the Department of Psychiatry at The Uniformed Services University of the Health Sciences in Bethesda, Maryland. She serves as the Director of the Office of Public Education and Preparedness at the Center for the Study of Traumatic Stress (CSTS). Ms. Vineburgh is an expert in health communication, health marketing and public education. She has created numerous public education campaigns that have generated national and international attention: Fight the Bite, the nation's first health campaign for Lyme Disease awareness; Courage to Care, an electronic campaign addressing the well-being of deployed soldiers and their families; and Can a Depressed Parent Be a Good Parent, You Bet, the nation's first campaign on parental depression sponsored by Children's Hospital Boston; Ms. Vineburgh's paper, "The Power of the Pink Ribbon: Raising Awareness of the Mental Health Implications of Terrorism" in the journal *Psychiatry* influenced public policy and led to Maryland's proclamation of National Resiliency Day on September 11, 2004 (E-mail: nvineburgh@usuhs.mil).

Preface:
Rapid Response to Workplace Disasters
Is an EAP *Essential*

Rapid response to episodes of workplace violence, natural disasters and acts of terrorism has become a critical component of employee assistance programs. However, ability to respond quickly and effectively is dependent on the development of an effective response plan in anticipation of a man-made or natural disaster which has become an all-too-common occurrence in the workplace. A well thought-out disaster response and management plan is also essential to restoring a sense of order and normalcy to traumatized employees and to re-establishing production and performance.

For many years employee assistance programs have been providing critical incidence stress management services (CISM) to employees that have been involved in, or witness to, workplace fatalities and accidents that are likely to traumatize workers and impair quality of work, increase sick leave and health and mental health claims.

This volume contains ten articles that constitute best practices and essentially represent the state of the art in crisis preparedness, crisis response and trauma management in the workplace.

In the first article Co-Editors Rich Paul of ValueOptions and Christina Thompson of Magellan Health Services summarize a series of interviews with internal and external EAP program managers. Paul and Thompson explore how the employers and their EAPs were impacted by the September 11th, 2001, terrorist attacks. They also examine techniques used by EAPs to actively engage employers in the development of disaster preparedness planning and responses in the aftermath of September 11th.

[Haworth co-indexing entry note]: "Preface: Rapid Response to Workplace Disasters Is an EAP *Essential*." Maiden, R. Paul. Co-published simultaneously in *Journal of Workplace Behavioral Health* (The Haworth Press, Inc.) Vol. 21, No. 3/4, 2006, pp. xli-xliv; and: *Workplace Disaster Preparedness, Response, and Management* (ed: R. Paul Maiden, Rich Paul, and Christina Thompson) The Haworth Press, Inc., 2006, pp. xxiii-xxvi. Single or multiple copies of this article are available for a fee from The Haworth Document Delivery Service [1-800-HAWORTH, 9:00 a.m. - 5:00 p.m. (EST). E-mail address: docdelivery@haworthpress.com].

David Benedek, Robert Ursano, Carol Fullerton, Nancy Vineburgh and Robert Gifford, a group of psychiatry faculty at the Uniformed Services University of the Health Sciences in Bethesda, Maryland, were involved in the aftermath of both the World Trade Center destruction and the attack on the Pentagon on September 11th, 2001. These scholars illustrate how the principles of a public health approach are applied to the emotional and behavioral consequences of terrorism to address resiliency, illness, distress, and risk behaviors to maximize return to health and work productivity.

Diane Stephenson and Dorothea Schneider, both with the Federal Occupational Health, Program Support Center, U.S. Department of Health and Human Services in Chicago, present a series of case studies that detail their own first person accounts of the Federal Occupational Health's EAP response to three consecutive and disastrous hurricanes that hit the state of Florida in 2004 and then by Hurricane Katrina, the most devastating and costliest hurricane on record to hit the Gulf Coast states of Louisiana, Mississippi and Alabama in 2005. Several thousand federal agency employees reside in these Gulf Coast states and lost both their homes and their workplace as a result of these natural disasters.

In the next article, Bern Beidel, EAP Director for the U.S. House of Representatives, discusses his program's response to the anthrax contamination that occurred in the mail rooms and office buildings in the nation's capital. Beidel also examines the valued role an EAP can play in helping the employer to manage human capital in the aftermath of such an event to re-establish order and promote continuity in the workplace.

Longtime colleagues and collaborators, Paul Maiden from the University of Central Florida and Lourens Terblanche from the University of Pretoria follow with an article on managing trauma in the South African mining industry. They also elaborate on how EAP professionals have adapted critical incident stress management techniques to respond to the workplace spillover of community violence that is so prevalent in South Africa.

Sally Bishop, Bob McCullough, Christina Thompson and Nakiya Vasi of Magellan Health Services explore the impact of repetitive episodes of workplace violence in the form of bank robberies, convenience store hold-ups, etc. They follow with a discussion of the importance of incorporating the concepts of resiliency in the development of appropriate trauma response techniques in high risk work settings.

Bob VandePol, Richard Gist, Mark Braverman and Lyle Labardee examine the advances in organizational crisis management and discuss the value and growing need for developing partnerships between employers and crisis managers as a means of securing around-the-clock access to crisis response teams. Integrating the crisis response team with established EAP services also ensures that a continuum of services is in place in anticipation of a crisis episode thereby insuring rapid and effective response to minimize the destabilizing impact likely to occur as a result of a major critical episode.

Jodi Jacobson's article explores the prevalence of compassion fatigue among professional helpers. Jacobson examines results from a national research study of members of the Employee Assistance Professionals Association (EAPA) who were assessed for risk of compassion fatigue and burnout, as well as potential for compassion satisfaction. Her research suggests that employee assistance professionals engaged in workplace trauma response are at low risk for burnout, but given the extent and intensity of their involvement, are at some risk for compassion fatigue. She also found that employee assistance professionals engaged in trauma response activities also have a high potential for compassion satisfaction.

CISM pioneer George Everly, Jr. and his colleagues present findings from a systematic review of nine workplace crisis intervention programs. Their results suggest that the workplace can be a useful platform from which to provide crisis intervention programs.

In the final article Kris Greenwood and her research team at Value-Options provide their findings from an exploratory study to examine how companies representing various industry types differed in the frequency of requests for critical incident services, the types of incidents that evoked the request, interventions used, and elapsed time between the request and provision of services. Their results demonstrated substantial variability in the types of incidents and the frequency of service utilization.

In the inimitable words of Franklin Delano Roosevelt, September 11, 2001, *is a day that will live in infamy.* Not since he spoke these words before the United States Congress after the bombing of Pearl Harbor on December 7, 1942, has the United States experienced a disaster and loss of life of such proportions. The world changed dramatically on that December day in 1942 and the world changed yet again on that September day in 2001. We will forget neither but we have learned from both. EAPs were well entrenched in most American businesses prior to 2001. Since that day however, EAPs and other trauma management specialists have become an essential element in helping employers prepare for and respond to a myriad of natural and man-made disasters that can and do occur in the workplace on what seems to have become all-too-frequent events.

R. Paul Maiden, PhD
University of Central Florida
School of Social Work

Employee Assistance Program Responses to Large Scale Traumatic Events: Lessons Learned and Future Opportunities

Rich Paul
Christina Thompson

SUMMARY. This article provides a summary of interviews with several national, regional, internal and external Employee Assistance Program providers as well as employers. The focus of the interviews was to ascertain both similar and dissimilar experiences of EAPs and employers in responding to large scale traumatic events. In particular, this article summarizes how the delivery of crisis response services has been impacted by the terrorist attacks of September 11th and how this has influenced the way in which EAPs and employers view the role of the EAP in responding to subsequent traumatic events. The experiences summarized herein reflect the fact that EAP has increasingly been a sought after partner in disaster preparedness planning and response post September 11th. In addition, this paper summarizes a common understanding that effective EAP responses to large scale traumatic events must involve a flexible approach using intervention methods best suited to the type of incident and that it must entail a dual focus on both the organization and the workforce. doi:10.1300/J490v21n03_01 *[Article copies available for a fee from The Haworth Document Delivery Service: 1-800-HAWORTH.*

The authors wish to acknowledge Bob McCullough and Mary Hill for their contributions to this article.

[Haworth co-indexing entry note]: "Employee Assistance Program Responses to Large Scale Traumatic Events: Lessons Learned and Future Opportunities." Paul, Rich, and Christina Thompson. Co-published simultaneously in *Journal of Workplace Behavioral Health* (The Haworth Press, Inc.) Vol. 21, No. 3/4, 2006, pp. 1-19; and: *Workplace Disaster Preparedness, Response, and Management* (ed: R. Paul Maiden, Rich Paul, and Christina Thompson) The Haworth Press, Inc., 2006, pp. 1-19. Single or multiple copies of this article are available for a fee from The Haworth Document Delivery Service [1-800-HAWORTH, 9:00 a.m. - 5:00 p.m. (EST). E-mail address: docdelivery@haworthpress.com].

E-mail address: <docdelivery@haworthpress.com> Website: <http://www.HaworthPress.com> © 2006 by The Haworth Press, Inc. All rights reserved.]

KEYWORDS. Employee Assistance Program (EAP), crisis response, critical incident, trauma

INTRODUCTION

The Employee Assistance field has often been the first line of defense in supporting organizations in developing and implementing effective disaster response plans. Equally as important is their contribution to supporting both the organization and the employees following the occurrence of a traumatic event. Since September 11th, 2001, and a recent sequence of natural disasters, crisis planning and response has taken on new meaning for Employee Assistance Programs (EAPs) and the organizations they serve.

The March 1993 car bomb explosion at the World Trade Towers in New York City followed by the April 1995 bombing of the Oklahoma City Alfred P. Murrah Federal Building represent incidents of terrorism that led to pandemonium in those workforces directly and indirectly impacted by these traumatic events. Since these two incidents, additional global terrorist attacks would force employers nationwide to re-evaluate their preparedness and response to such events. In a survey of human resource professionals following September 11th, Paul and Masi (2002) suggest that longer term goals and opportunities for EAPs include training opportunities as well as active participation in the development and implementation of crisis response plans and policies, including the promotion of greater coordination among company departments. To what extent has the occurrence of such incidents prompted employers to create or re-evaluate their disaster recovery plans? In addition, one critical area identified by human resource professionals in this study was improving effective communication channels within an organization to more effectively disseminate information and communication materials particularly should another disaster of the magnitude of September 11th occur again. This paper reviews some of the activities of organizations and EAPs including the extent to which such infrastructure enhancements were made as a result of the events of September 11th.

As well, while the response of EAPs and employers differ slightly from terrorist events and natural disasters, a significant number of natural disasters have required similar planning and a timely response. Moreover, within the last decade, EAPs have come to realize that serving the needs of a global workforce (whether this includes expatriates or host nationals) has required that EAPs are able to respond to traumatic events not just domestically, but throughout the world.

This paper summarizes interviews with several national and regional EAPs as well as internal EAPs, and their perception of how their business and their crisis response services have evolved over the last decade as a result of the types of traumatic events that have occurred. Additionally, interviews were also conducted with several employers to evaluate their perception of how their own business practices have changed following these events and their perception of the role and significance of having an EAP.

The most significant world events impacting U.S.-based employers over the last decade are reflected in Table 1. This table illustrates what EAPs have identified as the most influential events that have required

TABLE 1. Most Significant World Events Impacting U.S. Employers

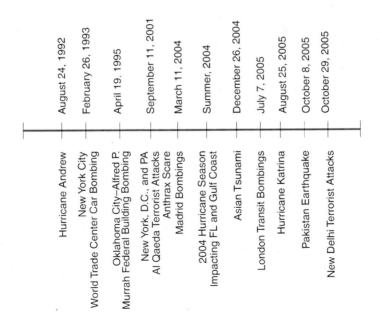

EAP involvement and subsequent delivery of supportive interventions to the workplaces they serve.

METHODOLOGY

This study explored the perceptions of EAP professionals and the corporations for whom they provide EAP services. The intent was to identify any trends or patterns related to the need for crisis response services from an EAP and employer perspective as well as the perceived helpfulness of such services. Moreover, both parties were asked to describe how their approach to workplace interventions following a traumatic event has evolved or changed as a result of more recent large scale incidents.

Both EAPs and employers were interviewed and asked a series of four questions that structured the interviews and allowed for expansion into broader discussions. The questions for EAPs are reflected in Table 2 and the questions asked of employers in Table 3.

TABLE 2

Interview questions of EAPs
1. How has your organization changed the way in which you view or offer crisis response services since the events of September 11th, other terrorist attacks and recent natural disasters?
2. How would you describe your theoretical approach to crisis response services pre and post these events? Has this changed at all, if so, how?
3. Have you observed any changes in the types of requests that you receive for crisis response support?
4. Have you observed significant changes in disaster preparedness efforts on the part of the clients you serve?

TABLE 3

Interview questions of employers
1. Where is your organization's primary location(s)?
2. How (if at all) have your expectations of your EAP changed in terms of the types of services or response support you require for traumatic events in the workplace following the events of September 11th, other terrorist attacks and recent natural disasters?
3. What do you see as being the most important value of offering EAP interventions as a response to a workplace critical incident?
4. What (if any) long-term impact do you believe these events have had on your organization as it relates to crisis response and disaster preparedness?

Open-ended questions were asked of participants because they tend to provide no structure for the answer; however, they were tightly focused in scope to elicit detailed information on perceptions related to crisis response services. Open-ended questions were also used because this effort represented only initial research among a small number of respondents. The eventual goal is that this study may be expanded, resulting in refinement of the research direction and with a more precise series of structured questions. The questions in Tables 2 and 3 were gathered through scheduled telephonic interviews lasting approximately 30 to 60 minutes in duration. Each interview included introductory comments by the interviewer on the purpose and scope of the study followed by the identified questions which led into less structured questions and answers.

RESULTS

This paper represents a collaborative effort on the part of Magellan Health Services and ValueOptions, two providers of behavioral health and EAP services. The experience of both organizations related to crisis response services was relatively similar in that both organizations serve companies that are national and international in scope and each were called upon to provide employer support to the large world events occurring over the last decade. Both organizations collaborated in interviewing other EAPs that represented a variety of EAP providers throughout the U.S. as well as sharing their own company's experiences.

THE EXPERIENCE OF LARGE NATIONAL EAPs

On September 11th news of the terrorist attacks on the Twin Towers was almost immediate. ValueOptions management team quickly pulled together a call to implement a disaster recovery plan for their New York City service center office. Shortly thereafter the same management team watched from a conference room as black billowing smoke rose from the recently struck Pentagon. On the actual day of the terrorist attacks call volume and overall service requests remained low; however, the next day the requests for services began early and continued for weeks and months to come. The account services team spent most of the day of September 11th reaching out and contacting customers to remind them that the EAP was prepared to consult with their management team and to support their employees. This outreach was prioritized with those customers located in New York and Washington, DC. In addition, efforts were made to initially identify the customers that had office space and/or contracted employees located in the Twin Towers and the Pentagon. Following the terrorist events of September 11th, ValueOptions responded with on-site trauma response services to many clients both directly and indirectly impacted. In the first several weeks following September 11th, over 3,200 hours of on-site services were provided in the form of crisis intervention, group critical incident debriefing and defusing services, individual counseling and management consultation. Moreover, many EAP staff members were deployed to "Ground Zero" to mobilize resources and coordinate response efforts. In addition, other supportive services were provided to clients including educational materials and access to the Achieve Solutions (EAP) Web site.

By the end of that same day, Magellan had received almost 200 requests for on-site services due to the terrorist attacks. In the month following September 11th, the company experienced nearly seven times its average monthly volume for crisis response services, responding to 2,315 separate event requests and providing 6,060 telephonic management consultations to over 275 clients and more than 78,000 individuals. Magellan staff, network clinicians and other trained professionals in the community provided 6,571 group debriefing sessions as well as 24,854 individual on-site sessions. During the months of September and October, these clinicians provided a total of 10,603 hours of on-site services to clients who had been impacted by the terrorist attacks.

To meet the significant need for education and information in the wake of the attacks, Magellan provided approximately 70 articles and tip sheets on a variety of topics, including how managers could respond to their employees' needs, coping with trauma, expected responses (symptoms, reactions), how to speak with children regarding the terrorist attacks, how to speak with children impacted by traumatic event(s), and tips on self-care. These materials were available via mail, e-mail, fax and through the company's Web site. To meet the significant need of its customers, Magellan opened access to the Web site, formerly available only to customers who had contracted for access, to all clients, resulting in a 400% increase in the number of hits to the site. Further, Magellan provided comprehensive clinical consultations that focused on the following themes: loss of fellow employees and family/friends, deep regret and sadness over the loss of police/firefighters, loss of a sense of security or trust, anger, fear, confusion, loss of resources, images of destruction and concern of what could be next.

The September 11th terrorist attacks tested Magellan's operational resources unlike any other event. The company decided early on to make crisis response services available to all Magellan clients, including those that had not contracted for EAP services. As call volume exceeded 200 requests per day for the crisis response intake team, many other Magellan clinical teams' experienced significantly decreased call volume, allowing the company to redeploy call center staff so that all calls were answered and serviced in a timely manner. At one point during the response, Magellan's crisis response team was being augmented by over 150 other staff that were conducting intake consultations and locating providers. Recognizing that Magellan's own staff was directly and indirectly impacted by the terrorist attacks and the level of response and in need of frequent support, company management ensured that crisis response services were also made available to Magellan employees as often as needed.

Due to the high volume of requests in the New York metropolitan area and the impact Magellan's local affiliates experienced, the company deployed internal resources to New York to assist in providing on-site services. Magellan's provider network management team contacted over 500 providers and identified 266 additional providers in the New York and Washington, DC, areas who had credentials to provide critical incidence stress management (CISM) services. In addition, Magellan marshaled clinicians from around the country to travel to New York to provide on-site management consultations, group and individual crisis response services, services to families and children and to assist local authorities in preparing crisis response services for first responders. Clients who had experienced direct loss of life were given top priority, followed by those who had been directly affected but experienced no loss of life, followed by those who were indirectly affected, but were still in need of crisis response services.

Beginning in mid-October, ValueOptions began conducting interviews with the key contacts and/or account liaisons that were responsible for coordinating and arranging trauma response services on behalf of their organization. The survey was completed through a telephonic interview with the key contact having been identified by a ValueOptions account executive. The purpose of the survey was to measure the satisfaction levels with the services provided by ValueOptions, and secondly to determine the organizational impact for both managers and employees.

The results below summarize the responses by 36 individuals in key management positions from 30 to 90 days following the terrorist attacks:

- The survey results indicate that of those organizations surveyed, educational materials, group crisis management, critical incident debriefing and defusing services, and online/Web services were utilized the most frequently in response to September 11th.
- 90% of participants rated the overall services they (managers) received as being extremely helpful to helpful.
- The services perceived as being most helpful for both employees and managers included: Group crisis intervention, critical incident debriefings and defusings, individual services, and management consultation.

Hard on the heels of the terrible plane crashes and destruction of September 11th, the country was forced to deal with more traumas–a series of bioterrorist attacks during September and October. The biochemical weapon was anthrax spores and the result was 11 confirmed cases of anthrax inhalation and five deaths. Significant fears spread throughout the country as suspected and confirmed findings of anthrax were located around the country. Within months of the first reported bioterrorism act, hundreds of postal facilities were evacuated due to suspected packages, multiple companies were tested for possible exposure and there were thousands of suspicious mailing incidents or threats.

For most EAPs, the anthrax attacks presented new, challenging reactions for service providers. Individuals located in affected areas presented with fear for their personal safety and the well-being of others. There was anger and mistrust of the information being provided by local public health authorities and the national Centers for Disease Control. There were fears about antibiotic treatment due to lack of knowledge, unpleasant side effects and the uncertainty of length of treatment. There was anxiety resulting from the need to change work locations because offices and facilities had been closed due to anthrax. And, there was grief related to the disruption of lives and the loss of friends/coworkers who had died from anthrax exposure.

The nature of the anthrax crisis demanded an unconventional response and EAPs rose to the challenge. EAPs deployed counselors to local hospitals and public health centers where antibiotics were being distributed. Individuals often waited in lines for hours to receive antibiotic treatment and counselors were there to walk the line and speak with individuals regarding their fears and concerns. In addition, EAP counselors were present at all work locations that employees had been transferred to while their home facility was being treated for anthrax exposure. Counselors held group and individual sessions and met with employees at their work stations in order to reach each individual. Further, counselors met with management in order to provide consultation on meeting employees' psychosocial needs and managing productivity expectations.

Even one to two years after the anthrax attacks, individuals were still exhibiting reactions–fear and anxiety regarding safety protocols lack of cohesiveness among co-workers and enthusiasm to return to the routine prior to the attacks. EAP remained a vital resource for employees and management during this time as local trainings were implemented for management and additional communication, including resources and tip sheets for self-care, was made available for employees and family members.

Employees returning to locations that had been closed due to anthrax exposure were provided ongoing EAP services for significant periods. For example, Magellan provided on-site EAP services around the clock for four months straight following the return of the workforce to one 24/7 worksite. EAP counselors provided individual and group sessions to employees and managers to consult on managing emotions, normalizing reactions and enhancing ongoing communication between parties. This EAP presence provided reassurance that employee and manager needs were important and that access to these services would be immediately available.

Even now, four years after the anthrax attacks, there is a heightened sense of fear and anxiety about any white powder substance found in or near a piece of mail. Many of the same reactions and concerns rush back to individuals and organizations at the possibility of an anthrax contamination. Throughout this incident, it was critical that EAP demonstrate an ability to adapt resources and be flexible to meet the needs of those impacted by anthrax including services that were typically thought beyond the scope of an employee assistance program.

Once the response to the terrorist and anthrax attacks had subsided, Magellan took the opportunity to review its internal procedures and capability to respond to large-scale, catastrophic events. Due to the magnitude of the event it was obvious that to be prepared for an event of this size or larger, several components need to be in place. Magellan asked several client companies to participate in a qualitative initiative on what, if any, additional needs they might have with a large-scale event. As a result, Magellan completed a Disaster Plan Quality Initiative that resulted in a barrier analysis and the formulation of an enhanced disaster plan. The measures included CISM audit scores, the number of requested events and satisfaction survey information. Satisfaction survey results are shown in Table 4.

Based on the feedback it sought, Magellan concluded the following:

1. The disaster plan should be tiered to reflect the level of severity of the event. Five (5) levels were formulated. As the need would grow, and become less manageable, it would then lend itself to go to the next level.
2. In addition to the expertise and capability of Magellan's centralized CISM unit, all company senior management/officers should be trained in the event that the unit was to be incapacitated and unable to provide the level of service needed.
3. Organizations may have unique needs and therefore would require individualized services.
4. A tracking system is necessary to handle such large volumes and specialization services required.

TABLE 4. Crisis Management Satisfaction Survey

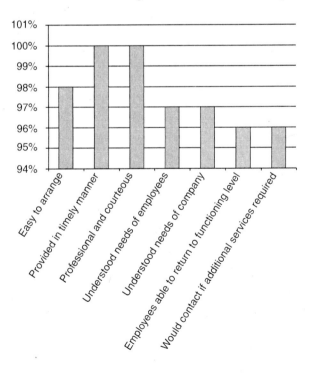

Each of the above steps required defining all aspects of each task. Among those were clearly written and consistent descriptions of all job tasks; up to date lists of contact people locally, nationally, internally and externally; a National Disaster Task Force comprising key individuals who could be called upon to provide leadership in the event of a very large disaster. The plan also involved extensive training for all levels of the organization which tested for reliability and readiness. Drills and mock scenarios were created to help the organization remain prepared, with each drill fine-tuning efforts that will improve the overall process. A refined follow-up tool also evolved to be used to reflect data needed to measure outcomes after an event.

One of the lessons learned following September 11th was that the success of an effective and swift response came by a willingness to partner and collaborate with others. The devastation was so far reaching that existing resources, communications and networks were disrupted. Harris Rothenberg International (HRI), ValueOptions' provider of Work/Life services, was significantly impacted as a result of their proximity to the terrorist attacks and yet despite that both organizations relied heavily on one another to support each other's business continuity efforts. This ultimately resulted in better service and support to both organizations' customers.

As is a common theme throughout this paper, ValueOptions' experience was not unlike other EAPs in that there was a clear realization that this was unlike any other workplace trauma and thus would require incredible flexibility. In addition, this event resulted in chaos within organizations, and consultation on how to lead in times of a crisis was of paramount importance. Several telephonic and on-site sessions were scheduled with executive management teams to assist them in remaining focused on leading and supporting their workforces during this unprecedented time. In addition, a great deal of energy was spent on supporting organizations to better understand the importance of frequent and effective communication strategies among their workforce. Content in the form of articles, tip sheets and trainings was continually being developed for employees and managers and distributed based upon the evolving and somewhat unpredictable needs of the workplace.

Finally, September 11th was the catalyst which increased the perceived importance by companies of the important role of the EAP both for employees but also the organization as a whole. Invitations to disaster preparedness planning and EAP involvement in other critical company committees or workgroups became the norm versus the exception. Moreover, ValueOptions recognized the importance of continually testing and refining internal national crisis response team efforts through frequent drills and planning meetings.

Interestingly, while Hurricanes Katrina and Rita represented a far different incident than September 11th, some of the tenants of a successful response were the same. The magnitude of the destruction left in the aftermath of Hurricane Katrina demanded a swift response. With resources deployed, ValueOptions focused on immediately modifying traditional crisis response efforts to focus on the immediate needs of individuals, including food, clothing and shelter. Many employers had very unique experiences and needs–from utility companies with employees restoring power while simultaneously discovering many of the deceased, to manufacturing companies trying to sustain business with many displaced and missing employees. In many ways the focus was on supporting the organization in formulating their response while consulting with managers and supervisors on how to best maintain a viable workforce. The support provided to employees was initially similar to that received by a soldier on the battlefield, to help them maintain focus to the immediate job they had to do. Workers given the mission to restore communities were given ongoing "inoculations" of psycho-educational information to help them cope with the effects of long term exposure to the devastation. At the same time a process was in place to remove workers when their safety or the safety of their co-workers was in danger due to lack of focus as a result of behavioral health issues. Best practices would support the idea that it is critical that EAPs proactively reach out to all of their customers to lend support and consultation on the ways in which EAP can provide assistance to employers. Immediately following Hurricane Katrina, many employers sought the expertise of their EAP to maintain a healthy and productive workforce. By utilizing the behavioral health expertise of an EAP to the overall organization's strategic response, many were able to maintain a safe and supportive environment for their employees during the days, weeks and months following this tragic event.

HARRIS ROTHENBERG INTERNATIONAL'S (HRI) EXPERIENCE

Harris Rothenberg International (HRI) is located in the heart of the business district of New York City on Wall Street and perhaps more than any other EAP was directly impacted by the events of September 11th. HRI acknowledges as well that what this event and other large scale disasters have reinforced is the understanding that no one crisis response intervention is the solution. HRI focuses on developing a structured intervention according to the specific situation. September 11th in particular, demonstrated how flexible and skilled one must be in crisis response but that having an established framework which assists in responding to such events is helpful but far different than having a pre-conceived idea of what needs to occur. HRI indicates that they approach each critical incident response like a puzzle and while they are well versed in trauma response theory and group dynamics, their response is always one appropriate for the particular situation. Everly (2000) notes that "crisis intervention services must compliment and augment natural recovery and restorative mechanisms." At HRI they may conduct any number of interventions but the ultimate goal is to support the employees in understanding their responses to trauma and addressing their immediate needs while proactively providing back to the organization information that can be used in a consultative manner to assist in the organizational response to the event.

Given the close proximity to the Twin Towers and having numerous clients located in these buildings, HRI has been a sought after partner for a number of clients in their disaster preparedness planning activities. Unlike feedback from some EAPs whose experience with clients outside of the most impacted locations (Washington, DC, and New York City) was that their customers had spent some time on disaster preparedness activities but then were unable to sustain this focus. HRIs experience has been that their customers have been vigilant in maintaining strong disaster preparedness plans with EAP involvement and consultation. HRI also believes that the events of September 11th has increased the recognition among customers that the EAP is an important resource in responding to both large and small scale events impacting the workplace. This is evident by the increase in requests they have received to provide proactive and reactive organizational support for crisis related events.

REGIONAL EAP EXPERIENCES

Workplace Solutions is a regional EAP located in the Chicago area and provides a slightly different perspective in terms of the overall impact of September 11th on their delivery of EAP services. Since September 11th the most notable change in the way in which crisis response services are viewed or offered is that the employers this organization serves are more aware of the types of services that are available and are more likely to call and request assistance. In addition, this organization has widened their repertoire in terms of their typical response. The Vice President of Operations noted that a great deal of what they do in providing on-site crisis response is grief work, for example, situations in which a co-worker has died. This organization now makes certain that they have more of a grief response orientation. In addition, they too acknowledged that their volume of requests for crisis response services has increased significantly since September 11th.

Unlike those EAPs interviewed that were in close proximity to the epicenter of the terrorist attacks, this group shared that while there was an increased focus on disaster preparedness planning following September 11th for a period of time, this focus eventually dissipated for the most part. One of their clients sponsored a half-day seminar on preparing for disasters, and it was well attended. Those in attendance at the workshop expressed that immediately following September 11th, they had good plans and intentions in terms of developing or enhancing their disaster preparedness. Unfortunately, the observation from this EAP was that organizations just did not follow through on these efforts.

For Worker's Assistance Program, a regional EAP located in Austin, Texas, the events of September 11th and other large scale events have had significant impact on how their organization delivers crisis response services. Most notably, they indicated an expansion of the role of their call center capabilities including having it function as a back-up communications hub. In addition, this and other events have required increased training of their internal staff as well as the need to increase the network of possible responders. Since they are located in Texas and were impacted by the '05 hurricane season, they have also increased their ability to link to the public emergency system. Their overall crisis response plan was beefed up significantly; their plan is now practiced and their system readiness is frequently tested.

In terms of their approach to crisis response services they noted that there has been less emphasis on the use of the Mitchell model exclusively, which may not fit for all events. While there is some confusion about the best approach, they have read the literature and modified their approach to best respond to individual and distinct events. While there has been criticism regarding the single session individual psychological debriefing and whether it is a useful treatment for the prevention of post traumatic stress disorder after traumatic incidents, such studies were unable to comment on the use of group debriefing, nor the use of debriefing after mass traumas (Rose et al., 2005). From their perspective, there is a need for a consensus on defining a crisis response. It becomes more confusing as it reaches the company level; an employer may ask for the highest level of response, which may not be the most appropriate for the situation. Many client companies' requests reflect provider recommendations. The recent hurricanes have exposed the weaknesses and brought us out of denial according to Worker's Assistance Program. The one bright spot through all of this is it has required a focus on resiliency and protective factors.

Since September 11th, Worker's Assistance Program has experienced an increase in intensity and frequency of requests, especially with each of the hurricanes. In general, companies are much quicker to ask for help for traumatic events and stabilization of the workplace. Often the requests are overreaction and ask for interventions that would not have been requested previously. While companies are not always sure what they want, or need, the good news is that there is increased sensitivity and awareness.

AN INTERNAL EAP PERSPECTIVE

Prior to September 11th, the anthrax attacks, and the recent catastrophic hurricanes, the focus of internal EAPs was counseling and clinical practice; however, there is now recognition of the need to provide organizational behavioral consultation. These events had a dramatic impact on the psychological well-being of employees and how they think of work. In all of these events, there was great disruption in the workplace that impacted human behavior beyond the single event period. The value of an internal EAP during these events was their assistance in structuring the human behavior response and helping the organization's management address their own actions in successfully supporting the resiliency of their employees. This internal EAP believes that companies now understand the importance of paying attention to human behavior and can no longer discount the human emotions. Companies look to the EAP to help structure management's response to human and organizational behavior, to buoy the needs of their employees, and to remain productive and competitive following a traumatic event.

Strongly supported by the two major unions, one of the more noticeable impacts for this EAP has been that the EAP is now in the organization's official response plan and not just an afterthought. This is the model of connectedness that external EAPs need to strive for in their work with their client companies–to be more than just the response to an event, but also to be a part of the crisis planning for organizational continuity assistance after an event.

AN EMPLOYER PERSPECTIVE

For a large national retail organization their expectations about EAP involvement in crisis events had always been high, but the events of September 11th best reflected their reliance on the EAP. This employer viewed September 11th as an opportunity for the EAP to become a business partner and trusted consultant. Due to the unusual circumstances of September 11th, the corporation requested that the EAP make initial outreach to impacted family members. These services would typically be seen as beyond the role of a traditional EAP and were provided with an initial outreach by a clinician in the event a family member required immediate crisis intervention. Outreach to family members included discussions regarding available services and assessment of immediate family needs. Following this initial outreach by the EAP, follow-up outreach calls were provided by a designated HR contact. EAP clinicians remained on stand-by to consult as needed to the HR professionals or to provide front line support as needed. In the months that followed September 11th this company requested that the EAP hold forums for other impacted corporations and to discuss best practices and lessons learned from the terrorists' attacks for improved disaster preparedness.

Important to one employer was receiving consultation and direction from their EAP; however, instead of taking the stance of the employer assuming what employees need or the EAP telling the company how to respond, the services would be driven by listening to the needs of the impacted employees and then consulting with management on the appropriate services to provide. The employer did not view the consultation and direction as a one time event. Rather this became a series of listening, assessing, consulting, and planning sessions with key representatives from Local Management, HR, Benefits and EAP in a frequent feedback and strategy loop that rolled interventions out in phases and according to the unique needs or issues during that phase of the process. This occurred several times as the effected group approached additional milestones in the recovery process. Today, opportunities to build group cohesion still exist even though it has been four years since the attack. Feedback from managers indicated that all consultation and services were timely and appropriate: individuals felt heard, cared for and treated with dignity as opposed to being treated like a victim. This organization commented that their front-line staff receives a tangible presence that allows them to receive the support, attention and direction required following a critical incident.

As it relates to disaster preparedness, one employer shared that they recognized they need to house emergency numbers and employee data that is accessible in more than one location. In addition, they periodically review organizational procedures for disaster preparedness related to terrorist activities or large scale events. The company had previous experience with responding to natural disasters so certain procedures had been in place such as a Disaster Call Center to help manage human resource needs for extended recovery operations or catastrophic events. Additionally the company has established an emergency financial fund to assist employees impacted by critical incidents.

This employer noted that following September 11th each subsequent widespread disaster event has had its own "personality," requiring both EAP and Management to remain in "listen mode" and thus individualize the response to the needs of the employees as a whole. Different groups, or spheres, of employees may also have unique issues.

CONCLUSIONS

There were clearly certain themes that continued to surface from the series of interviews that were conducted. Most EAPs identified that the greatest difference over the last decade was the increasing number of requests for crisis response assistance since September 11th. Nearly all of those interviewed indicated that the EAP has increased in overall visibility with their customers as a key resource in responding to both small and large scale traumatic events. The experiences of September 11th and other large scale events appear to have raised the level of awareness of crisis response services among management and human resources representatives, resulting in many employers making an increased number of requests for support when traumatic events impact the workplace. Table 5 reflects the experience of three large employers served by ValueOptions and the overall increase in crisis response on-site hours delivered three years prior to and after September 11th. This experience was consistent with that of other EAPs interviewed.

Along with the recognition that no two traumatic events are ever identical, all of the EAPs interviewed emphasized the importance of having an infrastructure that was prepared to respond to large scale disasters–recognizing that existing networks and resources are likely to

TABLE 5

	# of Employees	Average Number of Annual On-Site Hours Requested for Three Years Prior to September 11th	Average Number of Annual On-Site Hours Requested for Three Years Post September 11th
Employer A	35,000	26	233
Employer B	151,000	58	85
Employer C	173,000	31	98

be disrupted in one form or another. Each of the programs interviewed described ways in which they are now better prepared following September 11th to be able to mobilize resources remotely if necessary and to develop support materials and interventions that mirror the evolving needs of the workplace.

Another common theme was that most EAPs interviewed acknowledged that they used a variety of theoretical approaches and techniques in responding to traumatic events. This was recognized as both a positive and negative. The reality of crisis response is that no two incidents are ever exactly the same. As a result, a variety of different interventions may be appropriate. All of the EAPs interviewed indicated that while this has always been the practice, it was in many ways reinforced following the events of September 11th and Hurricane Katrina when responders had to suspend traditional thinking related to crisis response interventions.

Jeffrey Mitchell (2003) summarizing a variety of research on crisis interventions indicates ". . . our first big problem is that everyone talks about 'debriefing' and means something different. This is going to be a monumental problem to overcome and no viable solution has appeared to date." In addition, he suggests "there is much support for the concept of a comprehensive, systematic and multi-tactic approach for early intervention." This process of assessing and individualizing the intervention or approach in a multi-disciplinary manner has been repeated with other widespread natural disasters with success for a coordinated and flexible recovery response over the life cycle of the disaster and restoration of employees to full workplace functionality. In this approach the EAP becomes a resourceful entity that remains with employees and their managers in a flexible and attentive manner to normalize, support, and encourage them throughout their recovery journey. The downside to this multi-theoretical approach is it opens the door for criticism regarding how to measure the impact and success of one intervention technique over another and to what extent research reinforces the selection process of one intervention over another. Tehrani, Cox and Cox (2002) reinforce this indicating that "employers are becoming increasingly aware of the risks to employee wellbeing associated with the traumatic incidents that occur in the workplace. Despite this increased organizational awareness of the need to protect employees from the damaging effects of traumatic events, there has been little provision to help organizations to evaluate their management systems and post trauma interventions." Despite such criticism over the last several years, employers have continually turned to the EAP for assistance in managing traumatic events. In the future and the unfortunate likelihood of the occurrence of other large scale disasters, the role of the EAP will be a critical one. EAPs will continue to be an organizational tool used for proactive consultation and disaster preparedness planning as well as offering flexible and customized responses to meet the health and productivity needs of the workplace.

REFERENCES

Everly, G.S. (2000). Five principles of crisis intervention: Reducing the risk of premature crisis intervention. *International Journal of Emergency Mental Health*, 2, 1-4.

Mitchell, J. (2003). Crisis intervention & CISM: A research summary. www.icisf.org International Critical Incident Stress Management Foundation. 56.

Paul, R., & Masi, D. (2002). Organizational impact: Assessing the needs of employers. *EAPA Exchange*, 16.

Rose, S., Bisson, J., Churchill, R., & Wessely, S. (2005). Psychological debriefing for preventing post traumatic stress disorder (PTSD). The Cochrane Collaboration Database of Systematic Reviews.

Tehrani, N., Cox, S., & Cox, T. (2002). Assessing the impact of stressful incidents in organizations: The development of an extended impact of events scale. *Counselling Psychology Quarterly*, Vol. 15, No. 2, 191.

doi:10.1300/J490v21n03_01

Responding to Workplace Terrorism: Applying Military Models of Behavioral Health and Public Health Response

David M. Benedek
Robert J. Ursano
Carol S. Fullerton
Nancy T. Vineburgh
Robert K. Gifford

SUMMARY. The behavioral health response to the September 11th, 2001, attack at the Pentagon illustrates the principles of a public health approach to the emotional and behavioral consequences of terrorism. This model applies public health principles and consultation. It addresses resiliency, illness, distress, and risk behaviors to maximize return to health and work productivity. In this approach, multidisciplinary teams conduct a program of health surveillance, health education and informational briefings at sites within the workplace and to key leaders. The composition of these teams would differ in other civilian settings and should include an integrated response from security, employee assistance, human resources, communications, and leadership. However, the principles of the approach would remain consistent: identify individuals and populations at high risk for post-attack distress reactions or illness, integrate family support into workplace support, promote individual and

---

[Haworth co-indexing entry note]: "Responding to Workplace Terrorism: Applying Military Models of Behavioral Health and Public Health Response." Benedek, David M. et al. Co-published simultaneously in *Journal of Workplace Behavioral Health* (The Haworth Press, Inc.) Vol. 21, No. 3/4, 2006, pp. 21-33; and: *Workplace Disaster Preparedness, Response, and Management* (ed: R. Paul Maiden, Rich Paul, and Christina Thompson) The Haworth Press, Inc., 2006, pp. 21-33. Single or multiple copies of this article are available for a fee from The Haworth Document Delivery Service [1-800-HAWORTH, 9:00 a.m. - 5:00 p.m. (EST). E-mail address: docdelivery@haworthpress.com].

community resilience, and refer individuals as necessary for further assessment and treatment. doi:10.1300/J490v21n03_02 *[Article copies available for a fee from The Haworth Document Delivery Service: 1-800-HAWORTH.
E-mail address: <docdelivery@haworthpress.com> Website: <http://www.HaworthPress.
com> © 2006 by The Haworth Press, Inc. All rights reserved.]*

KEYWORDS. Terrorism, military applications, workplace response,
behavioral health, public health

INTRODUCTION

In the United States, the workplace has been a frequent target of terrorist attacks. The September 11th, 2001, terrorist attacks targeted the
World Trade Center and the Pentagon. The 2001 anthrax attacks centered on the U.S. Postal Service mail distribution centers, and Congres-
sional and Media office buildings. The 1995 Oklahoma City bombing
of the Alfred P. Murrah Federal Building destroyed a large office complex. Each of these events demonstrates the vulnerability of occupational settings to terrorist attacks.

In response to acts of terrorism such as the September 11th attacks on
both the World Trade Center and the Pentagon, and also in response to
recent natural disasters such as Hurricane Katrina, the United States has
increasingly combined the deployment of civilian and military resources. The events of September 11th heralded a new paradigm dis-
solving the boundaries between homeland security and national defense
to ensure the safety and health of our citizens in their communities and
at their workplaces.

Historical experience with behavioral health response to workplace
terrorism and recent advances in our understanding of the emotional
and behavioral responses to traumatic events suggest that there may be
specific approaches and specific interventions that will reduce the negative impact of terrorism in the workplace. Using a military model for
public health intervention, this article will describe a systematic approach to behavioral health response in the aftermath of a terrorist attack and outline a series of interventions based on such an approach that
can be used by civilian responders in workplace settings. This approach
contributes to individual recovery, but more importantly, fosters *community* resilience–the ability of the community (e.g., workplace) to return to healthy and adaptive functioning after traumatic disruption. In

this approach multidisciplinary teams use a program of health education and informational briefings–occurring at the workplace and outside of traditional health care settings–to promote adaptive responses and diminish post-terrorism distress, grief reactions, and risk behaviors. The approach also integrates worker family support into its workplace response. The multidisciplinary teams of this model perform outreach within the workplace community. By doing so they are able to locate sub-populations at high risk for post-traumatic illness or complicated distress reactions and to overcome barriers to health care access. The teams are also in a position to identify and coordinate appropriate referral for persons who may require further medical or mental health treatment.

A MILITARY MODEL FOR PUBLIC HEALTH/ MENTAL HEALTH RESPONSE TO TERRORISM

In the aftermath of terrorist attack, psychological injuries–like physical injuries–must be addressed in a timely manner. Mental health care must be provided, not only in hospitals or clinics, but also in close proximity to chaos and destruction, where traditional medical resources may be scarce. The disciplines of military and disaster psychiatry address such care demands in non-traditional environments and in mass casualty situations where resources are overwhelmed (Benedek & Ursano, 2005). As the reality of terrorism and the potential for mass casualties within our own national boundaries becomes increasingly likely, military psychiatry highlights the importance of the integration of mental health and public health. The coordination of the efforts of these diverse groups of care providers to assure needs are met and that no sub-group of victims is overlooked is a critical aspect of military and disaster psychiatry.

The September 11th attack on the Pentagon created a sudden and dramatic need for a focused medical response to casualties. In the early phases of recovery operations military medical leaders drew on experience from previous disasters, from experience with terrorist attacks in the United States, and on existing knowledge of behavioral health symptoms in the aftermath of traumatic exposure gleaned from experience with soldiers from the first Gulf War. At the direction of the Army Surgeon General, Army behavioral health consultants in psychiatry, psychology, and social work established an organized plan to address the behavioral health needs of survivors and their families and the military communities of the Pentagon and other rescue and recovery unit communities (Orman et al., 2002).

This Pentagon plan identified resources to provide for the behavioral health needs of involved communities, addressed health care delivery issues, and provided mechanisms for necessary health surveillance. The team of consultants recognized the possibility that many persons physically injured or exposed to the death or injury of others might either desire counseling or benefit from treatment as a result of symptoms arising from exposure to the attack (Ursano & McCarroll, 1990). These consultants recognized the likelihood of the emergence of traditional psychiatric disorders such as Acute Stress Disorder, Posttraumatic Stress Disorder, and depression as recovery efforts continued and the need for sustained availability of resources after recovery efforts concluded (Ursano et al., 1995). The team also identified the potential for the emergence of grief-related distress or complicated grief in a community forced to anticipate the deployment of many of its members to wage what has become known as the "global war on terrorism" (Prigerson et al., 1999; Horowitz et al., 1997). Finally, the consultants recognized the strong relationship between traumatic exposure and medically unexplained physical symptoms. The emergence of "mysterious" post- war syndromes such as the Gulf War Syndrome (Engel & Katon, 1999; Strauss, 1999) and the well-documented findings of increased somatic complaints and disability in survivors of the Murrah building bombing were of considerable concern to the consultants (North et al., 1999). These syndromes can undermine public confidence in the government's ability to protect its citizenry and in so doing serve the goals of terrorism (Holloway & Benedek, 1998). Thus, the plan these military medical consultants implemented–subsequently known as Operation Solace–sought to minimize the occurrence and severity of known psychiatric disorders, to prevent the emergence of a post-attack syndrome of otherwise unexplained somatic symptoms, and to encourage collective and individual mourning. The plan ambitiously undertook these objectives in the face of increased operational tempo in a workplace where the products and services are oriented to national defense and security.

Operation Solace planners first stratified, according to risk, potentially impacted military communities from highest to lowest as follows: injured or physically impacted, family member of someone killed or injured, work colleague of someone killed or injured, emergency responder (military or civilian), other Pentagon employees/visitors during and after the attack, and the national capital region population at large.

Levels of intervention for all risk groups were identified as: community-based, workplace-based, primary care, or specialty mental health clinic-based. Operation Solace sought to optimize the identification of persons requiring each level of care by concentrating resources necessary to identify and assess vulnerable persons in the central circles while still providing outreach resources across all domains of response.

The fundamental manner in which Operation Solace attempted to overcome barriers to health care access was by approaching affected Department of Defense community members *in the workplace* and engaging them as they entered the primary care system for any type of medical care (Orman et al., 1999). Because Pentagon employees have access to the Tri-care network of civilian health care providers (as civilian employees are insured by civilian managed care providers) Tri-care was also integrated into this plan to address health care needs. The most important component of both the immediate and sustained mental health response to the attack was the forward deployment of health professionals. These personnel provided outreach services to offices within the Pentagon and to surrounding civilian offices (which became temporary work facilities for surviving military personnel displaced by the destruction of their offices in the attacks). The professionals (including psychiatrists, psychologists, social workers, mental health nurses and technicians from all branches of the military service) were organized into multidisciplinary teams that fanned out through the Pentagon and surrounding buildings in close coordination with military chaplains. These interventions, defined as "pre-clinical," allowed the team members to engage affected military communities in their work environments in an informal and supportive manner without requiring the collection of identifying data or the opening of medical records. The approach assured maximal access while minimizing premature "medicalization" of appropriate distress reactions or grief.

At the requests of key leaders, the team conducted informational briefings regarding stress response and management, the use of home and workplace support networks, discussing the tragedy with children, and the availability of individualized evaluation and treatment resources put into place after the attack. Pre-clinical team members provided guidance to workplace supervisors, division or section leaders, and senior military and civilian leadership on principles of grief leadership (see Table 1).

Grief leadership refers to actions leaders can take and behaviors that they can encourage and role model to promote mutual support amongst employees sharing common losses (Ingraham, 1987; Wright & Bartone, 1994). Key leaders actively participated in the briefings. At the suggestion of the response teams, these leaders role modeled the sharing of grief and the process of acting as mutual supports for one another in the workplace. While teams were comprised primarily of mental health professionals or paraprofessionals, services rendered were primarily along the lines of preventive health education, enhanced communication, "non-medicalized" support, and identification of those in need of additional assistance.

This public health approach served as the organizing principle directing team movement and concentrating resources. A public health approach focuses on health promotion (raising awareness of the risk) and prevention (interventions to mitigate the risk), in addition to treatment. One of the primary objectives of a public health approach is to protect and enhance "population health," a term that referes to the overall health of a community, organization or group, rather than of an individual (Institute of Medicine, 2003). The Pentagon approach focused efforts on correct identification of high-risk groups and implementation of secondary and tertiary prevention strategies targeting the most vulnerable populations (see Table 2).

Pre-clinical outreach visits were implemented using a "concentric circle" strategy with earliest and highest levels of support afforded to those people who had offices within the destroyed wedge of the Pentagon (and those who were displaced from that part of the building). Support was then allocated to people located in neighboring wedges, followed by first responder and body handler communities, and those who occupied offices near the Pentagon at the time of the attack (see Figure 1). Members of local military units who deployed to provide initial medical response and support to recovery efforts at the Twin Towers were also identified as part of this outreach, and were afforded similar visits upon their return. High levels of specialty staff resources were maintained throughout the holiday season (December and January) and tapered progressively as referrals based from outreach diminished.

In addition to support teams, a Family Support Center was established in the days following the attack. Here, legal assistance, casualty affairs assistance, Red Cross, military relief services, and adult and child mental health counseling were made readily available to family members of attack victims. Temporary lodging, daycare, and child-schooling services augmented the resources of this center based on the unique needs of the community it serviced. The Family Support

TABLE 1. Grief Leadership Actions After Terrorist Attack

Leader Actions	Community Effects
Public announcements and appearances	Provides useful, accurate information; Reestablishes a sense of order/control
Press briefings	Reassures families, others; dispels rumors
Calm demeanor	Provides model behavior
Establishes controls, policies	Provides framework for organizing volunteer efforts efficiently
Organizes memorial services	Demonstrates respect for dead and care for families
Attends funerals, grieves	'Gives permission' for others to grieve
Announces/endorses assistance programs	Shows concern, establishes climate of healing, community support
Provides guidance without excessive policy/ rules	Communicates trust in others' abilities; fosters cooperation, initiative
Describes loss in positive terms: (e.g., heroic sacrifice, an opportunity to learn), recognizes contributions of survivors and helpers	Redirects community energy into rebuilding efforts
Outlines goals for future	Reorients to future objectives; facilitates preparedness for future challenges/losses

Adapted from: Wright KM and Bartone PT, "Community responses to disaster: the Gander plane crash," in Ursano RJ, McCaughey BG, and Fullerton CS, eds., *Individual and Community Responses to Trauma and Disaster: The Structure of Human Chaos,* Cambridge University Press, 1994.

Center, like the pre-clinical outreach teams, served as a referral source for additional individualized counseling as these needs were identified. Treatment was provided at the 10 primary care clinics (including the health care clinic at the Pentagon itself–which was staffed with additional mental health specialists after the attack) across the national capital region and coordinated at remote locations on a case-by-case basis.

As the pre-clinical visits and Family Assistance center identified individuals requiring more immediate higher levels of intervention (and referred those individuals to available resources) these sources also developed a voluntary registry of persons considered at higher risk for subsequent difficulties. These higher risk groups included the children, spouses, close friends, supervisors, or subordinates of someone killed in the attack, persons who sustained physical injury

TABLE 2. Principles of Intervention in a Workplace: The Pentagon Attack Model of Public Health Applied in the Workplace After Terrorist Attack

Pre-clinical, multidisciplinary team approach
Identify high risk groups
Target mental health, resilience, distress and risk behaviors
Identify barriers to care and services
Health education for prevention, assessment, and referral
Informational briefings (leader participation)
Grief leadership
Integrate family support into worker/workplace support

FIGURE 1. Operation Solace Outreach Model

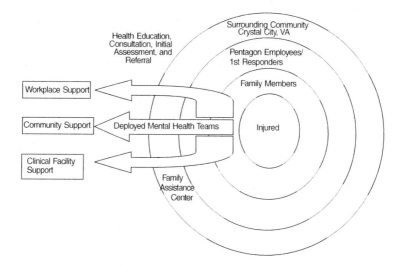

during the attack or evacuation, and those with a history of prior psychiatric illness. Case managers identified within the initial multidisciplinary teams or hired during the operation followed up with these individuals as the weeks and months passed after the initial operation to ensure that emerging difficulties were identified, evaluated, and treated as necessary.

APPLYING MODELS OF MILITARY RESPONSE TO THE WORKPLACE

How would we categorize or describe the populations affected by the September 11th Pentagon attack? Nearly one-half of the Pentagon's 24,000 plus employees are civilians. The building itself sits at the edge of a civilian business and shopping district (Crystal City, Virginia). Despite restricted access to the Pentagon, Washington, D.C.'s underground mass public transportation system has a public stop located directly below the complex. If the plane had crashed into a civilian office high rise in Crystal City, would the response have been very different?

The military response after the September 11th terrorist attacks on the Pentagon illustrates a response model across affected communities that can be applied to civilian workplaces. In a terrorist disaster within corporate or business settings, the application of public health approaches to identifying affected groups, and those in need of mental health intervention, is equally appropriate. However, in the corporate setting, the resources available for the planning and implementation of such a response may be very different from those in the military.

FIGURE 2. Corporate Resources in Terrorism Response Management

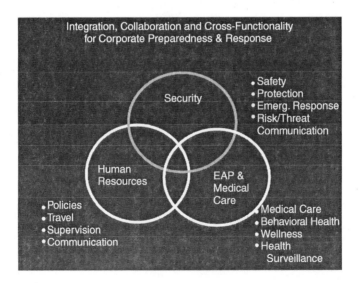

In an exploration of larger corporate preparedness, Center for the Study of Traumatic Stress of the Uniformed Services University School of Medicine, the United States' federal medical school, identified a number of functions involved in crisis management. These corporate assets include: Employee Assistance, Medical/Occupational Health, Corporate Security, Human Resources, Communications, and of course, senior management (Ursano et al., 2005). Many corporations integrate these functions to address the management of employee health and safety in the aftermath of disaster (see Figure 2). With the exception of Medical/ Occupational Health, personnel within these divisions are rarely health or mental health professionals. Nonetheless, many of the persons in these divisions are responsible for employee education, communication, and employee support programs within corporate work settings. Behavioral health professionals should therefore play an important role in educating their colleagues about behavioral response plans and seek to identify and train these resources proactively.

One model of early intervention after disaster recommended by expert panelists is psychological first aid (Watson & Shalev, 2005; National Child Traumatic Stress Network and National Center for PTSD, 2005; Ritchie, 2003). A component of psychological first aid is the establishment of a sense of safety (e.g., through evacuation or protection from re-traumatization). Other components include: facilitation of social connectedness, fostering optimism, decreasing arousal, and restoring a sense of self-efficacy (Center for the Study of Traumatic Stress, 2005) (e.g., through psycho-education, basic relaxation training, and cognitive reframing). Programs of intervention based upon the principles of psychological first aid can be developed and implemented within previously identified corporate resources. Psychological first aid is evidence informed and its principles are in keeping with the previously described military/public health model of response. Education and training in its principles are necessary, but the conduct of psychological first aid requires neither specific mental health expertise nor medical degree. It is intended to be implemented by lay persons. Further research on specific psychological first aid interventions will aid in developing this critical aspect of immediate care.

From within corporate resources, multidisciplinary teams should be assembled after a disaster or critical incident. As security and safety are reestablished in workplace settings, teams based on the integrated military medical model can fan out in concentric circles from the epicenter of a terrorist attack (e.g., site of a suicide bombing, or site of dispersion of a chemical agent). These teams would and identify subgroups that lost family members and/or coworkers. The teams' task would be to engage members of these communities at the workplace in a supportive, non-intrusive manner, offering educational briefings, consulting with leaders and encouraging them to demonstrate the appropriate expression of shared grief through rituals and through their own behaviors (see Table 1). The teams that include mental health care providers would provide informal individual counseling (and appropriate referral) and establish a family resources and assistance center, a model also previously used by affected NYC corporations through their behavioral health providers. Efforts should concentrate resources first in areas where the largest groups of vulnerable or affected populations are identified, and must remain responsive to the potential needs of lower risk-stratified groups through established appropriate networks to available primary and specialty care clinics. Resources can be tapered over time as utilization diminishes–but would be increased during anniversary or holiday periods. An attack involving a corporate workplace would necessarily draw upon not only its own resources, but also contracted and outsourced health services and local responders if appropriate. If the attacks were large scale, multiple business and community resources would be involved in the response.

Local and state governments, in consultation with FEMA would respond to a workplace terrorist attack according to our Federal Response Plan. With appropriate planning, the resources of the community (e.g., schools and other public facilities to serve as triage or care centers), workplace teams, and primary and specialty care across affected communities within and outside of the workplace exposed to the terrorist attack can work in a unified manner to respond.

CONCLUSIONS

The lessons learned from military experience with natural and human made disasters should inform civilian public health interventions in the planning and aftermath of workplace terrorism. Studies of the extent to which specific interventions or combinations (e.g., cognitive behavioral therapy, other exposure-based therapies, pharmacotherapy, or psychological first aid) utilized in public health approaches will actually prevent the development of ASD or PTSD, address complicated grief, or mitigate depression and other distress reactions in their infancy. Even as best practices become clarified on the basis of further study, optimal promulgation will rely on thoughtful identification of the numerous potential communities (including workplaces) and an understanding of the range of distress responses that individuals within these communities may develop. A public health approach to workplace terrorism should employ teams of workplace or corporate resources in outreach efforts. Given the significant roles that Corporate Security, Human Resources, Employee Assistance, Corporate Communications, and Medical/Occupational Health play in corporate planning for response to terrorism, members of these divisions should form the basis for such teams. Multidisciplinary teams trained in advance, with the assistance of mental health professionals, could be rapidly deployed after a terrorist attack. As occurred in the aftermath of the Pentagon attack, these teams could provide workplace management, employees, and their families with coping skills and techniques. Through health education and workplace briefings they could deliver pre-clinical preventive management to affected subgroups, diminish the negative consequences of distress reactions, and promote adaptive grief responses. Finally, they could help to appropriately identify high risk groups and refer individuals in need of additional counseling or medical care. This public health approach supports leadership and assists employees and their families, and in so doing fosters workplace resilience.

REFERENCES

Benedek DM, Ursano RJ (2005). "Military and disaster psychiatry," in Sadock BJ & Sadock VA, eds., *Comprehensive Textbook of Psychiatry*, 8th edition. Baltimore, MD: Williams and Wilkins.

Center for the Study of Traumatic Stress (2005). "Psychological First Aid: How You Can Support Well-Being in Disaster Victims" (fact sheet). www.usuhs.mil/psy/CSTSPsych1stAid.pdf

Engel CC, Katon WJ (1999). "Population and need-based prevention of unexplained symptoms in the community." In Institute of Medicine. Strategies to protect the health of deployed U.S. forces: medical surveillance, record keeping, and risk reduction. Washington DC, National Academy Press.

Holloway HC, Benedek DM (1999). "The changing face of terrorism and military psychiatry." *Psychiatric Annals*, 29(6): pp. 373-375.

Horowitz MJ, Siegel B, Holen A, Bonanno GA, Milbrath C, Stinson CH: "Diagnostic criteria for complicated grief disorder." *Am J Psychiatry*, 1997; 154: 904-910.

Ingraham LH (1987). Grief leadership. In "The human response to the gander military air disaster: a summary report." Division of Neuropsychiatry Report No. 88-12. Washington DC: The Walter Reed Army Institute of Research, pp. 10-12.

Institute of Medicine (2003). "Preparing for the psychological consequences of terrorism: A public health strategy." Washington D.C.: The National Academies Press.

McCaroll, JE, Ursano RJ, Fullerton CS et al. (2001). "Effects of exposure to death in a war mortuary on posttraumatic stress disorder symptoms of intrusion and avoidance." *Journal of Nervous and Mental Disease*, 189, pp. 44-48.

National Child Traumatic Stress Network and National Center for PTSD, Psychological First Aid: Field Operations Guide, September, 2005. www.ncptsd.va.gov/pfa/PFA_9_6_05-final.pdf

North CS, Nixon SJ, Shariat et al. (1999). Psychiatric disorders among survivors of the Oklahoma City Bombing, *JAMA*, 282, pp. 755-762.

Orman DT, Robichaux RJ, Crandell EO et al. (2002). "Operation Solace: Overview of the mental health intervention following the September 11, 2001 Pentagon attack." *Military Medicine*, 167 (supple 4), pp. 47.

Prigerson HG, Shear MK, Jacobs SC, Reynolds CF 3rd, Maciejewski PK, Davidson JR, Rosenheck R, Pilkonis PA, Wortman CB, Williams JB, Widiger TA, Frank E, Kupfer DJ, Zisook S (1999). "Consensus criteria for traumatic grief: a preliminary empirical test." *Br J Psychiatry*, 174: pp. 67-73.

Ritchie EC (2003) "Mass violence and early intervention: Best practice guidelines." *Primary Psychiatry*, 10(8): pp. 43-48.

Strauss SE (1999). "Bridging the gulf in war syndromes." *Lancet*, 353, pp. 162-3.

Ursano R, Fullerton C, Kao T et al. (1995). "Longitudinal assessment of posttraumatic stress disorder and depression after exposure to traumatic death." *Journal of Nervous and Mental Disease*, 183, pp. 36-42.

Ursano RJ, Vineburgh NT, Gifford RK, Benedek DM, Fullerton CS (2005). "Workplace Preparedness for Terrorism." (Report of Findings (unpublished) to Alfred P. Sloan Foundation).

Ursano, RJ, McCarroll JE (1990). "The nature of the traumatic stressor: Handling dead bodies." *Journal of Nervous and Mental Disease*, 178, pp. 396-398.

Watson P, & Shalev A (2005). "Assessment and treatment of adult acute response to traumatic stress." *CNS Spectrums*, 10(2), pp. 96-98.

Wright KM, Bartone PT (1994). "Community responses to disaster: The Gander plane crash," in Ursano RJ, McCaughey BG, and Fullerton CS, eds., *Individual and Community Responses to Trauma and Disaster: The Structure of Human Chaos*, Cambridge University Press, 1994, pp. 267-284.

doi:10.1300/J490v21n03_02

Case Studies of Federal Occupational Health's EAP Responses to Natural Disasters

Diane Stephenson
Dorothea U. Schneider

SUMMARY. Employee assistance professionals have increasingly been called upon to address the emotional and mental health needs of customer organizations and their employees in response to large-scale natural or man-made disasters. In doing so, employee assistance program (EAP) professionals must use a repertoire of responses that encompasses a broad range of interventions, generally anchored in an understanding of and focus on the organization and its culture, mission, management and labor concerns, and other critical characteristics. The EAP's fallback response to a crisis affecting the workplace is often a critical incident stress debriefing or close variant of it. However, EAPs can best serve their customers at all levels with interventions attuned to an understanding of the workplace culture gained through a consultative relationship with management, while factoring in the nature of the disaster, the length of time and characteristics of the disaster's aftermath, and the nuances of the employees' physical and emotional needs throughout the entire disaster response and recovery process.

This article highlights these issues through the presentation of two case studies, gained from the hurricane response activities of the Federal Occupational Health (FOH) EAP. FOH, a service unit within the U.S. Department of Health and Human Services' Program Support Center,

[Haworth co-indexing entry note]: "Case Studies of Federal Occupational Health's EAP Responses to Natural Disasters." Stephenson, Diane, and Dorothea U. Schneider. Co-published simultaneously in *Journal of Workplace Behavioral Health* (The Haworth Press, Inc.) Vol. 21, No. 3/4, 2006, pp. 35-58; and: *Workplace Disaster Preparedness, Response, and Management* (ed: R. Paul Maiden, Rich Paul, and Christina Thompson) The Haworth Press, Inc., 2006, pp. 35-58. Single or multiple copies of this article are available for a fee from The Haworth Document Delivery Service [1-800-HAWORTH, 9:00 a.m. - 5:00 p.m. (EST). E-mail address: docdelivery@haworthpress.com].

doi:10.1300/J490v21n03_03

has 60 years of experience working in partnership with its federal agency customers to deliver comprehensive occupational health services to improve the health, safety, and productivity of the federal workforce. FOH's EAP contracts with vendor organizations to provide direct employee assistance, work/life, and related services to more than 1.3 million federal employees. The first case study describes (from the first person perspective) an on-site, multi-focused EAP intervention at a federal facility. The second case study describes management consultation with the U.S. Postal Service in response to major hurricane activity. doi:10.1300/J490v21n03_03 *[Article copies available for a fee from The Haworth Document Delivery Service: 1-800-HAWORTH. E-mail address: <docdelivery@haworthpress.com> Website: <http://www.HaworthPress.com> © 2006 by The Haworth Press, Inc. All rights reserved.]*

KEYWORDS. Crisis management, disaster response, deployment, EAP, natural disasters

CASE STUDY NO. 1:
ON-SITE ORGANIZATIONAL AND INDIVIDUAL INTERVENTIONS

The Background

On August 29, 2005, the powerful blows of Hurricane Katrina were felt, not so much in Florida as initially feared, but in other Gulf Coast states–Mississippi, Louisiana and Alabama. The disaster carried all the features that increased stressfulness related to traumatic incidents, namely, physical harm, separation from loved ones, separation from home, damage/destruction to home, and multiple losses. Additional potent features followed; continuing new sources of injury, harm, and insecurity from flooding and continued high waters; chaos and the breakdown of social order; a refuge from the storm (the Superdome) that added additional trauma; lack of communication; and the overwhelming feeling that little was happening to ameliorate the destructive after-effects for the victims. Time seemed to be standing still when response and support were needed by the victims, some of whom also bore the role of responder or rescuer.

Just a few days before (August 24 and 25), several disaster response experts presented a Behavioral Health Awareness Training for Terrorism and Disasters as Hurricane Katrina was storming and swirling, gaining intensity, and threatening Florida, where one of the training instructors lived. Throughout the training, Dr. James M. Shultz of the Disaster Epidemiology Emergency Preparedness Center at the University of Miami kept checking weather reports and anxiously expressed his concerns about the possibility of Hurricane Katrina hitting Florida and wreaking havoc in his own community.

The training emphasized certain points (Shultz & Flynn, 2005), points which became poignantly real several days later:

- Features of disasters that determine stressfulness depend upon: the scope of the destruction related to injuries, deaths, damage; the physical harm to self or loved ones; the disruption of support systems such as separation from loved ones, displacement, disruption of home, work, or school; the intensity and duration of the impact; if there are multiple extreme events; if there are multiple losses such as home, basic necessities, personal items, vehicles, jobs, schools, health care, community and social support.
- Psychological casualties always outnumber medical casualties.

The first author had an opportunity to work directly in the affected site as an EAP responder. A week after Katrina struck, the first author was deployed to provide psychological support to persons working for a federal organization in an office building in Slidell, Louisiana; an organization that suddenly went from focusing on an information technology (IT) mission to providing a "Safe Haven" for hurricane responders and some victims. What follows is a first person account of this experience.

Slidell is just north of New Orleans across the eastern edge of Lake Pontchartrain. Slidell was severely hit by the hurricane and by the subsequent flooding. Reportedly, 80 percent of the housing stock suffered damage. The office building that was to be the home and work setting for the EAP responder for the next several days had become a safe haven for the organization's employees who remained in the area, some of their family members, as well as for responders and rescuers who lived in or came to the area to help. This refuge evolved at the site due to several fortuitous circumstances: It was on high enough ground to be spared from flooding; had its own generator because of the IT focus; had some kitchen facilities; and, critically, had two showers each for men and women. But, most of all, it was able to serve as a shelter and staging location because of the dedicated employee and management staff who offered their friendly and unending support to rescuers and responders.

Many of the factors cited by Schultz (2005) that cause increased disaster stress were present after Hurricane Katrina in this situation: deaths, injuries, widespread damage, displacement from home, complete disruption from daily life including all school and community activities; disruption of support systems; multiple losses such as homes, cars, possessions; and displacement of loved ones. Additionally, in the early days after Hurricane Katrina struck, there was lack of communication both within and outside the affected areas. And, the news that was heard engendered a strong sense of insecurity and uncertainty as to whether and when help would arise. There was a fear of general lawlessness and lack of law enforcement in the affected areas, creating additional threats to the safety and security of family, possessions, and self.

The Setting

My charge at Slidell was voiced in a few words: Provide support to the responders. I was the "embedded EAP," sleeping on a cot in what, in normal times, was someone's work cubicle, across the workspace from a family that acquired a couple of cubicles for mom, dad, and two small children. I had no office and no place to "set up shop." Outside contact via landline, cell phone, or Internet was at times nonexistent, or limited and spotty at best. Fortunately, several joint-use computers with satellite access were set up toward the end of the week I was there and were available for critical communication. This Internet connectivity allowed persons to access the Federal Emergency Management Agency (FEMA) for "blue roof" service, housing registration, and other services. ("Operation Blue Roof" is FEMA's program for installing blue plastic sheeting on roofs that have been damaged by hurricanes in order to mitigate additional damage that could result from rain.) I had access to a copy machine for my handouts and informational sheets. My work was done at the lunchroom tables, the outside patio or parking lot, in the halls, the occasional office I could appropriate, or on folding chairs under a live oak tree.

A senior employee of the facility picked me up at the Baton Rouge airport. He let me know that my presence was not requested by the facility employees themselves, but by their central office, which was far away from the ravages of Katrina. Central office thought the Slidell office could benefit from EAP help; the employees did not necessarily hold the same view. In fact, my presence might take time away from their newfound mission. The comments were understandable in the situation–caregivers give care, they do not need care.

On the way from the Baton Rouge airport to Slidell, we saw uprooted trees, billboards blown to new locations, roofs missing, and trees splitting homes. Once in Slidell, my host drove past neighborhoods–one totally devastated except for the big, new house on the hill, looking bereft, but somehow managing to stand on alone. We had to show identification to local police or military guards before entering any subdivision. Looters, sightseers, opportunists, and wanderers were not welcome. My host showed me his children's wooden climbing gym, now lodged at the entrance to the subdivision, as though welcoming children to an upside down fun park three blocks from their home. Already, eight days after the hurricane and flooding, homeowners had started the clean up. Lined up along the street we saw rolls of wet, moldy carpeting, upholstered chairs, smelly refrigerators, and unusable appliances and furniture waiting to be hauled off to who knows where. Plywood signs with the handwritten words Boil Water were set against poles at many major intersections. There was no electricity except for those who had their own generators and of course no street lights. You had to stop, look, and listen at all intersections. There were long lines of cars leading to the abandoned discount store, now used as a FEMA site for the distribution of water and ice. Posted at the site were other handwritten signs with such entries as: "missing, black lab, answers to Micky, contact . . ."

I foraged in a shed behind the office building for bedding that had been dropped off by the military–cots, sleeping bags, blankets as well as personal supplies and donated clothing. I organized my space in my cubicle (a sense of personal space in a situation like this becomes very important) and headed off to my main workstation, the lunchroom.

Although all employees of the facility had been accounted for, not a lot was known about their family members and how they may have been impacted. Employees of the facility, who in their other lives were administrative and IT staff, suddenly became cooks feeding over 800 people a day and providing shelter for 200 persons per day. Someone had written "Club Fed B&B" in large block letters on a whiteboard propped at the entrance to the lunchroom, bringing a smile to all who entered this federal facility. Someone had managed to hook up three or four washers and dryers outside the loading ramp. Others took up the role of laundry workers for, what the handwritten sign termed, the "Fluff and Fold"–a sorely needed and much valued task for those who, in the stinking heat and humidity, were trudging through debris, maintaining security in the neighborhoods, caring for abandoned pets, or performing on the search teams. Others seeking refuge, cleaned up the lunchroom, made coffee (a never-ending task), assured security, cleaned lavatories, or talked and laughed with the responders. I camped out with the rest, pouring coffee and wiping tables and dishing up food.

City of Slidell public works staff and police, staff from the Slidell Memorial Hospital, Louisiana State Police, Arkansas State Police, Greenville County South Carolina EMT, Noah's Wish, Greater Houston Rescue Dogs, FEMA, and the U.S. Marine Corps represented a few of the groups of responders and supporters who received comfort, stayed, slept, and/or ate at the facility. Responders received nurturing at the safe haven. Food, water, air conditioning, a place to sit and relax, and, for those who needed a home, their own cot and a hot shower, a place to talk, or not talk, about their experiences, their worries.

With little privacy and few resources, the setting is totally different from any kind of "traditional" EAP setting. Your clientele are the same persons that you eat with, wash up with, and cross paths with in the hallway in your pajamas or sweats. Although all of the activities engaged in could be considered under the rubric of critical incident stress management support services, in the broadest sense, some other terms used to describe these kinds of EAP/psychological activities and functions are: embedded social worker/psychologist/EAP (military term), psychological first aid, organizational and individual psychological surveillance, supportive counseling, problem-solving, and cognitive behavioral approaches.

One refugee, as he was chain-smoking outside, told me that his home was destroyed. He couldn't locate his wife who was seriously ill and supposed to find safety up north somewhere. Later, he found out she heard he had died. "For a dead man, I'm doing pretty good." Several persons felt guilty because "we only lost shingles off our roof and had a little flooding."

What does the EAP do? Listen; see if individuals need a bottle of water, a snack, or use of a Blackberry with a spotty connection; inform them that the computer connections had just been set up and they might be able to communicate with family and get registered with FEMA; let them know where to find me and other resources; give handouts; normalize emotional responses; listen more.

One person observed that we were "in a bubble." For the most part, there was little outside communication. No TV, no radio. This situation led to both an actual lack of communication with the outside world and with the facility's headquarters office, as well as a psychological separation, which created apprehension and misunderstandings, as well as a strong sense of self-reliance.

A number of the responders were victims themselves. Their homes were destroyed, their families evacuated to places far away. It was hard for them to communicate with family, or worse, they had not heard from family members and feared they were lost. While working to provide support and care for the rescuers and other responders, they had their own losses to face. Several told me that their helping roles gave them the emotional energy to maintain themselves despite their own losses; they were able to refocus energy and worry on something helpful and purposeful. They were helping others, performing a life-sustaining mission.

I had a conversation with a mother who, along with her husband and their two-week old baby, took refuge in the building. She was conflicted because she knew that the baby brought great joy and the hope of new life to the other people staying in the facility. Yet, she had to be especially careful to protect the infant from any infections or illnesses carried by the responders. She needed to take care of herself and the baby first. She sought ways in how to give weary responders the pleasure of seeing the infant, while remaining at a physical distance from them.

My greatest concern for these employees and other responders was their reduced attention to their own basic needs–primarily sleep and down-time. Fortunately, food was plentiful, as was bottled water, ice, and coffee. Local restaurants all closed due to damage, loss of staff, and lack of electricity, donated food from their freezers and storage shelves. So, the content of the meals ranged from steaks and hamburgers cooked out back by the staff of the facility over huge grills, to spaghetti and sausage, rice, grits, and canned foods. Whatever the food was, it was heartily eaten by all. The focus was on meat and starches. Fresh fruits and vegetables were very hard to come by.

One person had just gone back to the family home for the first time. What the hurricane did not destroy, the flood did–the family Bible, pictures of the children when young, and a collection of rare books. But what hit this person most while returning to our refuge was seeing people trudging wearily down the street–people with all their possessions in a shopping carts looking for water and safety and rest. Another observed, "I believe that the empathy we feel for others who are much worse off than we helps drive much of the altruism you witness."

In a situation like this, it is not unusual to hear a manager state that they are working with minimal rest or time off, so that "my employees do not feel the way I do." And, the importance of leadership in such a crisis cannot be underestimated in establishing common goals, a sense of urgency, and identifying and leveraging the talents of all available resources. In this situation, the management team was working around the clock. They were deeply motivated to continue to manage this new, critical mission of the organization. As "safe haven" managers, they assured that all within their scope of care were safe and secure. They followed the maxim the group had zeroed in on in the first days of their transformation from an IT office to the Club Fed B&B–"Do the right thing in the right way for the right reasons." With the management staff, the EA professional spent time listening, looking at the situation from different angles, shared observations, recommending interventions, and doing some reality testing: can you be all things to all people in need? Also focusing on manager self-care–do you have any down-time at all? When are you sleeping? What connections and communication are you able to have with your own family? What support can I give?

At the lunch tables were a number of Marines, some seeming too young to be there, but who had already lost members of their group when they were in Iraq recapturing Fallujah. A young Marine was very conversant about post-traumatic stress disorder (PTSD), discussing his adjustment back to the U.S. after being on the battle line: "What they need is an adjustment-to-the-U.S. class; we did okay adjusting to going to Iraq, but coming back to the U.S. was a different story." An employee of the organization succinctly observed, "We lost homes and possessions; they lost comrades in support of freedom. This, in a way, fuelled many of us to work harder."

Several individuals had to leave their pets in their homes after the flooding had subsided, returning every night to give clean water and food and attention, to make sure the pet-door worked and that pets weren't overcome with heat. Some did this only to find pets gone after well-meaning souls had removed them to temporary animal shelters without leaving a note for the owner. The dog or cat was a friend, a comfort. Talking about the pet was a safe focus for personal fears and anxieties about what would happen next. Where would the family live? What work could family members get since many employers were closed down? What would happen to them and their trusty pets, which were now separated from them?

A representative from a public service department, who may never have been characterized as cheerful, used the opportunity at the safe haven to recount with great bitterness his stories of rescue–they didn't like how I helped them into the boat; they didn't like the boat; they asked why I didn't come sooner; they're so ungrateful. He was caught in these discouraging and obsessive thoughts. We talked outdoors a long time, moving from venting, to explaining, to exploring, to problem-solving. What would give him some distance from the issues and unending days and hours on the job? Then, conducting an informal screening–Where are you sleeping? Do you have any space of your own? Are you eating? Anyone to talk to? Do you end up getting tears in your eyes as you're doing your work? Ever encounter anything like this before?

Outside of this setting, our EAP only served a small portion of the population passing through the facility. I tried to track down the EAP numbers for the different groups of responders bunking in the facility, as well as some general support numbers for them to use once they left. I prepared a flyer with critical numbers including our number for those who didn't know who or where to call. I placed them in the lunch-room, along with other tip sheets like: What Should I Tell My Children; Survivors of Disasters; Coping with the Aftermath of a Flood; Hurri-cane Disaster Relief; Assistance for Children after a Hurricane; and Su-pervisors and Union Representatives Guide to Helping Employees. I distributed the informational sheets to employees at the daily 9 p.m. staff meetings. Even though all insisted that their children were doing fine, I suggested they take the handouts, keep them in mind. Children come up with questions, comments, behaviors that can surprise us par-ents, and catch us off guard not knowing how to respond. I noticed other handouts joining mine at the front table, as well as Bibles in camou-flage-colored covers. A number of individuals came up to me later, say-ing they happened to glance at, then read, a handout. What did I think about this concern, or that?

The rescue and responder setting promotes a macho "do not worry about me, I just keep doing my job" attitude and approach. The situation calls for it, and the responders with this mentality either self-select the role and/or cloak themselves in the role as is demanded by the situation. At the same time, most formal responder groups now also receive train-ing in the psychological aspect of disasters, in post-traumatic stress dis-order, and have received or become familiar with some form of critical incident stress service. This is a positive step that at least allows for the discussion of the psychological effects of disasters.

Spirituality and religious beliefs became visible and reassuring to many during the aftermath. One particularly eloquent man offered an oral prayer every evening that many persons chose to participate in. People in a disaster response situation may benefit from an identified quiet area in which to pray, meditate, reflect, and find some peace.

Summary of EAP Activities and Interventions

At Slidell, formal group critical incident stress debriefings were not held and were not determined to be helpful or productive at the time. The disruption due to the hurricane and flooding was still very immediate and continuing to occur. Staff were finally hearing if all their fellow employees were accounted for; responders were continuing to search homes; persons were just beginning to go back to their homes to be confronted by the damage; families were separated.

My focus was on attending to individual and team needs in a flexible and non-prescriptive way. Specific activities then included:

Organizational Screening

This involved assessing group resilience, adaptive functioning, and the mutual social support of the group. In this case the group included the employees of the facility who provided physical care and shelter for themselves and responders, as well as some of the family members of employees, and the responders who took shelter there. Group functioning is critical in a situation of this nature since lack of social support is linked to a heightened risk for stress disorders.

In this instance, the employees as a team were functioning adaptively. They had each other and a strong management structure to provide support. They pitched in to provide physical support, were organized and purposeful, and took on new and different roles. Management provided direction, support, care, and vigilance. The facility head led informative group staff meetings every evening to assure that information was shared. Many of the employees and family members were former military. They knew the importance of following a structure and system, which provided an additional sense of security and feeling that "things were under control" here, even though they may not have been under control outside the grounds of the facility. The employees and the facility itself provided social, emotional, and physical support as well as a sense of safety and security to the responders who slept, rested, talked, and ate at the facility. Although working hard and without much opportunity for respite, the team had created a natural support system, reducing the risk of stress disorders in themselves and the responders.

Surveillance for Mental Health and Substance Abuse Issues and Screening for Symptoms

This involved maintaining ongoing surveillance of all persons encountered for heightened mental health issues, then conducting on-site psychological screening of those with heightened symptoms and/or circumstances. In this setting, you will use your clinical and organizational surveillance and assessment skills every moment you are on-site. You will need to take additional steps when your professional assessment so indicates, making it important to identify all potential organizational, medical, and mental health resources.

Consultation with Management

Consultation with senior and middle management covered observations and issues about the situation, specific persons they had concerns about and would like the EAP to monitor, the interaction of the disaster with other issues going on at the workplace (in this situation, the disaster came on top of distressing news about a facility closing), and the manager's own self-care. The EAP gives feedback to and discusses with management the workgroup's functioning and needs, group emotional issues, and actions to take to support positive and adaptive coping. Often, it gives managers a sense of security just knowing a mental health professional is "on the ground," if needed. The EAP and senior management also plan EAP follow-up and next steps, as well as longer term emotional health needs of employees and employee groups.

Psychological First Aid

These activities were generally done informally, either individually or with informal groups (e.g., people working on the same task, gathering in the halls, smoking on the patio, eating in the lunchroom). Working on-site as an "embedded EAP" involves utilizing the core actions and perspective of psychological first aid. Make your presence known, be visible, be available, and follow the lead of the persons you are working with. Select a private room, secluded corner, or outdoors area that you and the individual can go if privacy is needed. With reference to the Field Operations Guide developed by the National Center for PTSD (2005), the core psychological first aid actions taken in this situation included: ·

- *Non-intrusive contact and engagement.* When the EA professional is on-site 24/7, visible and living among the responders and victims, the EA professional can be approached casually and conveniently by anyone who wishes to talk. If others on-site have badges and/or T-shirts identifying their roles and affiliations, the EAP should follow the same protocol. This helps give you legitimacy and normalizes your role alongside other support and response roles. It is convenient and easy to sit at the lunch table and begin conversations with the others. Offering a bottle of water, soap and towel to those returning from a 14 to 18 hour day working at a disaster site may provide comfort as well as the small boost needed at that moment. Make yourself known, and show that you are approachable and can be called on anytime.
- *Provide emotional comfort.* Sometimes just your presence, or giving a phone number to call should it be needed, or listening meets a need. Due to your presence at staff meetings or your contact with management, you may have access to useful information that the others needing support at your site may not have heard. Sharing appropriate information can give a greater sense of security and order to the recipient.
- *Stabilization.* Oftentimes, the effects of the accumulation of the devastation, the fatigue, and the immediate sense of hopelessness can overwhelm a distraught individual. This is normal and common. The counselor can calm, support, and stabilize.
- *Practical assistance.* At my site, practical assistance sometimes just amounted to letting individuals know that the computers were set up and connected in the conference room, that the "blue roof" persons from FEMA were coming on site the next day, and similar practical pieces of information.
- *Connection with supports.* Giving phone number and Internet access information on helpful Websites, EAP, medical, and disaster assistance is both practical and supportive. I also enlisted the assistance of the responders themselves to help me find the EAP and other resource numbers for the various responder groups that domiciled at the facility. In addition to helping me, searching for the EAP number served to remind the responder that his or her own EAP was available.

Supportive One-to-One Counseling

Counseling that focuses on personal reactions, symptoms, and coping strategies related to the impact of the disaster serves to normalize stress reactions and support self-efficacy. Cognitive behavioral approaches can be utilized to help persons identify their reactions and symptoms, look at any maladaptive beliefs, and problem-solve adaptive responses and reactions.

Educational Information

Handouts and discussion about such topics as the range of expected responses to traumatic exposures, stress reactions, longer term concerns, coping, and resources serves to strengthen personal coping strategies. It is important to assure that individuals have the EAP phone number, understand they can call anytime for counseling and consultation, know the EAP's range of services, and realize that the services are available during and following the disaster, when secondary issues may arise. Although many responder groups voice support for psychological support, individual responders generally say it is good for others, but they may still be apprehensive about availing themselves of services, especially during the early days of the response. So, give information and resource numbers that they can take with them. Have your material out and available, whether it seems people are taking advantage of it or not.

The Importance of Maintaining Boundaries

As mental health professionals, we are sensitive to issues of boundaries in our professional relationships with our clients. In a traditional work setting, we have our offices; we set times to meet with clients; we have comfortable boundaries that accompany those structures. In a setting where you share food and living quarters under basic conditions without privacy and you are the only mental health or medical worker on site, the situation is quite different. It is important that the EAP responder maintain a professional role appropriate to the situation and not add to the stress or discomfort of those with whom we are working. This means engaging in supportive listening and the other activities addressed in a friendly, steady, and accessible fashion, but not being overly chummy or overly commiserating. To maintain boundaries while having a personal outlet and obtaining needed support for yourself, consult daily with a colleague by phone or e-mail. Maintaining a private journal may help release personal tensions. Wearing a T-shirt, polo shirt, or vest with the name of your EAP or similar identifier can help, in a subtle way, to remind yourself and others of your specific role in that situation.

Identify a "Champion" in the Organization

In a situation like this, it is critical for the EA professional to quickly identify and leverage a champion in the organization. That person will be invaluable in understanding the dynamics, nuances, people, and background of the situation. Not having such information or support will make the EA responder's job more difficult. The earlier that connection can be accomplished, the greater success the EA responders will have in gaining the cooperation and trust of those whom they are there to serve.

EAP as Part of the Disaster Plan

An individual who generously helped me quickly gain an overview of the dynamics observed that the initial defensiveness I observed was in part due to the fact that I was sent by the headquarters office. The process of introducing the EA professional into a disaster situation would be cleaner and less encumbered with such issues if each organization's disaster plan clearly includes the participation and involvement of the EAP and all are made aware of this before a disaster strikes.

Practical Tips

Most EAPs involved in critical incident response efforts have kits with supplies, handouts, and other materials packed and ready to go at a moment's notice. In addition to the contents of the kits and standard travel supplies, when an EA professional may be living on-site under very basic circumstances the following tips may be helpful.

- Have your work identification badge with you, and arrange to get any other ID badges from the organization you are visiting as soon as you are able.
- Take at least one paper copy of all appropriate handouts, flyers, and business cards with you, since you may not have computer connectivity to download them. A CD or flash memory device loaded with your handouts is convenient if you will have electricity.
- Wear cargo pants or something else that is durable, dirt and wrinkle proof, and has lots of pockets.
- Response team members coming to help out in other location wear T-shirts with their team's identification on them (e.g., Los Angeles

Police Department, Noah's Wish, etc.). You and your team should also have T-shirts, polo shirts or vests with appropriate identification.

- Take bug spray, sun screen, a sleeping bag sheet, easily transportable food products used everyday (instant coffee, tea bags), vitamins and medication! (A large percentage of responders pick up colds and flu; allergies are likely to be heightened.)

- If you have more than one cell phone or wireless connection devices that use different service providers, you may want to bring all, since connections for some service providers will go through, others not. Possession of a satellite phone could be most helpful.

- At sites that become centers for hurricane support and response, we recommend establishing stress management centers at the earliest possible moment, so the center becomes quickly identified and known by staff and management. Responders are more apt to seek out a stress management center, rather than EAP counselor's office. These stress management centers are different from standard EAP offices in several critical ways. First, although the centers house an EAP counselor's office, their scope is considerably broader than that. The stress management center can contain the following: a relaxation room with cots or couches, CD players, and soothing CDs; a private, quiet room for prayer, meditation, silence; counselor office; a "memory wall" with butcher paper and markers that persons can put their thoughts, memories, hopes and prayers on; a "library" with copies of all your tips sheets, resource numbers, critical incident guides. In your center, you can also hold stress management groups, group and individual debriefings, grief groups, and supportive counseling, relaxation or meditation training groups, and other presentations or educational groups. (Recognizing that space may be an issue at some sites, rooms will need to be multipurpose.) With this setup, the center quickly becomes a "destination" associated with comfort and support for response staff.

On-site EAP presence after a disaster is valuable to management, employees, responders, and to those supporting response, rescue, and recovery efforts. The EAP can help reduce stress effects, support adaptive coping, regularize responses and activities, and restore touchstones on a short term, immediate basis. Though perhaps not as critical as food, water, or sleep, EAP support in the early days following a disaster helps create the necessary environment and perspective to normalize an abnormal situation and to stabilize the foundation for adaptive recovery.

CASE STUDY NO. 2:
THE EAP'S DISASTER RESPONSE
FOR THE U.S. POSTAL SERVICE

Background

In 2004, and again in 2005, we experienced the trauma of multiple major hurricanes in the United States. Hurricanes Charley, Frances, Ivan and Jeanne pummeled Florida in quick succession in the late summer and fall of 2004, creating a mosaic of physical destruction thorough the state but with a relatively limited loss of life. Property damage was extensive, and the misery toll was high due to lack of electricity in some areas for a prolonged period. Extended loss of electricity has a profound impact on the quality of life. Lighting, air-conditioning, traffic lights, running water, gasoline pumps, and communication systems are all affected by loss of electricity. In 2005, we had catastrophic Hurricane Katrina affecting Louisiana, Mississippi and Alabama, followed by Hurricanes Rita and Wilma in the Gulf States and Florida. What made Katrina particularly catastrophic was the breakdown of several levees in Louisiana resulting in extensive urban flooding. The death toll and destruction of housing and infrastructure in coastal Mississippi and Louisiana, especially in the City of New Orleans, are hard to fathom.

One of our key customers, the U.S. Postal Service (USPS), was significantly affected by these hurricanes. As a federal organization that provides an essential service to the public, the Postal Service must secure the mail and get its operations up and running as quickly as is safely possible, despite structural damage to facilities, flooding, lack of electricity and a workforce that is also personally affected. The USPS provides universal service to all households, so it has facilities throughout the region, ranging from large plants that employ thousands, to one-person post offices.

To understand how we provide EAP critical incident stress management (CISM) services to our Postal customer, a brief review of the structure of the program and the customer may be helpful. FOH has an agreement with USPS to provide comprehensive EAP services to its employees. The USPS EAP is a joint program with management and the two largest postal unions, the National Association of Letter Carriers and The American Postal Workers Union. FOH contracts with a vendor agency that provides all the direct service field staff and a national service center. FOH manages the vendor in its delivery of EAP services. USPS consists of Districts (typically a large metropolitan area or a state),

Areas composed of several states, and Headquarters. FOH EAP provides at least one full-time EAP consultant in each of approximately 80 Postal districts. Our EAP consultants work in close consultation with their USPS district human resources (HR) manager, and union leadership to ensure that services are customized. In some districts we additionally have EAP clinicians dedicated to the account. In all districts we use EAP affiliates as needed to supplement our dedicated field staff. We have a national CISM team, consisting of volunteers from among all our EAP staff consultants, clinicians and regional supervisors. Members of the CISM team are deployed when a large-scale response is required. FOH also has a team of national consultants that are the liaison to the customer's Area offices, while FOH senior management interfaces with USPS headquarters.

In 2004, because the hurricane impact was so extensive, we revised our practice and deployed an FOH national consultant to the affected districts to manage the EAP response. This worked well, and we have subsequently incorporated it into our model: An FOH national consultant and/or a CISM team leader from our vendor is sent to the affected District or Area in order to coordinate and manage the response. When multiple districts are affected we may deploy several individuals to manage the various responses, as well as relying on our district EAP consultants to manage some of these.

Because of the nature of the work at the Postal Service, mail carriers are only at their post office for a few hours in the morning when they prepare the mail for their routes; clerks, who serve customers at the Postal counter, also have limited opportunities to be pulled away from their duties. Plants and some other large facilities may have 2 or 3 shifts and be operational round the clock. Thus our typical type of intervention at a Postal site for many kinds of critical incidents consists of management and union consultation, brief defusings and informational talks called stand-ups, rather than formal, lengthy debriefings. In the case of the death of an employee, we also offer grief groups to co-workers. When on-site, we also typically conduct a walk-around to talk individually to employees who are interested in further contact.

The Assessment Visit Approach Developed for Hurricanes Charley, Rita and Ivan

In 2004, we monitored storm and hurricane predictions closely. In anticipation of the first major hurricane, we distributed EAP tip sheets to some districts. These focused on personal preparation for and recovery from hurricanes for employees and their families. During our response that year we developed many more informational handouts in response to the needs we were hearing about. Accurate but brief practical tip sheets about government and community resources such as FEMA, Red Cross, and others were particularly appreciated.

Immediately after the first hurricane (Charley) hit, FOH deployed a national consultant to the affected Florida district and met with the local district HR manager to identify needs. There were 41 facilities directly affected in her district–some facilities were heavily damaged, others were without power and would begin working on generator power shortly. The HR manager wanted us to visit all these facilities immediately with the goal of helping them to take care of their people. This was a daunting task, since it required swift deployment of staff over a large, significantly damaged geographical area within a short period of time only days after the hurricane had hit.

To meet this need, and to work within the constraints mentioned, we developed a new response strategy which we called Assessment Visits or, affectionately, "The Hug and Touch Tour." This involved sending each CISM responder on a pre-determined driving route for about a week, so each could visit numerous facilities a day. Because carriers would be on their routes in some places when we visited later in the day, our goal was not to do traditional critical incident stress debriefings (CISD) or even to talk with each employee. Rather, our goals were: (1) to assess the human situation at each affected facility and identify needs that could be met with return visits or other interventions; (2) to serve as an ambassador for the organization to help show its caring for employees; (3) to provide information about resources including but not limited to the EAP, and to strongly encourage affected employees to make an appointment for EAP counseling typically through our affiliate network; (4) to provide emotional first-aid to employees; and (5) to offer supportive coaching to managers and union representatives about handling the stress. We accomplished these goals by consulting on-site with management and union leadership, conducting brief stand-up talks, doing walk-arounds to offer to talk individually with employees, and leaving written materials. These assessment visits were very well received by managers, union representatives and employees.

We worked closely with all levels of the customer organization, union and management at the District, Area and HQ levels–to keep them informed of the plan and response, to learn about needs from them as well, and to develop new informational handouts and communication strategies. At one point the customer even provided some unusual resources to us–they provided us a camper trailer to house a counselor when we couldn't find lodging.

In some locations that had very extensive damage as well as a sizeable workforce, Postal operations relocated to large tents that were set up as temporary facilities. In some cases we provided daily on-site visits to these heavily affected worksites.

Of course, in 2004 we had multiple hurricanes affecting most of Florida. We replicated this "Assessment Visit" response for each of the hurricanes. As a result we made over 300 visits to Postal sites in a 2-month period using our local district EAP staff, our CISM team, and affiliates. In addition we used our vendor's national service center to make over 400 outreach telephone calls to additional facilities to assess needs.

Consultation to the Customer and Follow-Up

One of the key services that are provided during a CISM response is consultation to management. We have learned that our customers value the *qualitative* data we glean from our encounters at our on-site visits. This data is comprised of themes, tones and opportunities or recommendations. These themes, tones and opportunities may be specific to a work unit, a facility, or they may be generalized across many facilities. It is essential to maintain confidentiality as one shares the synthesized data with the customer.

For example, in the aftermath of the hurricane, one initial theme we heard was the gratitude that employees felt toward the organization for the water, food and supplies they were providing people to help make it possible to work. Sharing positive themes helps reinforce the positive things that management is doing.

A tone is the general feeling among employees that we might be encountering. It is usually predictable at some time after a critical incident that the tone in a workplace will go from shock and sadness to anger. By alerting management to a change in the tone at a facility, management may be able to intervene to mitigate a negative tone.

An opportunity is a suggestion or recommendation to management in response to a theme. For example, when we observed inconsistent rumor control, resulting in confusion, anger and distrust, we reflected this back to management as an opportunity to improve rumor control. Sometimes a simple suggestion by the counselor can make a big difference. As an example with regard to rumor control, a counselor suggested that the manager briefly meet every morning with his/her supervisors to identify "today's rumor" and "today's fact." The manager was then able to do a quick stand-up talk each morning to keep misunderstandings down. We also recommended there be a liberal leave policy, whenever possible, during the recovery phase.

Sharing themes, tones and opportunities carries some risk. It is essential to have a very good understanding of one's customer, and to have the relationships in place so that the information can be "heard." There are some caveats to consider: (1) be acutely aware of the potential political impact of the information you share and the various audiences who may access the information; (2) share the information with the appropriate levels of management; (3) do not blind-side the manager in charge of a facility or unit by sharing information up the line before you have shared it with him/her; (4) present the information in a way that is helpful rather than judgmental; (5) make your recommendations (opportunities) realistic–do not suggest something that the customer cannot do or that is impractical; and (6) understand the importance of labor union support.

By working closely with the customer, opportunities developed to allow the EAP to be a part of the customer's review and planning teams. For example, in some of our districts, the resident EAP consultant has become an ad hoc member of the district's threat assessment team and/or emergency management team. In that role they are ideally placed to review, critique and evaluate with management the response to the event and the back-to-work routine after the event. Typically the goal is to review what went right, what went wrong, and to identify solutions for crisis mitigation, preparedness/prevention, response and recovery.

One result of our assessments was that we identified facilities that needed return visits. In a few locations we also provided a counselor on site for extended periods because of their special needs or cumulative trauma.

One of the key elements of the follow-up is to urge the organization and its managers and union representatives to monitor how employees are doing, and to encourage them to refer to the EAP when they notice problems. It is our experience that employees often will not be ready to seek out EAP counseling services right away–especially when they are displaced and dealing with immediate needs for shelter, food and basic services. It is later, when EAP is no longer at the site that managers need to encourage EAP use, and that EAP promotion information may be most needed. So we created some informational messages to managers on these topics.

Our EAP counselors also provided extensive follow-up outreach during the year to the most severely impacted areas. We recognized with our customer the long-term recovery needs of their employees. People who had serious home damage or had lost their homes needed ongoing support and understanding. Financial counseling workshops were offered in some locations to assist people as they worked through their recovery.

Counselors also did what they could to emotionally prepare the workforce for the next hurricane season. They provided information on developing a personal family disaster response plan, distributed government information on evacuations, and so forth. After the hurricanes of 2004, we reviewed which communication links with the customer needed to be strengthened, so that EAP information could go out in a timely and effective way. For example, we learned that getting information out to facilities in advance of hurricane season was important. Once a hurricane hits and electric power is lost or people are dispersed, distribution of information is much more difficult. We developed additional handouts on stress management and hurricane recovery tips for the next season.

Our key management team reviewed our EAP response and identified what went right and what went wrong. We also held feedback sessions with our responders that identified logistical challenges and the need to provide more timely support and debriefing for responders.

Some of the questions we asked ourselves and our customers as we did this internal review were:

- Did we have the right staffing, the right level of services, and the right speed of response?
- What were our logistical challenges and how can we overcome them?
- Was our partnership with our customer solid, and where do we need to strengthen that partnership?
- How do we support our EAP responders, and what can we do better to support them?

Our review after last year's hurricanes reinforced the value of a national critical incident response team that is composed of staff EAP counselors and managers who volunteer for deployment out of their normal duty stations to help with a critical incident response of a large magnitude. As a result, we recruited additional members and strengthened the team. A workgroup developed recommendations to improve logistics, safety, incentives/rewards, and timely debriefing for responders. Those recommendations were in place and retraining had been done when the 2005 hurricanes hit, and that put us ahead of the curve in responding this year.

Further Customizing the Response in the Gulf Coast for Hurricane Rita

In 2005, we felt we were well prepared to respond again to multiple major hurricanes using our Assessment Visits model. So with Hurricane Katrina on the horizon, we sent out EAP information to our customers in advance, stayed in close contact with them, put our trained CISM team on stand-by, and waited. What we never anticipated was the level of destruction and displacement of people caused by Hurricane Katrina and the flooding of New Orleans in its wake. As of January 22, 2006, the death toll resulting from Hurricane Katrina and the aftermath stood at 1,103 deaths and 3,259 people missing and unaccounted for. The failure to completely evacuate New Orleans, the loss of infrastructure and the size of the impact overpowered local, state and federal resources. Whole communities in coastal Mississippi such as Waveland, Pearlington and Picayune were devastated, and the Alabama coast had major damage as well. Hurricane Rita soon followed, hitting near the Texas/Louisiana state line and devastating the rural western coastal area of Louisiana.

As a result, we had to deploy on multiple "fronts." EAP teams were deployed to Alabama, Louisiana, Mississippi and Texas to organize and implement the assessment visits and other services. Logistical challenges were substantial, though not unanticipated. Simply finding housing and car rentals for our responders seemed to be a Herculean task, though we managed with some creativity and the forbearance of our responders.

As we implemented the assessment visits, we soon realized that additional components would be needed to support the workforce and to offer emotional first-aid to the traumatized evacuees. A large segment of the Postal employee population in southern Louisiana was displaced. Several hundred employees were displaced to Houston, where we partnered with USPS human resources to create a Postal Employee Resource Center (PERC). This became a telephonic outreach center to displaced employees in Houston as well as providing support to employees who came to the PERC. In various locations in Texas, Postal human resources, union leaders and EAP partnered to make visits to shelters to try to find Postal employees. We also alerted all of our staff throughout the U.S. to work with their district HR managers to conduct outreach to displaced employees that might have evacuated to their states.

We also encountered employees with secondary trauma, that is, the stress of repeatedly hearing the agonizing stories of loss from others. EAP thus provided support and defusings to Postal personnel who had the challenge of locating employees and providing them with key employment information. We also offered debriefings to Postal workers who were deployed to shelters to do change-of-address work with the evacuated population. We attempted to pay close attention to managers–who often worked 7 days a week and rarely seemed to complain. These were staff whose job it was to account for all employees and deal with all the personnel issues, as well as managers who were focused on getting operations up and running. Outreach to managers and union representatives were done wherever we found them.

Our EAP office in New Orleans was in a high-rise building that was closed for more than six months due the infrastructure damage caused by the flooding. With the generous help of our customer, we were able to relocate our staff to temporary quarters and created a PERC in Baton Rouge, which became a "drop in" center as well as a staging area for our CISM responders. We also developed plans to partner with the USPS medical unit nurse to do outreach visits. Though we ended up doing our visits separate from the medical staff for logistical reasons, we were able to share good information with each other that enhanced the services we provided.

As we conducted our Assessment Visits now using two-person teams, we realized that the level of devastation in some communities, the separation of family members from one another, and the loss of homes and possessions by so many of the employees would require a longer-term and more intensive EAP involvement on-site than we had ever provided before. In Mississippi, for example, our roving teams made repeat visits to facilities and established firm relationships with key personnel. As the assessment visits started to wind down, we determined that a transition phase was necessary in order to "hand-off" these newly developed relationships in a way that would be comfortable for our customers. We did this by identifying key affiliates in the affected locales and introducing them to the facility managers with whom we had developed relationships. In this way were able to hand-off the relationship to the affiliate and increased the comfort of the managers in working with our affiliate. As the EAP team leaders left the district, they also transitioned the coordination of ongoing services back to the district EAP Consultant.

Though our EAP staff made over 400 site visits in four states in 2005, the work is not yet done. It will be a long time before there is a return to normal for those who are still displaced from their homes and communities. Though our Postal employees are working, many are doing so away from the place called home. Our challenges will be to find ways that EAP can continue to evolve so as to meet the unique and long-term needs of these employees. By working closely with our customer (management and union) and listening to the needs of employees, we hope to find solutions.

NOTE

Specific details related to personal experiences have been altered to maintain confidentiality. The authors' views do not necessarily represent the views of the federal agencies discussed, Federal Occupational Health, or the United States Postal Service. The authors express their deepest thanks to the field staff, supervisors and managers who participated in the hurricane response. We hold in our hearts those whose lives have been changed forever by the disaster and appreciate the openness of our agencies and employees who allowed us to come in and work with them.

REFERENCES

National Child Traumatic Stress Network and National Center for PTSD, September 2005. Psychological First Aid: Field Operations Guide, SAMHSA.

Shultz, James M., Flynn, Brian W. Behavioral Health Awareness Training for Terrorism and Disasters, University of Notre Dame, August 24-25, 2005.

doi:10.1300/J490v21n03_03

An Integrated Approach to Expand
One Federal Government EAP's Role
Beyond Disaster Response

Bernard E. Beidel

SUMMARY. In view of the world events of the past several years, the demand on organizations to have dynamic disaster preparedness and management systems in place is growing exponentially as the immediate and long-term effects and the potential disruptive impact of natural disasters, acts and threats of terrorism, and other crisis situations has increased for organizations, the workplace and the work force. Whether the employer is an international private sector enterprise, an independent labor organization, a governmental agency, or a small non-profit entity, the demands on work organizations and their employees is extensive in times of crisis or when responding to a specific disaster or traumatic incident, whether natural or man-made. As evident by the advent of an entire industry of consultants and organizations providing disaster preparedness, planning, response, and management services, the workplace has indeed become the playing field for a patchwork of disaster and trauma related services and strategies, many of which are disparate and disconnected from the very work force upon which the execution of the disaster response plan or the continuity of business operations is dependent. This author will build upon the conclusions of a recent study indicating that the "human capital" dimensions of disaster preparedness and management are often overlooked in such planning and execution efforts, while advancing the idea that employee assistance

[Haworth co-indexing entry note]: "An Integrated Approach to Expand One Federal Government EAP's Role Beyond Disaster Response." Beidel. Bernard E. Co-published simultaneously in *Journal of Workplace Behavioral Health* (The Haworth Press, Inc.) Vol. 21, No. 3/4, 2006, pp. 59-87; and: *Workplace Disaster Preparedness, Response, and Management* (ed: R. Paul Maiden, Rich Paul, and Christina Thompson) The Haworth Press, Inc., 2006. pp. 59-87. Single or multiple copies of this article are available for a fee from The Haworth Document Delivery Service [1-800-HAWORTH, 9:00 a.m. - 5:00 p.m. (EST). E-mail address: docdelivery@haworthpress.com].

doi:10.1300/J490v21n03_04

programs provide not only a logical but an ideal fit for that void. By offering some examples from one federal EAP's evolving efforts in this area, the author will offer a discussion of various approaches, strategies, activities, and partnerships that an EAP affords the employee assistance practitioner–a collection of capabilities that are inherent in the very conceptual framework and fundamental premise on which EAPs in the workplace have been built, and of the possibilities that can be realized as that EAP becomes well-positioned and fully integrated into the workplace, bringing value to and providing vital resources to the work organization and the work force in preparation for, response to, and management of disasters, traumatic events and other crisis situations to which more and more employers and labor organizations around the globe are prone–ultimately enhancing the value of the EAP to the organization and to their collective continuity of operations planning and execution. doi:10.1300/J490v21n03_04 *[Article copies available for a fee from The Haworth Document Delivery Service: 1-800-HAWORTH. E-mail address: <docdelivery@haworthpress.com> Website: <http://www.HaworthPress.com> © 2006 by The Haworth Press, Inc. All rights reserved.]*

KEYWORDS. Employee assistance services, EAP, disaster preparedness, disaster response, disaster management, emergency preparedness, emergency management trauma response, human capital, continuity of business operations

INTRODUCTION

In its April 2004 report to the Congress of the United States, entitled *Human Capital: Opportunities to Improve Federal Continuity Planning Guidance*, the General Accountability Office (GAO), formerly the General Accounting Office, summarized its series of interviews with disaster response, preparedness and management experts from private sector businesses, federal agencies and other public sector organizations, by emphasizing two key human capital principles that the experts indicated should guide all organizational business continuity efforts: (1) "demonstrate sensitivity to individual employee needs and" (2) "maximize the contributions of all employees to mission results" (GAO, 2004, pg. 3). In its corresponding review of the disaster and emergency management literature–a review which included industry journals, federal guidance, and specific codes and standards, and that prompted the subsequent extensive interviews of industry experts–

the GAO identified a glaring gap in that "the available literature was limited in its attention to human capital" (GAO, 2004, pg. 2).

As a term that has come into more frequent and preferred usage in both the specific human resources field and the general business environment, "human capital" within the context of disaster preparedness, response and management speaks to the very core, fundamental premise and vital presence of any viable employee assistance program or service delivery system. A sample definition from the human resource literature itself reflects the compatibility of the need for a "human capital" focus in disaster management and the corresponding capabilities and potential contribution on this front of the long-standing employee assistance tradition. Specifically, in *The Human Resources Glossary, Second Edition*, Tracey defines "human capital" as follows:

> Contrasted with financial capital or equipment capital. The assets of wealth of an organization embodied in or represented by the hand, minds, and talents of its employees. Also describes what an organization gains from the loyalty, creativity, effort, accomplishments, and productivity of its employees. Said to contribute more than one-half of an organization's productive capacity. It equates to, and may actually exceed, the productive capacity of machine capital and investment in research and development. (Tracey, 1998, pg. 243)

When considering Tracey's definition, the critical elements of "human capital" in work organizations parallel the foundational concepts and tenets of the employee assistance field, namely that employees and their labor brothers and sisters are the core assets of any organization—assets to be valued, supported and, particularly during times of individual or organizational difficulty, helped and maybe even salvaged through a defined regimen of workplace based "employee assistance" services and the corresponding collection of specific strategies, which Roman and Blum (1985) defined as the "core technology of employee assistance programs."

As articulated in their seminal article on "The Core Technology of Employee Assistance Programs," and later augmented in Roman's article on the "Seventh Dimension" of the "EAP core technology" (1990), EAPs offered employers and employees a unique partnership in the workplace and a distinct blend of services and strategies to address the challenges posed to both employer and employee, or union and member, when an employee's productivity became negatively impacted by problems and situations of either a personal or work-related nature. These six, and later seven, components of the "EAP core technology" are "found nowhere other than in an EAP, either individually or in combination. Thus, the components of an EAP's core technology . . . are not found in other programmatic efforts in work organizations, either individually or in combination" (Roman & Blum, 1985, pg. 16).

Since its earliest of beginnings, the employee assistance field and profession has offered employers–large and small, private and public–a dynamic collection of strategies that address the convergence of performance, productivity, illness, behavior, and human dimensions in the workplace and their collective manifestations for the work organization and the work force. With the escalation of threats against and within work organizations, and the corresponding stress and strain on employers, labor organizations and employees, EAPs are often in an enviable and potent position in the organization to provide critical leadership in and direction to the organization's overall disaster preparedness, trauma response and ongoing incident management, bringing to bear the unique set of skills, perspectives and capabilities that are essential for leading the organization and the work force through the human dimensions of any disaster or trauma–the same skills and capabilities that are historically the hallmark of the employee assistance profession.

To frame this discussion, however, two critical perspectives are helpful–one with its roots in the specificity and well-defined standards of the employee assistance profession; the other arising out of the more general assessment conducted by the GAO of the vital elements or actions that appear critical to assure that the organization addresses the vital human capital considerations that, while often overlooked, are identified by the experts as critical to the organization's success in responding to, managing during and recovering from a disaster. While the events of September 11th 2001, the escalation of global terrorism, the infiltration of domestic and work-related violence into the workplace, and the ever present and unpredictable reality of devastating natural disasters have prompted many organizations to develop disaster preparedness and management plans, the continuum of services, capabilities and resources is only complete when the business, public agency or labor organization takes that same perspective to their focus on helping the organization and its work force–its human capital–plan for, test against and execute its continuity of business operations and functions under a variety of scenarios and circumstances.

A Framework for Appreciating the Emergence of the EAP's Role in the Organization's Disaster Preparedness and Management, and in the Continuity of the Organization's Ongoing Operations

Consistent with its evolutionary roots and its responsiveness to the unique productivity and performance problems presented to American industries, businesses and labor organizations in the 1940s by employees and union members who manifested the problems of alcohol abuse and alcoholism in the workplace, the employee assistance profession again recognized the challenge of responding to individuals, work groups and eventually the larger organization when they were individually or collectively affected by a traumatic incident in the workplace or a larger disaster in the community. While a defined crisis intervention and response methodology had initially been developed and honed during the 1970s in the United States in the more homogeneous world of emergency responders and other rescue, fire service and law enforcement personnel (Mitchell & Resnik, 1981), the employee assistance field soon developed a significant interest of its own in the adaptation and application of this emerging approach for responding to critical incidents in the workplace. Mitchell and Resnik (1981) provide an excellent overview of this evolving emergency response approach to crisis, while specifically offering a wonderfully segmented discussion of the application of the approach under varied, yet defined, emotionally charged situations. For instance, whether dealing with a suicidal person or a multi-casualty situation, they offer the unique perspective of applying a crisis response methodology "to assist emergency service personnel in dealing with average people, within the 'normal' range of behavior, who are suddenly thrown into a crisis as a result of a high level of stress in their lives" (Mitchell & Resnik, 1981, pg. 1). The appeal to EA professionals and EAPs is obvious–a methodology for addressing the issues that arise when individuals are jettisoned from their routine and normal range of experience, and thrust unprepared into the emotional upheaval and unpredictability of a traumatic incident, a sudden disaster, or an act of violence or terrorism. As the advantages of proactively responding to "normal people dealing with abnormal situations" became more evident, the application of this defined methodology to the broader workplace was a logical evolution.

With the escalation of workplace violence, the devastation wrought by a variety of natural disasters, and the growing reality that acts of terrorism and the threat of terrorism were becoming potential and formidable players around the globe in both the private and public sectors, more and more corporations, businesses, labor organizations, and governmental agencies throughout the world were turning to their EAPs in times of crisis–looking for solutions at both the micro or employee level, as well as at the macro or larger organizational level. Specifically, with this growing demand from its organizational and individual clients, the employee assistance field recognized the infusion of the critical incident stress management methodology and defined protocols as an appropriate expansion of its core employee assistance services in order to offer the most comprehensive continuum of disaster and trauma response services. Although employee assistance professionals recognized the need for and sought a more proactive response to trauma, crisis and violence in the workplace, the employee assistance field was challenged with the appropriate adaptation and application of these specific protocols to the more heterogeneous world of business and labor organizations. Throughout the final two decades of the twentieth century, it became increasingly common for internal EAPs and Member Assistance Programs (MAPs) to provide critical incident stress management (CISM) services to their respective business and labor organizations. Similarly, more and more external EA services or vendors were marketing CISM in their standard book of EAP business or as part of their broader continuum of workplace services. But taking its cue from the early, ongoing and evolving work of Mitchell and Resnik (1981), Everly and Mitchell (1997, 1999), Mitchell and Everly (1996), Mitchell (1983, 1988), and others in the critical incident stress response field, EA practitioners recognized as well that the workplace and the work force demanded this comprehensive continuum of services that went beyond the immediate and short-term response to the individual employee or union brother and sister, to a full range of critical incident stress management (CISM) services. As applied to EAPs and the employee assistance field, the "comprehensive" framework for CISM advanced by Everly and Mitchell in their seminal work on CISM resonated loudly with EA professionals as they employed the methodology with individuals, work groups and the larger organizations they served:

> This volume represents a new era in crisis intervention. It is the first book ever written on Critical Incident Stress Management (CISM) as a comprehensive crisis response program. By comprehensive, we mean an integrated, multi-component intervention system that spans the entire crisis spectrum from pre-crisis preparation and on-scene support services through post-crisis intervention and follow-up mental health dispensations, as necessary. . . .

CISM is a programmatic approach to reducing the frequency, duration, severity of, and impairment from, psychological crises. (Everly & Mitchell, 1999, pg. xiii)

In fact, the emergence of critical incident stress management (CISM) as a practical methodology with potential application beyond the emergency services arena alone prompted the corresponding and specific interest in the demonstrated value of this approach to crisis response. In response to this expanded interest and the growing application of the approach, Everly and Mitchell (1997, 1999) produced their comprehensive review of the foundation, development, mechanics, and standards of care for effective CISM, including in their second edition a considerable review of the expansive empirical research on crisis intervention. Merely two years after its initial publication, the authors prefaced the second edition with an acknowledgment of the growing interest in and expansive use of the CISM methodology:

Although it has been only two years since the first edition was published, we felt a second edition was needed. This need was created by virtue of a dramatic increase in the expressed interest in, proliferation of, and empirical investigation surrounding, crisis theory, crisis intervention, and specifically Critical Incident Stress Debriefing (CISD) and Critical Incident Stress Management (CISM). Even though the field of crisis intervention has been in existence over 90 years, there exists considerable disagreement and confusion surrounding the most basic of definitions. Obviously, when a field cannot agree upon basic definitions, it has difficulty in communication, research, and standardization of practice.

This text was created to assist in the resolution of definitional dilemmas and the creation of operating standards through the refinement of operating definitions and protocols. In addition, this revision provides an updated review on research issues and findings relevant to the entire field of emergency mental health. (Everly & Mitchell, 1999, pg. xi)

Although the critical incident, workplace stress and employee assistance literature has become replete with further discussions of this continuum and its demonstrated value within the workplace and in sustaining the organization's human capital investment, if you will, particularly during times of prolonged disaster or crisis response, the work of Everly and Mitchell (1997, 1999) remains the most concise history on the development of CISM as a comprehensive methodology, and the hallmark and essential guidance for the effective application of the methodology in the workplace by EA professionals individually and by the EAP field at large.

For the purposes of this discussion, however, the foundational impetus and initial framework for EAPs to embrace this critical incident response paradigm can be found in two of the basic program standards for EAPs promulgated by the Employee Assistance Professionals Association as part of its program standards.

> The employee assistance program shall remain alert for emerging needs and may add new services when they are consistent with and complementary to the employee assistance program (EAP) core technology. (EAPA, 1999, pg. 4)

And:

> The employee assistance program shall offer responsive crisis intervention services to employees, eligible family members, and the organization. (EAPA, 1999, pg. 16)

Consistent with both the spirit and specific focus of these individual standards, and in keeping with their collective intent, EA professionals recognized that the emerging influence of disasters and critical incidents in the workplace and the EAP's ability to meet the corresponding challenges, demanded that the profession and the field look beyond its own discipline for the services and strategies that could be adopted or adapted to respond to and address these growing and largely unprecedented issues in the workplace. The elevation of the importance of critical incident stress management (CISM) as a viable component in the employee assistance service continuum was evident in 1998, when the Employee Assistance Professionals Association (EAPA) depicted CISM as one of the diverse range of specific workplace-based services provided by EAPs consistent with the "EAP core technology," and distinctive from those services that are more reflective of and responsive to the managed care and health care interface with EAPs. As depicted in Figure 1, critical incident stress management represented a significant contribution to the comprehensiveness of the EAP's response to the emerging needs of the modern workplace and the challenges presented therein by the escalating incidents of workplace violence, trauma and

FIGURE 1. Employee Assistance Programs (EAPs) and Health Care (HC)/Managed Care (MC) Laws (a)

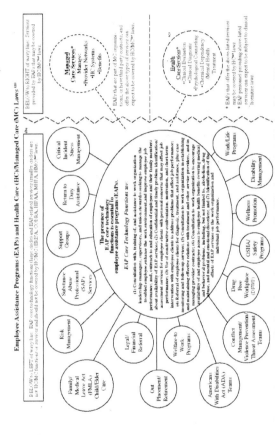

Employee Assistance Programs (EAPs) and Health Care (HC)/Managed Care (MC) Laws [b]

[a] Health Care/Managed Care Laws: ERISA = Employee Retirement Income Security Act (1974); COBRA = Consolidated Omnibus Budget Reconciliation Act (1986); FMLA = Family Medical Leave Act (1994); HIPAA = Health Insurance Portability and Accountability Act (1996); MHPA = Mental Health Parity Act (1996); HMO = Health Maintenance Organizations acts
[b] EELOW that provide capitated functions/services that do not fall under ERISA's "employee welfare benefits" definition
[c] EAPs that provide prepaid, natural HC services/right-of-way laws, where individual benefits can be at risk, may fall under HC/MCⁿᵈ laws
[d] EELOW is LEFT of way/line: EAP functions that are core and should not be covered by HC/MC laws

67

disaster–and more recently with the threat and actuality of national and international terrorism.

As with the employee assistance field's evolution from a pure alcoholism and alcohol abuse focus in the 1940s and 1950s, to the broader "employee assistance" focus that emerged in the late 1960s and early 1970s and that carries through to the present, the critical incident response field has likewise evolved to a broader "trauma and disaster" focus today. The ultimate effect on work organizations and other employers around the globe is a fundamental and practical realization that their very survival and ability to sustain the continuity of their organization and operations, and their specific capability to fulfill their service delivery and product development commitments, depends solely on their preparations for and actual execution of the strategies to usher their employees through a disaster or trauma, and to sustain and support them in its wake as the organization and its work force, not unlike the phoenix, rises from the organizational, administrative and operational ashes–often both figuratively and literally. While disaster preparedness and planning, and response and recovery management is big business in this age of terrorism and in the face of random violence, for many organizations, their ability to successfully navigate both the immediate and frequently prolonged challenges of the event and its aftermath will ultimately come down to the ability of its EAP to assist on multiple dimensions and levels–from responding to the individual employee injured in a disaster; to comforting the family member who has lost a loved one at the hand of a violent act of a co-worker; to consulting with the shop steward struggling to muster her remaining contingent of labor brothers and sisters who have lost many of their colleagues in an industrial accident; to consulting with the highest executives in the organization as they plan to temporarily relocate employees and operations as they rebuild the business, recover its infrastructure and sustain its viability, productivity and profitability. Nothing cuts more to the heart and fabric of an organization than its ability to take the proverbial disaster punch, and yet not only recover, but emerge stronger and more agile than before. And time and time again, EAPs have been in the corner serving as the individual employee's "cut man" and the organization's "manager"–helping to put the fighter back in the ring, if you will.

So, while the employee assistance field's standards provide the primary leg upon which EAPs stand in response to natural disasters and other traumatic events in the workplace, the employee assistance profession's philosophical foundation of focusing on the multifaceted human dimensions in the workplace is the other, whether focused on enhancing the productivity of the work group, improving the job performance of an individual employee, or helping the organization foster an environment that supports the employee's ability to balance the demands of their personal life with the realities of the work world. With this duality serving as the basic foundation for the balance of this discussion, the focus on the GAO's six recommended organizational actions provides an ideal and specific framework for looking at how one federal EAP has attempted to integrate the program itself and its core EAP services into the larger organization's disaster preparedness, response, management and recovery activities. As enumerated in Table 1, and as exemplified through one federal EAP's experiences throughout the balance of this discussion, these six key actions provide ample opportunities for other EAPs to demonstrate and exercise their broader value to the organizations and work forces they serve.

As previously stated, these six action steps derive from the opinions and experiences of human capital or emergency management and preparedness experts from across the public and private sectors. The action steps are illustrative that "the continuity process . . . extends beyond the goals of life safety and the performance of essential operations" (GAO, 2004, pg. 9). In considering these specific action steps in the context of an EAP's role in the organization's disaster preparedness and management, it is also beneficial to see them as an EAP preparedness checklist as well. Specifically, EA professionals can serve themselves well and bring real benefit to their EAP and its ability to fully serve an organization's needs during and after a disaster by using these six action steps as a touchstone against which they benchmark their own preparedness and that of their program. In other words, how well does the EAP itself stack up against these six critical activities?

As further presented by the GAO in their report, the experts they paneled went on to identify two specific principles that they recommend guide these organizational actions to address the human capital considerations in any organizational continuity planning and implementation processes.

> The first is recognizing and remaining sensitive to employees' personal needs during emergencies when shaping the appropriate organizational expectations of employees. The emergency event that activates continuity plans may also cause emergency events in the personal lives of individual employees. Similar to an organization placing its highest priority on the safety and well-being of its employees, employees may have high-priority responsibilities to

others. These personal responsibilities may limit employees' ability to contribute to mission accomplishment until these other obligations are satisfied.

The second principle experts identified is maximizing the contributions of all employees, whether in providing essential operations or resuming full services. This should be done within the limits of an employee's ability to contribute given the situation, as described in principle one, and within the limits of the organization to use those contributions effectively. According to the experts, the experience of organizations during emergencies has been that employees remain motivated to contribute to organizational results, which is increasingly felt the longer the emergency continues. Enabling employees to contribute promotes more effective delivery of essential operations and more rapid resumption of full operations. In addition, in extreme disruptions of employees' personal circumstances, providing purposeful activities helps avoid the debilitating affects of a disruption on employees, including job-related anxiety and post-traumatic stress disorder. (GAO, 2004, pgs. 9-10)

As assessed against these principles, the ultimate challenge and critical starting point for any EAP is assuring that its own EA professionals are themselves prepared to respond and contribute to the organization's overall response to the needs of its work force in advance of, during and after a disaster and as it carries out the organization's recovery and continuity of operations. The old adage of "physician, heal thyself" is an all too true and real expectation of the EA professional and the EAP itself as they prepare for and carry out their professional and programmatic responses to the demands of disaster preparedness and management. The best approach for any EAP to take well in advance of a disaster or traumatic situation is to have an independent employee assistance service in place for its own EA professionals and EAP support staff. During such extreme traumatic situations and prolonged emergency or crisis response scenarios in the workplace–times of extreme demand on an EAP and the EA professional–the question often arises, "who debriefs the debriefer?" Considering the realities of terrorism, violence and disasters around the globe, today's global workplace and every small, mid-size and large organization's and employer's need for effective disaster preparedness and management capabilities demands that every EAP have a ready answer to that question and a realistic and practical plan to carry it out–a plan that fully support its own EA practitio-

TABLE 1. Key Organizational Actions to Enhance Continuity Efforts

Demonstrate top leadership commitment	• Instill an approach to continuity planning that includes human capital considerations • Allocate resources and set policies • Set direction and pace of recovery
Seek opportunities for synergy	• Integrate continuity efforts with broader decision making • Consider how continuity investments benefit other program efforts
Maintain effective communication	• Build relationships through two-way communication • Establish roles, responsibilities, and expectations • Develop redundant communication vehicles
Target investments in training and development	• Raise awareness of continuity efforts • Build skills and competencies to increase flexibility • Foster a culture that values flexible employees who are empowered to make effective decisions
Leverage the flexibility of human capital	• Enable employees associated with resumption activities to contribute to mission results in alternate assignments • Sustain the contribution of employees associated with essential operations • Maintain organizational knowledge of staffing requirements and availability
Build process to identify and share lessons	• Create a learning environment • Make learning explicit and shared

Source: General Accountability Office (GAO). *Human Capital: Opportunities to Improve Federal Continuity Planning Guidance*. GAO-04-384. Washington, DC: April 2004, pg. 4.

ners and program supports personnel as the EAP responds to and guides an organization and its work force through the very situation that may directly affect the EAP and its EA professionals as well. In their earliest of works on critical incident stress and disaster response, Mitchell and Resnik (1986) addressed this issue in the context of "crisis worker," offering a menu of practical steps and a checklist of strategies for identifying responder stress and the potential associated burn out and mitigating its effects, particularly in an extended or prolonged period of response.

Similar to the concept of "aftershock," as first postulated by Andrew Slaby to characterize "any significant delayed response to a crisis" (Slaby, 1989) experienced by individuals, the responsibility rests with the EAP to prepare its EA professionals and other personnel for the demands of the larger response to the organization and the work force–almost serving as a form of inoculation against the very strains and stresses that the EAP will be called upon to guide the organization through and about which it will be providing guidance to the organization's leaders. As Slaby borrows from geology to describe the psychological aftershock of trauma as comparable to the aftershock of an earthquake, which frequently causes the most damage by striking already weakened structures (Slaby, 1989, pg. xiv), today's organization's are fully served when the EAP has built resiliency into its own operation and personnel–hopefully positioning itself to withstand the potential, and often delayed, psychological and organizational aftershocks of prolonged disaster response, management, recovery, and continuity of operations efforts. The reader need look no further than the prolonged efforts at Ground Zero following September 11th 2001, or the continuing recovery underway across businesses and communities throughout the northern Gulf Coast of the United States in the aftermath of Hurricanes Katrina and Rita that struck that area in the fall of 2005, to realize both the challenges for EAPs and EA professionals in supporting and assisting the organizations, work forces and individual employees and families over an extended period of time. But in providing such support and a specific focus on the human capital dimensions of the organization's preparedness, response and management efforts, the EAP has the opportunity to model the very behavior it advocates for the organization and all of its personnel.

Using the six organizational actions advanced by the GAO as a guide, we can look at one federal EAP's efforts over the past few years to fully integrate its service and its personnel into the fabric of the larger agency's disaster preparedness, response and management activities.

1. Demonstrate Top Leadership Commitment

When first pressed into response to the Capitol Hill anthrax incident in October 2001, the EA professionals of the U.S. House of Representatives' Office of Employee Assistance (hereafter referred to as the EAP) were poised to assume their traditional employee assistance roles to support the personnel of the House in the aftermath of the incident, to include providing consultation, assessment, short-term support, referral, and follow-up services, typical of any "EAP core-technology" and workplace based employee assistance service. With the EA professionals on the team having extensive critical incident response and management experience in the law enforcement, transportation, health care and legislative communities, the EA professionals were already familiar with the application of the CISM services across a breadth of occupations and work groups. CISM protocols were in place and had been applied to other situations that the employee assistance team had responded to on prior occasions.

What quickly became evident, however, was that responding to the workplace and the overall organization in the aftermath of the anthrax situation would be like no previous incident. With the entire Capitol Hill campus evacuated, the entire work force displaced, and the U.S. Congress shut down for the first time in its history, the challenges to the institution of the U.S. House of Representatives and to its work force were unprecedented. The employee assistance team was quickly called into action by the leadership of the organization to assume roles that had more to do with the continuity of the institution's ongoing operations, than traditional employee assistance and defined critical incident response.

The leadership of the organization quickly called upon the employee assistance team to serve as the lead in managing the organization's response and sensitivity to the human capital dimensions of the displacement from the normal workplace surroundings, through the establishment of and relocation to alternate work sites, and ultimately to the replication and resumption of normal operations, although they would hardly be considered routine considering the magnitude of this disruption and prolonged aftermath of this unprecedented intrusion into the personal and work lives of every employee in the House. The mere fact that the EAP itself was dislocated and unable to return to its own office space for well over six weeks brought to the employee assistance team an immediate need for a lasting lesson in continuity planning. Prepared for a traditional employee assistance response, but quickly charged with the organization's human capital focus, the employee assistance team recognized the limitations and inadequacy of its current response plans, and the corresponding futility of their prior response experiences. While recognizing that this incident was unprecedented for the EAP, it was also an energizing experience for the team, providing each of the EA professionals involved the opportunity to broaden their skills and abilities as the front people in the organization's day-to-day communication effort with the work force. The incident actually presented the EAP with new avenues to demonstrate its value to the larger organization by not only filling a critical internal communications role, but in helping bridge the informational chasm that can often exist between the leadership of an organization and its general work force during times of crisis and upheaval.

But with the directive to take the human capital lead for the organization's response, came the commitment of the organization's leadership to provide the resources and venues for keeping the human capital focus in the lens of the House's overall response to and management of the incident. From allocating office space to the employee assistance team that placed it in immediate proximity to the institution's leaders, to positioning and promoting the EAP team as the primary communications conduit between the employees and the institution's leaders and the incident command team, the leadership of the organization quickly demonstrated that the EAP was a vital member of the overall management team and a critical player in keeping the human capital focus throughout the process of response, recovery and ultimately, the resumption of operations. Within the first few days of the management of the event, the Office of Employee Assistance moniker had been replaced and the employee assistance team renamed the "human matters" team–reflecting the EAP's new and more broadly defined role and demonstrating not only the critical commitment that the organization's leadership was making to the organization's human capital, but the trust and confidence they placed in the EAP to carry out this critical mission as the organization and the EAP, along with so many other internal and external operational partners and stakeholders, navigated this uncharted territory. While the EAP had enjoyed a well-established and recognized position in the organization prior to this incident, there is no doubt that the incidents that occurred in October 2001 further integrated the EAP into the organization's fabric and placed it at the table as the organization's leaders and incident managers deliberated over and made critical decisions regarding the resumption of operations and the return of employees to a less than fully restored workplace.

In the five years since the anthrax incident, the EAP has assumed an ongoing role as part of the organization's ongoing business continuity and disaster recovery operation, most recently participating in the planning and execution of the response to personnel and offices impacted by the historic hurricanes of 2005, and focusing primarily on the human capital issues involved in the organization's response to the individual employees, the managers for whom they work, and their respective families. As part of the organization's ongoing disaster response and recovery management group, the employee assistance team has been charged with developing the organization's overall human capital continuity plan to identify and address the related human capital and work group issues critical to the success of sustaining ongoing operations under a variety of circumstances and situations–ultimately assuring the leadership's commitment to foster an organizational culture where human capital interests are the focus, work and responsibility of the entire organization throughout the disaster planning, preparedness and recovery phases of incident response, as it sustains its operations in these uncertain times.

2. Seek Opportunities for Synergy

As reflected by the panel of disaster response, preparedness and management experts interviewed by the GAO as part of their study of strategies to fully understand the human capital dimension of continuity planning and to optimize the organization's human capital as the primary resource in times of disaster response, technological threats, or other acts of terrorism or workplace violence, one of the contributing factors in the overall success and effectiveness of any organization's response and continuity efforts is their ability to find the synergies with other decision making and operational efforts (see Table 1). This is an area where EAPs traditionally excel and have a considerable experience in working with a variety of internal and external resources. The viability for many businesses and organizations in today's competitive marketplace and in the climate of tighter operational budgets and leaner work forces is to optimize the performance of the organization through more effective team development and execution and the transparent management of those teams and their projects and services across the breadth of an organization's operations. As many EA professionals recognized in the field's earliest years as it advocated for a more progressive and proactive approach in the workplace for dealing with the problem of employee alcohol abuse and alcoholism, the success of those efforts would ultimately rest with the EAP's ability to find those opportunities for synergy with other organizational entities and partners, whether that be the labor representative committed to saving the job of a union sister or brother, or the supervisor interested in salvaging the experience, knowledge and investment in the employee made by the company.

In today's complex world and with the reality that many organizations are leaner on both the personnel and financial levels, effective disaster preparedness and management is reliant on the organization's ability to achieve this synergy. So how does the EAP contribute to this synergistic approach?

The first step is fully assessing and understanding the resources available in the organization and among the work force–certainly not new territory for any EAP or EA professional. As the U.S. House of Representatives' EAP has experienced through its work over the past five years in the capacity of disaster planning and preparedness, the movement of the organization to a firm continuity of operations footing has presented the EAP with an exceptional framework for better understanding and alignment of its comprehensive services to the organization, which ultimately demonstrates the EAP's value across new dimensions. For instance, as the EAP has participated in a number of drills, exercises and tests of the plans over the past few years, it has also been able to capitalize on the expertise of a number of internal and external subject matter experts in the area of disaster response and management. Through these multi-dimensional exercises, involving a variety of organizational entities and disciplines, the EAP has been better able to test out with these other organizational partners which of its CISM services and capabilities are best aligned to the organization, at what particular time and under what particular circumstances. Specifically, while the continuum of CISM services includes "pre-incident preparation, individual support, demobilizations and group informational briefings, defusings, critical incident stress debriefings (CISD), family support, and mental health follow-up" (Everly & Mitchell, 1999, pg. 15-18), the EAP best serves its organization and its work force by achieving the optimum alignment and execution of these varied interventions depending upon the specific and unique circumstances and duration of the event, the preparedness of and impact on the individuals and work groups involved in the event, and the overall context of the organization's culture and approach to its day-to-day management of its human capital.

In preparing an effective disaster preparedness plan, the EAP needs to pose a series of questions of its professionals in an effort to identify both the realistic and unrealistic expectations of its services and to capitalize on those resources and partners that can further enhance its benefit to the organization. A few possibilities are advanced here:

- How do our services align with the organization's response to the varied stages of the disaster: rescue; response; recovery; continuity assurance? In short, what is our role on an immediate (e.g., at the scene), short-term (e.g., responding to those traumatized), mid-range (e.g., managing the work group in the aftermath of the disaster), and long-term (e.g., assimilating the experience into future preparedness efforts) basis?

- If we employ CISM strategies to respond to and support employees and union members during and in the aftermath of the disaster, what is our consultative role with the leadership and management of the company and the union?
- As the organization develops the larger disaster preparedness and response plan, what is the EAP's role in driving the human capital issues and focus at all levels and throughout all departments in the company?
- Where are the allies of the EAP in or outside the company–the other change agents and strategic partners that understand the value of the EAP and see the benefit in working with the EAP in preparation for, response to, and recovery from any disaster or other traumatic event?

A great example of this synergy is found in the EAP's experience during the response to and resumption of business following the anthrax incident in the fall of 2001. The EAP deployed a variety of traditional CISM strategies to respond to the unique circumstances of the event, but learned through the process that not all of the approaches resonated with the individuals involved. While some employees working in offices where potential exposure to anthrax-tainted mail existed were comforted with the medical testing and medication regimen provided in response to their assessed exposure risk, other employees found that process in and of itself additionally stressful–almost hinting at the "second injury." In many cases, the strategy employed by the EAP was contingent on a number of factors including the age of the employee, longevity with the organization, proximity to their support system, and pressure from family and friends regarding continued employment on Capitol Hill. The following excerpt from a recently published report on focus groups conducted with Capitol Hill employees following the anthrax incident in 2001 reflects the varied perspectives of and reactions to a number of different interventions employed by Capitol Hill employee assistance programs and other mental health practitioners in the aftermath of the event. While the number of participants ($n = 28$) in the focus groups was limited, their comments offer an important initial glimpse into and resounding evidence of the importance of this synergy and the alignment of interventions, resources and strategies to the people, needs and partners of the organization. At the same time, however, some of the comments and perspectives expressed reflect the importance of the EAP addressing the expectations of the organization and the work force as it prepares and plans for any disaster response and as it aligns itself with the rest of the organization in its continuity planning.

> Early psychological interventions to help workers cope with their feelings about the anthrax incident in the workplace received mixed reviews. Some comments were quite critical. "The Employment [sic] Assistance Office set up group therapy sessions . . . most of these people have been to a couple of those. I didn't think of those as very productive at all." "The way [this] psychologist approached it, it was, 'So, tell us about your feelings' or . . . 'That's normal,' every time we said [anything] . . . 'That's normal.' Don't just tell me that what I'm feeling is OK. Tell me why I'm feeling what I'm feeling." Others were more positive. "We went to a really good one that talked about coping skills." Some felt their own emotional support of one another was more helpful. "We all talked [to each other] about what we are doing to get by, but in a lot of ways we were getting therapy from each other. . . . So, yeah, there's psychologists out there who are experts on trauma, but we are experts on this trauma. . . ."
>
> In focus group comments, early psychological interventions did not receive particularly high approval ratings. Whereas some people felt that techniques such as relaxation were helpful, others wanted them better tailored to their needs. Even though their feelings were identified as "normal" for people in the context of extreme stress, these feelings were not normal in their usual experience, and therefore simple reassurance about the normalcy of their feelings was inadequate. (North, Pollio, Pfefferbaum, Megivern, Vythilingam, Westerhaus, Martin, & Hong, 2005, pgs. 84 & 86)

Clearly the message of "normalcy" related by the one psychologist referenced above may have been lost in his or her apparent failure to acknowledge the uniqueness of this particular event for the employees and to realize the limited experience of the individual involved to appreciate the "why" of the feelings, no matter how normal for the event. What the experiences of this limited group also reflects is that building resiliency into the organization's ability to meet disaster response demands and to carry out the organization's continuity planning and execution really comes down to building resiliency at that individual employee and union member level. Any EAP's ability to find organizational partners to assist in aligning and even carrying out its continuum of CISM services enhances its ultimate ability to match those services to the specific and often changing needs of the work force as it moves from planning and preparedness, through response and recovery, and ultimately to the continuity and sustainment of operations and the organization's human capital. Such synergy and alignment enables the EAP to benefit from the breadth of perspectives and interests across the organization as it attempts to meet the needs of the individual employee, manager and work group with the services and resources that are ideally suited for those particular needs at that specific time. Through this unique blend of partnerships, services can be better matrixed across the organization, creating an environment where multiple operations benefit from each other's knowledge, experiences and skills. For the EAP, such synergy provides additional opportunities to demonstrate value to the organization, while also setting the stage for a fuller integration into the organization–at the strategic, operational and human capital levels.

3. Maintain Effective Communication

If the world of disaster preparedness and crisis response has taught us anything, it is that communication is the vital ingredient in the development of any successful plan and in its full and successful execution. The organization and the work force are best prepared when they are well informed. As evident in the wide range of our own personal and professional experiences with crisis and trauma, it is far easier to deal with the known than the unknown, even when the imminent is somewhat challenging. This element for maximizing the human capital capability in disaster preparedness and continuity planning is familiar territory to the employee assistance field. EAPs have historically been grounded in a foundational belief that individuals and organizations are able to make the best decisions when they have the most complete information on the options before them. One of the basic tenets at the root of an EAP's confidential assessment process is the concept of "informed consent"–assuring that the individual has the complete information about any prospective disclosure prior to their actual consent to that disclosure–which epitomizes the EAP's sensitivity to the importance of information and its effective communication throughout the organization and with the work force in any disaster preparedness, response and management situation.

Again, the experiences of the House of Representatives' EAP during the anthrax incident exemplifies the vital role that the EAP can play for an organization in providing a forum for and the strategies to achieve this communication goal. As part of its "human matters" responsibilities, the EAP initiated a process of tracking all the questions and feedback that its professionals received as they conducted briefings, educational programs, status updates, and other informational dissemination activities over the course of the many weeks following the initial anthrax exposure on Capitol Hill. As referenced earlier, the EAP was able to serve as a conduit to the organization's leaders and the incident command team by channeling the questions and input from the work force upward, and doing so with absolute anonymity. In turn, the organization's leaders recognized the value in getting these very specific questions and gaining the real-time understanding of what was on the minds of the employees as the event continued to unfold and information changed over time. The questions and feedback initially posed by the employees became the specific topics for ongoing communications back to the employees from the organization's leaders and the incident command team. This process eventually morphed into a daily cycle of question solicitation and informational briefings to respond to the specific questions raised by the work force. Through the use of varied and diverse communication approaches and redundant communication vehicles (e.g., conference calls; e-mail; recorded messages at call-in centers; voice messages; print mailings; flyers and posters; Websites), the EAP found itself at the hub of the two-way communications effort within the organization–bringing the human capital perspective and sensitivity to the very messages that the EAP was crafting for the organization on a daily basis in response to the questions and inquiries raised by the work force. All of which was achieved through the close and ongoing partnership with other entities within the organization and those others serving as part of the response team assisting the organization. In the years since the anthrax response, the organization recognized the inherent value in this internally focused communication effort and further enhanced the process by establishing a communications team solely focused on this level of communications engagement during times of disaster and crisis response, and as part of the organization's continuity of operations. The lessons learned on the communications level during the anthrax incident have paid long-term dividends in the organization's ongoing communications efforts on a day-to-day basis–with the added bonus of fostering the ongoing partnership between the EAP and the organization's team and providing the regular interface between both teams that will ultimately benefit the organization in sustaining a human capital focus in its future disaster preparedness and continuity assurance efforts.

4. Target Investments in Training and Development

Since the tragic events of the fall of 2001, and with the subsequent acts of terrorism and violence in workplaces and communities around the world since then, one area of particular focus to most organizations is their need to foster an environment and an organizational culture that engages employees in the development of their own resiliency and that of the organization. As is evident in any disaster preparedness and continuity of operations planning, the best laid plans are only executable if the personnel are available and able to carry out the plan. This is the rub with any preparedness or continuity effort, and the crux of the report by the GAO. Employees at all levels need to be aware of and active participants in the continuity efforts of the entire organization, understanding the critical importance of their own flexibility in responding to varied scenarios, under a variety of circumstances, and possibly from a variety of different venues.

Before the EAP can assist the organization's work force in making this transition, it must first enable its own EA professionals to make the transition. While resiliency can be advanced through the building and development of additional skills and competencies beyond one's routine work responsibilities, it can also be enhanced through technical capabilities. For instance, since the events of 2001, the EAP staff has been fully outfitted with the technical capabilities (e.g., wireless networked laptops) to conduct business from any location. Perhaps more importantly, however, the staff has had the chance to incorporate off-site functionality into its routine business practices, giving the EAP the opportunity to test system and operational capabilities before circumstances demand that ability in the future. As part of the larger organization's continuity planning team, the EAP is also playing a vital role in defining the continuity training and plan testing requirements for the organization, with a specific focus on the human elements that are involved in moving a work force into a constant state of readiness and fostering the corresponding organizational climate that promotes employee engagement, participation and resiliency to see the value that preparedness brings to bear each day through the enhancement of the employee's performance and the expansion of their perspective and role in the larger organization.

5. *Leverage the Flexibility of Human Capital*

As the GAO observes in their report, the events of September 11th 2001, while presenting unprecedented challenges to many organizations, also "give ample evidence of the dedication and flexibility of federal, state, and local government employees in providing services to the American public" (GAO, 2004, pg. 16). This statement is equally true for the collection of private sector businesses and labor organizations affected, particularly those directly impacted by the strike on the World Trade Center towers in New York City. And the experiences of the employee assistance profession at Ground Zero and at the Pentagon that day and for many weeks and months thereafter bear testimony to the GAO's observation and bring forth valuable lessons for the larger employee assistance community. Indeed, the operational word was "flexibility."

With the unprecedented and catastrophic dimensions of those events, many of the EAPs "on the ground," so to speak, had to quickly adapt and respond in corresponding unprecedented fashion. Traditional CISM protocols had to be modified as the events continued for a prolonged period of time and as individual employees, responders, family members, and organizations continued to endure the intensity and actuality of the events far beyond the timeframe that most EA practitioners had been oriented to. So, as formal debriefings were put aside as the event "continued" for many individuals, EA professionals found themselves developing new strategies to provide more informal and "comfort-based" services to those impacted at the scene. As time moved on, the traditional CISM services advanced by Everly and Mitchell (1999) were augmented by many services and functions devised by EAPs in response to or in anticipation of emerging and changing needs at the site or at remote corporate locations. The demonstrated flexibility and value of so many of these responding EAPs enriched their position in their organizations in terms of subsequent disaster preparedness and continuity planning. Similar to the experience of the House Office of Employee Assistance in the aftermath of the anthrax incident, when it found its immediate value to the organization in the role of communications conduit, many of these EAPs realized their value in providing services through non-traditional and often untested ways. Their ability to be a critical player in their respective organization's response and at the heart of the organization at this most vulnerable of times demonstrates the inherent ability in EAPs in general to leverage their own human capital in order to contribute to the immediate and prevailing needs of the larger organization. That can only be accomplished through the resiliency and flexibility of EA professionals who embrace and have the competence and ability to carry out a concept of continuity of operations that covers the spectrum of services from the "EAP core technology" to the full range of critical incident stress response and management capabilities.

Specific evidence to the significance of this resiliency in the larger employee population of an organization is provided by North and her colleagues in their discussion of their focus group study of the specific effects of the anthrax incidents on Capitol Hill employees in the fall of 2001.

> Despite the disruption, workers said they pulled together and refused to allow derailment of their work, a testament to the resilience of this population. The 9/11 attacks a month earlier may have had both sensitizing and habituating effects in people's response to trauma and in the context of other stressors in individuals' lives. . . . The social support of exposed individuals for one another identified in these discussions should not be overlooked as a valuable source of strength to complement formal mental health interventions. (North, Pollio, Pfefferbaum, Megivern, Vythilingam, Westerhaus, Martin, & Hong, 2005, pgs. 85-86)

In the context of moving a workplace and a work force beyond disaster response and on to the establishment and execution of continuity of operations, this resiliency is a critical element in optimizing the human capital of an organization as its major organizational asset. When well integrated, the EAP of any organization is logically poised to help the organization build that resiliency long before the disaster strikes, the violence erupts or the threat of terrorism arises. By building on the commitment of the organization's leadership to engage the full potential of its human capital, and then to develop, foster and promote the synergy and partnerships, communication strategies, and training and educational programs to cultivate resiliency among its own EAP staff and the larger work force, the EAP demonstrates its larger and more universal value to the organization. In building its own resiliency and that of its EA professionals, the EAP has the capability to function as the critical partner and, at times, the actual trailblazer in helping the organization navigate this critical transition from a reactive and solely responsive mode, to a more proactive and continuous learning one–ultimately positioning itself and its host organization to not only engage, but to more fully realize the ultimate potential of its human capital assets during these most demanding of times. And in doing so, the EAP and the organization's leaders create the vital partnership with the work force in fostering the environment where each disaster, trauma or other critical incident serves as a valuable experience and resource in building the resiliency and flexibility of the EAP, the organization and the work force–moving ever closer to the goal of maximizing the organization's human capital assets and their role in effective continuity planning and ongoing execution.

6. Build Process to Identify and Share Lessons

For EA practitioners, this final organizational action should be no stranger. Several of our "EAP core technology" functions are contingent on the EA professional's ability to foster a "learning environment" in which individuals can learn something about themselves in order to make adjustments in their thinking or change behavior in order to correct a performance problem or a personal situation. The very premise on which the employee assistance field is based maintains that if presented with the facts and the reality of their job performance or personal situation, most employees will respond to that information positively by addressing the cause and attempting to learn through this performance confrontation and subsequent problem assessment process. In reality, EA professionals create this environment in any number of their interfaces in the workplace. Whether conducting an assessment with a depressed employee, advising a manager on the approach to take in confronting an employee with an extensive pattern of missed deadlines and unexplained absences, or consulting with the corporate and union leadership on the impact on the work force of a recent incident of workplace violence, the EA professional's effectiveness in each of these core functional areas is often contingent on his or her ability to foster and sustain a personal and organizational "learning environment." For many employees, managers, shop stewards and leaders when they first approach the EAP, they are frequently seeking information, often long before they are seeking solutions. As a result, the initial role of the EA professional is one of a "teacher." While that can be in the more traditional sense since many EAPs provide a variety of educational programs and training services in the workplace, it is usually on a more one-to-one basis and through a more subtle transaction. This ever present and long-standing role of the EAP and EA professionals more than fits the GAO's call for a process to identify and share lessons learned as a critical part of ensuring that the human capital resources of an organization are optimized in the continuity planning and execution efforts.

While the GAO offers specific suggestions for organizations on the use of various measures to support "data-driven decisions" (GAO, 2004, pg. 19), they report that according to their panel of experts, "having a framework prior to a disruption helps to gather data important to evaluating the effectiveness of human capital approaches during a disruption" (GAO, 2004, pg. 19) in services and operations. Consistent with the addition of the "seventh dimension" (Roman, 1990) to the "EAP core technology" calling for an evaluative component to any employee assistance effort, EAPs should be well positioned to serve as models to the larger organization in applying the lessons learned through their day-to-day assessment and consultation services and through their critical incident stress management experiences to the organization's disaster preparedness and management efforts and to the organization's ongoing continuity of operations.

CONCLUSIONS

The employee assistance field has a long tradition of charting new territory in the workplace and in work organizations. From the earliest roots of the profession when it was often frowned upon to raise the issue of alcoholism in the workplace to taking on the issue of drug addiction and the related fight of adequate insurance coverage, to meeting the unprecedented challenges of the escalation of workplace violence and global terrorism, Employee Assistance professionals have often been at the forefront in tackling the most difficult of issues for employers and employees, businesses and governmental agencies, labor representatives and their union brothers and sisters. With a strong history of advocating for and providing services in support of better performance in the workplace, whether at the individual employee or larger work group level, EAPs have continued to evolve as the needs of the workplace and the realities of the world of work have changed. With the emergence of the threat of and actuality of global terrorism and seeming epidemic and somewhat epic dimensions of recent natural disasters around the globe, EAPs have once again prepared for and responded with the expansion of services into the area of critical incident stress management (CISM) methodologies and related support systems and strategies. In citing the recent report of the General Accounting Office (GAO) as a framework for enhancing human capital continuity efforts in organizations, this discussion has raised the consideration that EAPs are once again–by virtue of their proactive approach to problem solving, their traditional human capital focus, their history of targeted and responsive service delivery, and their well-integrated position in the organization–poised to play a critical role in helping the organization and the work force assure that the organization's disaster preparedness, response capabilities and continuity of operations are consistently focused on general human capital considerations and reliant on those human capital capabilities unique to each organization.

REFERENCES

Employee Assistance Professionals Association (EAPA). (1998). Employee Assistance Programs (EAPs) and Health Care (HC)/Managed Care (MC) Laws. In *Member Resource Directory*. Arlington, VA: EAPA.

Employee Assistance Professionals Association (EAPA). (1999). *EAPA Standards and Professional Guidelines for Employee Assistance Programs–1999 Edition*. Arlington, VA: EAPA.

Everly, G.S., Jr. & Mitchell, J.T. (1997). Critical Incident Stress Management–CISM– A New Era and Standard of Care in Crisis Intervention. In G.S. Everly, Jr. (Ed.) *Innovations in Disaster and Trauma Psychology, Volume Two*. Ellicott City, MD: Chevron Publishing Corporation.

Everly, G.S., Jr. & Mitchell, J.T. (1999). Critical Incident Stress Management–CISM– A New Era and Standard of Care in Crisis Intervention, Second Edition. In G.S. Everly, Jr. (Ed.) *Innovations in Disaster and Trauma Psychology, Volume Two*. Ellicott City, MD: Chevron Publishing Corporation.

Mitchell, J.T. (1983). When disaster strikes . . . The critical incident stress debriefing process. *Journal of Emergency Medical Services, 8, (1)*, 36-39.

Mitchell, J.T. (1988). The history, status, and future of critical incident stress debriefings. *Journal of Emergency Medical Services, 13, (11)*, 49-52.

Mitchell, J.T. & Everly, G.S. (1996). *Critical Incident Stress Debriefing: An Operations Manual for the Prevention of Traumatic Stress Among Emergency Services and Disaster Workers*. Ellicott City, MD: Chevron Publishing Corporation.

Mitchell, J.T. & Resnik, H.L.P. (1986). *Emergency Response to Crisis: A Crisis Intervention Guidebook for Emergency Service Personnel*. Ellicott City, MD: Jeffrey T. Mitchell.

North, C.S., Pollio, D.E., Pfefferbaum, B., Megivern, D., Vythilingam, M., Westerhaus, E.T., Martin, G.J., & Hong, B.A. (2005). Capitol Hill Staff Workers' Experiences of Bioterrorism: Qualitative Findings From Focus Groups. *Journal of Traumatic Stress, 18 (1)*, February 2005, 79-88.

Roman, P.M, & Blum, T.C. (1985). The Core Technology of Employee Assistance Programs. *ALMACAN*, March, 8-9, 16, 18-19.

Roman, P.M. (1990). Seventh Dimension: A New Component Is Added to the EAP Core Technology. *Employee Assistance*, February, 8-9.

Slaby, A.E. (1989). *Aftershock: Surviving the Delayed Effects of Trauma, Crisis and Loss.* New York: Villard Books.

Tracey, W.R. (1998). *The Human Resources Glossary, Second Edition: The Complete Desk Reference for HR Executives, Managers, and Practitioners.* Boca Raton, FL: St. Lucie Press.

U.S. General Accounting Office (2004). *Human Capital: Opportunities to Improve Federal Continuity Planning Guidance.* GAO-04-384. Washington, DC: April 2004.

doi:10.1300/J490v21n03_04

Managing the Trauma
of Community Violence
and Workplace Accidents in South Africa

R. Paul Maiden
Lourens Terblanche

SUMMARY. Community violence that spills over to the workplace is substantially impacting the quality of work/life in South Africa. Gold mining is one of the country's leading industries and also one of the most dangerous. Internal and external employee assistance programs are well represented in South Africa and are helping employees deal with the economic and psychological fall-out of community violence and work related accidents. doi:10.1300/J490v21n03_05 *[Article copies available for a fee from The Haworth Document Delivery Service: 1-800-HAWORTH. E-mail address: <docdelivery@haworthpress.com> Website: <http://www.HaworthPress. com> © 2006 by The Haworth Press, Inc. All rights reserved.]*

KEYWORDS. Community violence, mining accidents, South Africa, employee assistance programs (EAPs)

INTRODUCTION

Community violence in South Africa has a direct and severe impact on its economy and its workplaces. Community violence in the form of frequent car jackings, bank robberies, ATM robberies, street robberies,

[Haworth co-indexing entry note]: "Managing the Trauma of Community Violence and Workplace Accidents in South Africa." Maiden, R. Paul, and Lourens Terblanche. Co-published simultaneously in *Journal of Workplace Behavioral Health* (The Haworth Press, Inc.) Vol. 21, No. 3/4, 2006, pp. 89-100; and: *Workplace Disaster Preparedness, Response, and Management* (ed: R. Paul Maiden, Rich Paul, and Christina Thompson) The Haworth Press, Inc., 2006, pp. 89-100. Single or multiple copies of this article are available for a fee from The Haworth Document Delivery Service [1-800-HAWORTH, 9:00 a.m. - 5:00 p.m. (EST). E-mail address: docdelivery@haworthpress.com].

Available online at http://jwbh.haworthpress.com
© 2006 by The Haworth Press, Inc. All rights reserved.
doi:10.1300/J490v21n03_05

89

beatings, rape, burglary and homicides are having a substantial negative impact on the South African workplace. There were 22,000 recorded murders in 2000–more than those who were killed in car accidents (Steven, 2003).

In South Africa, workplace hostilities are reported to be *abnormally high*, with some surveys indicating that as many as four out of five workers have experienced hostile behavior at the workplace during their working life (Safety Council, 2005). In a recent study on *The Changing Workplace* (in South Africa), 78% of employees confirmed that they had been bullied or victimized at least once in their careers (International Labour Course, 2005). Sexual harassment is also a widespread problem in the South African workplace. An attorney from the Women's Legal Center, an Non Government Organisation (NGO), estimates that some 75% of women experience some form of sexual harassment and that 40% of these women had left their jobs or changed jobs as a result of the harassment (Bureau of Democracy, Human Rights and Labor, 2004).

Although workplace violence is reported to be increasing even in places that have been relatively safe, emergency service workers frequently face one form of violence or another, some more than others. For example, a study on ambulance staff in South Africa reported that 70% of them had been subjected to verbal abuse, 50% to physical violence, bullying and mobbing, 40% to racial harassment and 30% to sexual harassment (International Labour Course, 2005).

The result has been a marked decline in direct foreign investment and an estimated 25,000 professionals emigrating from South Africa annually, 60% of which is directly attributed to violent crime (Steven, 2003).

South Africa has a well-developed system of internal and external employee assistance programs all of whom are adept at handling trauma resulting from community violence that has spilled over into the workplace as well as work-related accidents, particularly those that have occurred in the gold and coal mining industry which is fraught with the dangers of sub-surface mining.

TRAUMA MANAGEMENT BY THE INDEPENDENT COUNSELING AND ADVISORY SERVICES (ICAS) AND THE CAREWAYS GROUP

ICAS and the Careways Group are two of the largest external employee assistance providers in South Africa (Terblanche, 2005). Both have had extensive experience in workplace trauma management some of which is unique to the economic and cultural climate of Southern Africa that is characterized by a high incident of community violence as well as tribal clashes resulting from territorial disagreements and long-standing traditional inter-tribal conflict.

ICAS, a UK-based firm, is a global provider of employee assistance and other behavior-risk-management services. They currently service approximately 150 organizations in Southern Africa covering some 200,000 lives. ICAS reported a trauma-debriefing incident where they were called to a client company compound following an outbreak of community violence. The episode was the result of complaints by local youth over the management of a company sponsored soccer club and the alleged killing of a youth during violent clashes with riot police at a blockade disrupting company business activities. Rampaging youth raided the company's facilities including a new ultra modern building and the company housing estate, causing substantial damage and financial loss to the company. They also set fire to fuel tanks, looted property, and in some instances assaulted and threatened individuals with knives and other street weapons. The company clubhouse was looted and torched and the house of several employees who lived outside of the compound was burned to the ground. The attack left four company personnel with injuries and required an urgent helicopter evacuation of a large group of spouses and children of local and expatriate workers. The violence lasted several days, resulted in five deaths, numerous injuries and prompted a government investigation.

Careways reported a rather unique situation where they conducted two consecutive trauma debriefings, the first being an industrial accident followed by a subsequent suicide of a maintenance supervisor who worked at the accident site. A Careways corporate client experienced a major gas tank explosion at chemical plant in a large rural community. The explosion claimed several lives and resulted in numerous injuries. Many of the surviving employees were afraid to return to work for fear of another explosion that might cost them their lives. A large number of contract workers were also afraid that they would lose their jobs because of the explosion. Careways went to the job site and over a three-week period conducted debriefing sessions for 852 employees at various chemical plant facilities. Thirty-five percent of these workers were contract laborers, not typically covered by the Careways service contract. However, the company decided to include all the workers in the trauma debriefing sessions.

Two months later Careways was summoned back to the chemical plant because of the suicide of a senior plant maintenance official. They provided trauma debriefing services to 152 employees who had worked with the maintenance supervisor. The employee suicide raised new concerns for the chemical plant managers, resulting in individual counseling sessions with 76 employees. Six other employees reported that they had sought out private therapy on their own to cope with the stressors of these two related incidents (Terblanche, 2005).

TRAUMA MANAGEMENT IN THE MINING INDUSTRY

South Africa's economy also relies heavily on its gold mining production. The gold and coal mining industry is one of South Africa's leading employers. It is also one of the most dangerous workplaces as demonstrated by several recent newswire articles reporting underground earthquakes, one of many hazards that accompany deep below ground mining operations.

Johannesburg:
26 Miners Trapped by Quake Hauled to Safety; 16 Missing

Rescue workers hauled 26 miners to safety in a frantic operation to save workers trapped underground by an earthquake that shook the northern parts of South Africa on Wednesday. The quake, which had a preliminary magnitude of 5, damaged buildings and caused scores of minor injuries. It was centered near Stilfontein, 125 miles southwest of Johannesburg. Sixteen miners were still missing, DRD Gold said; 3,200 have been evacuated. (Orlando Sentinel, 3/10/05)

Carletonville:
Rockfall Traps 10 in Mine in South Africa; 5 Dead

The death toll in a gold-mining accident rose to five when rescue workers pulled out the bodies of three miners trapped in the shaft. An underground earth tremor caused a rockfall Tuesday at the mine in Carletonville trapping 10. (Orlando Sentinel, 5/12/05)

These and other death and injury-causing accidents result in considerable physical and emotional trauma to the mineworkers. As a result, the mining industry has taken a lead in the development of post-traumatic stress programs.

Psychologists at the Chamber of Mines, a human resource consortium of mining houses (Badenhorst & Van Schalkwyk, 1992), were the first to implement trauma management programs called the Care of Pressurized Employees program (COPE). The impetus for their development was one of the most catastrophic mining accidents that occurred in 1987 after a methane gas explosion in the mineshaft severed a double-decker elevator cables sending 52 mineworkers to their death at the bottom of the shaft (De Beer, 1988). For many years prior, the Chamber of Mines developed safety systems within mines, provided first aid training, and distributed literature to the employees and trained workers on mine safety (Chamber of Mines of South Africa, 1989).

COPE was developed to provide a management system to "assist employees in coping effectively with the demands and pressures that adversely affect quality of life, health and productivity following traumatic mining incidents. COPE will provide employees who, experience difficulties in coping with the effects of trauma, early access to professional care" (Badenhorst & Van Schalkwyk, 1992). To promote the utilization of this trauma management program and to demonstrate management support of the program, the Chamber of Mines developed the following policy statement:

> The management of this mine supports the COPE program to assist the employees and their families to manage psycho-social problems which have adverse effects on their job satisfaction, quality of work, productivity and lifestyle. The following principles pertain:

- Personal information of the employees utilizing the program will be kept strictly confidential.
- Employees treated for trauma-related stress will receive the same consideration as those extended to employees with medical problems.
- Participation in the program will not prejudice an employee's job security or chances of promotion.
- Participation in the program is voluntary.
- Management reserves the right to recommend employees for assistance. (Badenhorst & Van Schalkwyk, 1992)

The COPE Program

The COPE program was conceptualized in three specific operational modes:

1. Providing care to employees affected by a past critical incident;
2. Providing care to employees involved in minor critical incidents;
3. Providing care to employees involved in major critical incidents.

1. Providing Care to Employees Affected by a Past Critical Incident

At the inception of the COPE program, it was determined that a relatively large number of mineworkers were likely experiencing some degree of post-traumatic stress due to a high incidence of injuries and death resulting from previous mining accidents. At the height of production of gold mining in South Africa, it was not uncommon to employ 25,000 to 30,000 workers in one gold field with three to four major shafts and dozens of sub-shafts. These shafts are fraught with danger resulting in injuries and fatalities occurring from sub-surface earth tremors and quakes, collapsed pilings, cave-ins, and methane gas explosions. Larger mining operations maintain separate accommodations for paraplegic and quadriplegic miners; disabled workers are unlikely to return to their rural villages as there are no rehabilitation services or facilities available nor are they able to maneuver around their village, as there are no paved roads, sidewalks or disabled access. The disabled miners living in the mine hostels are provided medical care, physical rehabilitation to the greatest extent possible and ongoing counseling through the employee assistance program (EAP) (to clarify–COPE is operated through the employee assistance program). The disabled workers are re-assigned new job responsibilities such as cutting and stitching miner overalls, making tracksuits for the mining house sports teams, and winding spools of electrical cables and light fixtures that were to be used to light the underground shaft tunnels.

The COPE program also provided identification, assessment and treatment of mineworkers whose injuries were not as apparent as those physically disabled workers but whose psychological trauma could be just as debilitating. This initial component also included mandatory employee orientation on the COPE program as well as access to the mine's EAP. Supervisors were also trained to recognize symptoms of mineworkers who may be suffering from post-traumatic stress and referral to the EAP for counseling. The focus of the supervisor training was identifying post-traumatic stress syndrome (PTSD) affected employees based on production and work performance criteria rather than clinical symptoms.

2. Providing Care to Employees Involved in Minor Critical Incidents

The second operational mode of the COPE program addresses the needs of employees involved in minor critical incidents. A minor critical incident is not defined in terms of the intensity of its effects on the organization, but it terms of the degree to which it disrupts employees inside the organization where it occurs (Badenhorst & Van Schalkwyk, 1992).

In the event of a minor incident, the ordinary support systems of both the organization and the mineworker are still intact and fully functional. Since many individuals involved in minor incidents exhibit no immediate stress reaction (delayed nature of PTSD), a program of proactive intervention was developed where key personnel managers at various mining sites were trained to follow up after the minor incident, identify workers involved as well as those on the periphery. Once these workers were identified, they were interviewed and where appropriate, referred to the employee assistance program and a COPE counselor for education and therapeutic services as necessary. Direct services were frequently provided by the EAP counselor due to the minor nature of the incident. However, on occasion there are situations requiring a community referral for more extensive services beyond the scope of the EAP.

3. Providing Care to Employees Involved in Major Critical Incidents

The third component of the COPE program was designed to meet the needs of organization and mineworkers involved in a major critical incident resulting in the disruption of the entire mine operation. The earthquake at the DRD gold mine in Stilfontein referred to at the beginning of this article is one such incident where the entire operation and existing support systems was adversely affected. Loss of life, significant worker injury and damage to facilities both above and below ground appear to be substantial. The premise of the third component of the COPE model is that major critical incidents in mines are unpredictable (impact of destruction on workers, material and existing infrastructure). The mode three management of critical incidents requires that mine management follow a previously established protocol in order to effectively manage the critical incident and its expected aftermath. During the major critical incident, an attempt is made to conduct trauma debriefing sessions to involved workers, observers, rescue workers and families followed by availability and referral for individual counseling as necessary.

During major critical incidents, affected individuals are managed in groups on-site by EAP staff. They also provide on-site consultation to mine management on human behavior issues concerning the macro management of the critical incident. Since trauma-related circumstances can make intervention impractical, the collective addressing of all involved through alternative mediums after the critical incident provides an opportunity to address the following issues:

- An atmosphere of motivation and coping with the critical incident is created.
- Mine management's acknowledgement of the human response to critical incidents is demonstrated.
- Rational perception of the events can be stimulated among all parties involved.

Employees and their families can be reminded of how to deal with and where to receive personal assistance regarding PTSD. The effective systems management of employees following exposure to a critical mining incident is dependent on important trauma management principles (Badenhorst & Van Schalkwyk, 1992). They are:

Simplicity. Any intervention strategy aimed at assisting employees following a critical mining industry should be as simple as possible as the following guidelines suggest:

- Physical comfort, consolation and protection from further harm
- Reunification with natural support systems, i.e., family, friends, coworkers
- Encouragement in the ventilation of feelings and experiences
- Stimulation of rational perspective (providing the real facts)
- Education regarding human reactions to trauma
- Stimulation of realistic and constructive activity
- Encouragement of coping behavior
- Focusing on inner strengths and potential
- Continuous stimulation of hope

Proximity. Support should be provided as close as possible to the mine-site disaster scene by utilizing individuals from normal support systems such as family, friends, coworkers or supervisors to render the necessary bio-psychosocial assistance.

Immediacy. Trauma management should be rendered as soon as possible after the mining critical incident has occurred.

Expectancy. Resumption of normal activities as soon as possible following the traumatic incident is the major objective of management. The expectation should be that recovery is possible through the utilization of personal coping skills and potential. A "sick person" status should not be ascribed to any employee who has been exposed to a traumatic incident (Badenhorst & Van Schalkwyk, 1992).

It is noteworthy to mention that the COPE's mining trauma management model includes family members in addition to the mineworkers. Large mining operations are usually located in remote rural locations with mine employees typically being housed in mining compounds or communities that are constructed and owned by the mining house. These compounds and communities are replete with grocery stores, a hospital and clinic, dining facilities, schools, and recreational facilities such as swimming pools, movie houses, social clubs, beer halls and taverns. As a child, the first author lived in a similar railroad depot community in a remote rural town of Choma, Zambia (formerly Northern Rhodesia). The Railroad Employee homes, as well as the local school, the grocery store, the outdoor movie theatre (consisting of a large wooden panel painted white and rows of benches behind the grocery store), the bank (housed in the train depot), and health clinic were all owned by Rhodesia Railroads. This concept is quite similar to the company towns created by earlier U.S. industrialists, such as George Pullman and H. J. Heinz, to accommodate the day-to-day needs of workers and to promote productivity.

In the South African mining industry, housing is often included in the compensation package and the layout is similar to the U.S. military base housing with accommodation being assigned based on position in the organization. Unmarried workers and mineworkers recruited from the neighboring countries of Botswana, Zimbabwe, Zambia, Lesotho and Namibia are housed in large single-sex dormitory-like hostels, each with its own dining, recreational and drinking facilities. Some mining operations also maintain housing for visiting family members as most of the miners work on contracts of nine months or longer and are working a considerable distance from their home community. Visiting family quarters were developed in response to the high rate of absenteeism among mineworkers who were homesick for their families and often abandoned their jobs to return home to tend to family issues. The mining houses found that they also experienced attrition due to a high rate of pedestrian road accidents of workers who had left the mine compound to travel to their home village (Maiden, 1999). As a result, families are intricately woven into the fabric of the mining industry in South Africa and are severely impacted when there are mining accidents resulting in injury or loss of life.

The wisdom of the decision to extend PTSD services to family members was evidenced in what is referred to as the Virginia mine dump accident that resulted in loss of life and significant damage to the rural community of Virginia, South Africa. South Africa's landscape is pock-marked by large above ground mine dumps that essentially contain the slough of the gold mining industry. These dumps are multiple stories high and contain residual clay, soil and ground rock left over from the gold extraction process. This clay-like substance is pumped in thick liquid form, layer upon layer into the mine dump and is left to dry in the sun. For safety reasons, it is important that each layer dries and solidifies before a subsequent layer is applied. In the Virginia mine dump incident there was a breach in one of the exterior walls that resulted in a mudslide that essentially consumed a substantial portion of the Virginia community. This accident occurred when many miners were far below ground and unaware of what had occurred. Upon coming to the surface, many workers found that they were without homes and some had lost family members. This incident dramatically affected an entire community.

The South African workplace is also substantially impacted by post-traumatic stress because of deaths from AIDS-related complications, one of the highest in the world. The South African population currently stands at 47 million with an HIV/AIDS prevalence of 10% (Xinhua News Agency, 2005).

Post-traumatic stress has also been identified as a national concern after the end of the apartheid era because of the experiences of ex-detainees, families of murdered political activists, awareness of abuse within the family, and the dramatic rise in violent crime outside the townships where the rates have always been high (Du Plessis, 2001).

CONCLUSIONS

Experience has demonstrated that a traumatic incident within a mining environment will have a significant impact on mineworkers, mine management, family members and the community or compound surrounding the mine. It is fitting then that attention is given to its effective prevention, and management by means of comprehensive interdisciplinary planning and intervention. The EAP services originally initiated through the Chamber of Mines to the South African mining industry has provided the best solution by offering those employees who have been traumatized in critical mining incidents, with an opportunity to resume a healthy personal life and a productive work life, free of the residual effects associated with trauma producing workplace accidents.

Since the inception of the COPE program, the Chamber of Mines Employee Assistance Programs was spun off to form the independent Centre for Human Development (CHD). While the Centre continues to provide EAP and critical incident debriefing services to many of the mining operations throughout South Africa they are also the external provider of services to numerous other employers in South Africa. The COPE model has been modified with critical incident services being provided to workers and employers who have been impacted by the rise in carjacking, home invasions, workplace robberies, and community violence that continues to plague South Africa. In recent years, because of the closings of a number of South African mining operations, the COPE program has also been incorporated into a mineworker retrenchment program (Historian, 1999). The Centre for Human Development recently acquired Human Dynamics, another South African EAP vendor, and formed the Careways Group, which is cited above.

A study by Harper (1999) on the development of workplace human services in South Africa indicated that of the top 100 companies surveyed in South Africa 42% had implemented an EAP. Of this group, 85% have incorporated trauma management training as part of their wellness education programs offered to employees and managers (Harper, 1999). In urban areas such as Johannesburg, Pretoria, Durban and Cape Town, street violence is a common everyday occurrence. Harper suggests that South Africa's "culture of violence" has resulted in many employers offering violence prevention and avoidance programs but also *post-violence stress reaction* programs to help employees deal with the aftermath of a carjacking, purse snatching, home invasion or other random street crime (Harper, 2000). She indicates that knowledge of managing post-traumatic stress is a fundamental requirement of all employee assistance and other human resource providers in South Africa. ICAS' experience in helping an employer respond to an episode of community violence is also a unique aspect of trauma management in the South African workplace.

REFERENCES

Badenhorst, J.C.C. and S.J. Van Schalkwyk (1992). Minimizing post traumatic stress in critical mining incidents. In Maiden, R.P. (ed.) *Employee Assistance Programs in South Africa.* New York: Haworth Press.

Bureau of Democracy, Human Right and Labor (2004). Country reports on human rights practices. February 25th. Retrieved from: *http//:www.state.gov.drl.rls.hrrpt/2003/27752/htm*

Chamber of Mines of South Africa (1989). *Mine safety division, mining survey.* Johannesburg.

De Beer, D.W. (1988). Critical incidence of the Kinross and Saint Helena mine disaster. *Institute or Personnel Management Journal.*

Du Plessis, A. (2001). Occupational social work in South Africa. In Maiden, R.P. (ed.) *Global Perspectives of Occupational Social Work.* New York: Haworth Press.

Harper, T. (2000). South Africa. In Masi, D. (ed.) *International Anthology of Employee Assistance Programs.* Washington, DC: Dallen, Inc.

Harper, T. (1999). *Employee assistance programming and professional developments in South Africa.* In Maiden, R.P. (1999) *Employee Assistance Services in the New South Africa.* New York: Haworth Press.

Hiestermann, G. (1999). A model for psychosocial management of retrenchment: The South African mining industry. In Maiden, R.P. (1999) *Employee Assistance Services in the New South Africa.* New York: Haworth Press.

International Labour Course (ILO) (2005). In focus programme on safety and health at work and the environment. Retrieved from: *http://www.ilo.org/public/english/protection/safewrok/violence/intro.html*

International Labour Course (ILO) (2005). Violence and stress in the workplace: Scope and impact of violence and stress on emergency services. Retrieved from: *http://www.ilo.org/public/english/protection/safewrok/violence/intro.html*

Maiden, R.P. (1999). *Employee Assistance Services in the New South Africa.* New York: Haworth Press.

Orlando Sentinel (2005). Johannesburg: 26 miners trapped by quake hauled to safety; 16 missing. March 3rd.

Orlando Sentinel (2005). Carltonsville: Rockfall traps 10 miners in South Africa; 5 dead. May 5th.

Steven, H. (2003). Turning the tide of violence in South Africa. Retrieved December 5, 2005 from IDRC Reports. Program Website *http://www.idrc.ca/en/ew-45629-201-1.*

Terblanche, L. (2005). CISM in the South African context. Technical report, Pretoria, South Africa.

The Changing Workplace (2005). Retrieved from: *http://www.safety-council.org/info/OSH/bullies.html*

Xinhua News Agency (2005). South African population grows to 47 million.

doi:10.1300/J490v21n03_05

Resiliency in the Aftermath of Repetitious Violence in the Workplace

Sally Bishop
Bob McCullough
Christina Thompson
Nakiya Vasi

SUMMARY. The definition and occurrence of traumatic events is expanding and impacts everyone's lives in some way. The degree to which a violent event impacts an individual, a group, a workplace or the community varies. Unfortunately violent events are all too common. Businesses are realizing the significance of violence as a workplace problem and the varying degrees of trauma that has a devastating impact on employee retention, workplace functionality and personal well-being. The events can include industrial or natural disasters; worksite accidents; organizational changes; suicide; homicides; robbery; assault; threats of violence and even terrorism. How prepared an organization is varies and may be correlated with how resilient individuals and the entire workplace are after workplace violence/trauma. This article focuses on what workplace violence and trauma includes, the effects of repeat events, how resilient people are while trying to prevent additional events if possible in the workplace. doi:10.1300/J490v21n03_06 *[Article copies available for a fee from The Haworth Document Delivery Service: 1-800-HAWORTH. E-mail address: <docdelivery@haworthpress.com> Website: <http://www.HaworthPress.com> © 2006 by The Haworth Press, Inc. All rights reserved.]*

[Haworth co-indexing entry note]: "Resiliency in the Aftermath of Repetitious Violence in the Workplace." Bishop, Sally et al. Co-published simultaneously in *Journal of Workplace Behavioral Health* (The Haworth Press, Inc.) Vol. 21, No. 3/4, 2006, pp. 101-118; and: *Workplace Disaster Preparedness, Response, and Management* (ed: R. Paul Maiden, Rich Paul, and Christina Thompson) The Haworth Press, Inc., 2006, pp. 101-118. Single or multiple copies of this article are available for a fee from The Haworth Document Delivery Service [1-800-HAWORTH, 9:00 a.m. - 5:00 p.m. (EST). E-mail address: docdelivery@haworthpress.com].

Available online at http://jwbh.haworthpress.com
© 2006 by The Haworth Press, Inc. All rights reserved.
doi:10.1300/J490v21n03_06

KEYWORDS. Violence, workplace trauma, repeat events, resiliency and adaptive strategies

INTRODUCTION

What Is Workplace Violence?

We need to be able to identify what is deemed violence since we do get exposed to many events that could be traumatizing. What would be considered violence falls into a continuum of a wide range of behaviors/ actions that can be physical or psychological and that, for some, may be considered as acceptable. The following chart outlines a variety of behaviors that would be included (Chappell & DiMartino, 1999):

Homicide	Scratching	Leaving offensive messages
Rape	Squeezing, pinching	Aggressive posturing
Robbery	Stalking	Rude gestures
Wounding	Harassment, including sexual and racial	Interfering with work tools and equipment
Battering	Bullying	Hostile behavior
Physical attacks	Mobbing	Swearing
Kicking	Victimizing	Shouting
Biting	Intimidation	Name calling
Punching	Threats	Innuendo
Spitting	Ostracism	Deliberate silence

Some of these behaviors may not be immediately thought of as violent but many individuals will experience or witness these types of acts in their lifetime. It is important to note that not all stressful events are violent or traumatic. You cannot go a day without an incident being highlighted by the media, whether locally or nationally.

Unfortunately many violent acts are not reported so the percentages that are reported to the workplace, law enforcement, etc., may, indeed, be higher. Depending on the intensity, not everyone responds the same way to a single event and events could have a cumulative effect which could take time until a reaction is triggered. Some of these acts and events will occur in the workplace. Not all of the occurrences will be tied to the workplace directly but that is where the problem is brought to light. Personal problems also come into play with how people cope. The following statistics tied to some of the examples of a few behaviors/actions that were listed in the previous chart are eye-opening. These are outlined in a fact sheet on *http://civil.nih.gov* which includes the following:

- Murder is the leading cause of workplace fatalities according to the Occupational, Safety and Health Administration (OSHA). The guidelines state that "Employers can be cited if violence is a recognized hazard in their workplaces and they do nothing to prevent it. Therefore, if the company has received notice that a former partner has threatened to harm an employee or has made attempts to harm an employee at work, the company will have a duty to protect that employee. This duty extends to the threatened harm, or any other harm that could logically flow from the threatened harassment, such as injury to other employees who attempt to protect the threatened employee (National Center for Victims of Crime, 1996).
- An average of 20 workers are murdered each week in the United States. The majority of these murders are robbery-related crimes.
- Workplace bullying is the deliberate repeated, hurtful verbal mistreatment of a person (the target) by a cruel perpetrator (the bully). The vast majority of bullies (over 80%) are bosses with the remainder being co-workers. Male bullies represent 50% of all bullies. When a target is female, 46% of the time her bully is also female. Bullying is more prevalent than sexual harassment and racial discrimination. One recent study estimates that approximately one out of five U.S. workers has experienced destructive bullying in the past year.
- Partner violence contributes to lost productivity due to premature death: Homicide is the number one leading cause of death for women on the job, and 20% of those were murdered by their partner at the workplace (Bureau of Labor Statistics, 1993).
- The National Institute for Justice estimates that from 1987 to 1990, domestic violence cost Americans $67 billion a year.
- An estimated one million workers are assaulted annually in U.S. workplaces. Most of these assaults occur in service settings such as hospitals, nursing homes, and social service agencies.

Workplace Violence and the Impact

On average, workplaces in the U.S. will see one employee killed and approximately twenty-five employees seriously injured in a week, by a current or former employee of the same company (Armour, 2004). Even though the violence itself can be a split-second event, the effects can last indefinitely. Although the majority of employees eventually recover from such trauma, a workplace incident may exacerbate the symptoms of those employees with pre-morbid depression or anxiety and other mental health issues (Armour, 2004). Financially, a workplace incident can cost an organization between $6.4 and $36 billion in lost productivity from employee resignations, a weakened public impression, costly insurance, added security, and other factors (Gray et al., 1999).

Based on this information, it is important to note that workplace violence is clustered among various types of settings. According to 1996 data, the highest risk of workplace deaths is placed on taxi drivers, compared with any other occupation. However, employees of health care, community services and retail settings are at an increased risk of non fatal violence. The retail and service settings account for more than half of workplace deaths and 85% of nonfatal workplace violence (Jenkins, 1996). According to a review of workplace violence literature, nurses are starting to feel increasingly prone to violence on the job. Reports from the Bureau of Justice mirror this sentiment with statistics of up to 429,100 nurses as victims of violence crimes each year between 1993 and 1999 (Doody, 2003). Employees working within human resources are increasingly seen as targets for violence due to their association with layoffs, work schedules, salaries etc. (Gray et al., 1999).

The U.S. Department of Health and Human Services' National Institute for Occupational Safety and Health (NIOSH) 1996 publication on violence in the workplace listed the following risk factors associated with workplace violence:

1. Contact with the public
2. Exchange of money
3. Delivery of passengers, goods, or services.
4. Having a mobile workplace such as a taxicab or police cruiser
5. Working with unstable or volatile persons in health care, social service, or criminal justice settings
6. Working alone or in small numbers
7. Working late at night or during early morning hours
8. Working in high-crime areas

9. Guarding valuable property or possessions
10. Working in community-based settings (Jenkins, 1996)

After a violent incident at a workplace, an organization's response is based on emergency procedures set in place within its policies. A response may include having a critical incidence team on-site, counseling, compensation and paid-leave for the victim in order to recover. Based on research conducted in 1999, researchers studied various organizations, including evaluating their workplace violence procedures. They found that out of 110 retail businesses they examined, only one had any type of policy on workplace violence. Given the prevalence of workplace violence, it is surprising that a setting faced with the likelihood of violence would not strongly protect its employees by developing and implementing procedures and provisions. As concerning, only five of the thirty-five health services business studies had some sort of provision in place for workplace violence (Gray et al., 1999).

These statistics demonstrate that this is a growing problem, so the question we must ask is–what must occur to tackle these concerns? There are several approaches, but some of the consistent themes include:

1. There must be education on what violence is, i.e., that it can be either by threat or actual harm to person or property.
2. No threats or harm will be tolerated and that must be clearly communicated to everyone at the workplace.
3. There must be a workplace violence policy. The role of management and supervisors in observing and reporting behaviors and acts must be clear. In addition, the level of Critical Incident Stress Management Services required will depend on the intensity of the need. The Workplace Violence Research Institute has compiled the following list of "Violence Prone Behaviors" for management to look for. As with any of the following, it is a pattern and intensity you are looking for:
   • Increased use of alcohol and/or illegal drugs
   • Unexplained increase in absenteeism
   • Noticeable decrease in attention to appearance and hygiene
   • Depression and withdrawal
   • Explosive outbursts of anger or rage
   • Threats or verbal abuse of co-workers and supervisors
   • Repeated comments that indicate suicidal tendencies
   • Frequent, vague physical complaints

- Noticeably unstable emotional response
- Behavior which is suspected of paranoia
- Preoccupation with previous incidents of violence
- Increased mood swings
- Has a plan to "solve all problems"
- Resistance and over-reaction to changes in procedures
- Empathy with individuals committing violence
- Fascination with violent and/or sexually explicit movies or publications
- Escalation of domestic problems
- Large withdrawals from or closing his/her account in the company's credit union
- Repeated violations of company policies (Mattman, 1998).
4. Training for everyone.
5. How to get the organization stabilized after the situation has passed.
6. Incorporate the lessons learned to help prevent other similar events.
7. Continued education, awareness and updating of materials, resources and always communicating that information.

Unfortunately, many behaviors and acts can and often do occur multiple times. We need to be aware of repeated events and what that reinforces for workers.

Responding to multiple incidents in the workplace can be extremely complicated when it comes to crisis intervention services. What makes a response to multiple incidents unique is not the type of incident that has occurred but the timeframe of the incidents. Examples of multiple incidents in the workplace could be a financial institution that experiences two robberies in a short period of time or perhaps a retail store that experiences a death during a natural disaster impacting the community. These examples demonstrate multiple incidents that have their own unique impact on an organization and may be addressed in a same crisis intervention response.

Magellan Health Services' CISM team has adapted similar consultation questions utilized by ICISF (International Critical Incident Stress Foundation) when assessing for a multiple incident crisis response to include:

- How many incidents have occurred?
- Can you describe the types of incidents with as much detail as possible?

- Provide the timeframe for the incidents?
- Describe the degree of exposure for each employee?
- Is there one incident on which individuals seem to be focused?

These questions, added to Magellan's existing CISM consultation, facilitate a comprehensive assessment of need and the opportunity to structure the appropriate level of service delivery from among the array of available services. The depth of this consultation allows the crisis incident responder to be prepared for issues that may arise while providing the service.

As part of the CISM consultation, clinicians ask if affected employees have experienced another critical incident within the previous 12 months. This has become an important part of the follow-up process because research and experience have shown that individuals with a recent history of trauma tend to have a more pronounced stress response with subsequent traumas and these individuals may require additional support. Notably, some company leaders recognized how this impacts employees and inquired about trends related to multiple critical incidents. Typically, approximately 13% of events in a quarter involve support to a group of employees that had experienced multiple traumas within the past twelve months. Often when CISM services are requested for a seemingly mild event, employees have already come near to exhausting their coping skills due to the impact of a prior traumatic experience and require additional support. Of note, in one quarter of the year, 14% of all robbery events occurred at bank branches that had been robbed within the past year. (Repeat robberies at other businesses, such as retailers, were rare.) A review of events with multiple traumas in the past quarter revealed that company leaders almost always made use of an on-site counselor. These services, without exception, were found to be helpful or very helpful by employees and company management. Recent findings revealed that 85% of employees had fully returned to previous levels of functioning.

Another Magellan customer, a large retail organization that deals with numerous robberies, has found that when responding to repetitious events, the following is beneficial:

- Response to repetitious events should be organized in a multi-disciplinary manner.
- The exposure and vulnerability of employees for repeated violence in locations, if not taken seriously, may result in resentment, anger, increased stress-related illness and high attrition.

- Preparation is vital. Provide a kit that is centrally located that provides a list of what to do. Include written materials to educate employees on common trauma response, general do's and don'ts for self care and the phone number to the EAP or other beneficial resources.
- Establishing a method to track and organize initial response and follow-up for events is strongly encouraged. Events may also be categorized by the level of severity of the violence and other stress factors co-occurring at a specific location. Preparedness and interventions may require adjusting according to the level of violence.
- Consider training a group of peer volunteers or regional corporate responders to address immediate post-event needs. Employees may want to go home after an event and have the EAP come in the next morning. Training for regional responders to pull the group together for a brief 15-30 minutes before departing the work-site may help stabilize the workgroup. Employees may need a chance to talk a bit, receive a little education and, very importantly, know that a plan is in place to address safety and the process of recovering from this event together. Volunteers may need to be formally trained in conducting a Defusing in advance of the event. The volunteers or regional responders should have access to an EAP or appropriate professional for consultation.
- If the organization has a Corporate Security Office where any and all incidents are reported centrally, consider establishing a protocol where Corporate Security will notify the EAP of the event, give basic information relative to the nature of the incident and the address and phone number of the affected location along with the name of an on-site manager or local contact person. The EAP can then make an outreach call to the affected location, provide immediate management-level consultation, clinical support to severely impacted employees, fax or e-mail materials as necessary and appropriately begin to discuss the need for any on-site intervention or support. The process of establishing an outreach protocol has been viewed positively in this retail organization as a proactive and supportive measure provided to them and the impacted employees by their employer.
- The organization's security services should provide a safety analysis and training to personnel. If there is no corporate security, request assistance from the local Chief of Police or division of the police/emergencies services that handle these events.
- Consider focusing stress resiliency training for employees in locations prone to repetitious violence.

When dealing with trauma, employees will react differently depending on the cumulative effects of intellectual abilities, interpersonal capabilities, creativity, productivity, ability to manage, change and respond to diversity. How this all comes together will directly relate to how resilient the workplace will be.

Defining the Concept of Resilience?

The concept of resilience refers to a "series of adaptive strategies employed by individuals to aid them in managing traumatic stress and coping with disasters and disruptive events" (Allen & Toder, 2005). These strategies may include using social support, accepting change, developing new skills as an aid towards self-development based on challenges, and seeing things in a long-term focus (Allen & Toder, 2005). Resiliency enables an adult to maintain relatively stable, healthy levels of physical and psychological functioning even after a highly adverse event (Bonnano, 2004).

According to the literature, interest in resilience was primarily connected with war trauma and post traumatic stress disorder (PTSD). However, after September 11th, with the sudden rise in fears over homeland security, research turned towards the development of resilience. The American Psychological Association (APA) and Discovery Health Channel partnered together in 2002 for a public education campaign called "Talk to Someone Who Can Help." This included a documentary, *Aftermath: The Road to Resilience*, that presented resilience as something that can be learned through an individualized journey. Accompanying the documentary were brochures and journal articles that were intended to be disseminated to communities in order to combat the burgeoning fears (Daw, 2002).

Research on resilience first emerged as a major theoretical topic around the study of children of schizophrenic mothers. Studies had suggested that despite their high risk background, these children still thrived, leading to an increasing interest in the reasons behind individuals' varied responses to adversity. Research then expanded to include adverse conditions such as socioeconomic disadvantage, maltreatment, poverty, community violence, chronic illness and other such catastrophic life events. The research conducted enabled researchers to come up with three factors that were implicated in the development of resilience: attributes of the children, their families, and their social environment (Becker et al., 2000).

However, because most research regarding coping with trauma has been from individuals that have experienced psychological problems or sought treatment, resilience has often been misunderstood as either extremely rare or as a pathological state (Bonanno, 2004). Bereavement theorists used to be highly skeptical of people who did not show strong reactions after a traumatic event. They viewed 'absent grief' or the absence of distress after the death of a family member, for example, as a pathological and rare response that stems from denial and avoidance (Bonanno, 2004).

Trauma theorists, on the other hand, are less suspicious about the absence of grief, but often ignore resilience. And yet, available research clearly shows that the majority of individuals exposed to such events do not show chronic distress but instead healthy functioning that looks similar to that of resilience (Bonanno, 2004). It is important to note that resilient individuals do experience some emotional pain and sadness, especially immediately after a loss. Nevertheless, the difference is that these experiences are brief and do not interfere with their normal functioning, or their ability to experience positive emotions (Bonanno, 2004).

Given that, though some theorists seem to ignore this vital concept, it is important to be able to identify resilient individuals. According to research, there are a few pathways that lead to a resilient individual: hardiness, self-enhancement, repressive coping, and positive emotion and laughter. Hardiness helps to shield an individual from extreme stress. The concept itself consists of three dimensions: being committed to finding meaning and purpose in one's life, believing that one can influence one's environment, and the ability to grow from both negative and positive experiences. Hardy individuals are more confident and look to social support as a means of coping, thus helping them with any distress they may experience. However, hardy individuals are able to minimize the amount of distress they might feel because they view potentially threatening situations as less stressful (Bonanno, 2004).

Self-enhancement, or unrealistic biases in favor of oneself, can score high on measures of narcissism and tend to be seen negatively by others; however, they are also linked to resilience (Bonanno, 2004). In a study of individuals in or around the World Trade Center during the September 11th attacks, self-enhancers were seen as having more active social networks and were rated as better adjusted by their close friends (Bonanno, 2004).

Repressive coping is also viewed as negative and maladaptive, and even correlated with long term health crises. However, these tendencies can also foster resilience after a trauma. Repressors show no relative distress emotionally after a traumatic event, however, they may show distress ways in indirect measures rather than through emotion (Bonanno, 2004).

Lastly, positive emotion and laughter, though rejected by some theorists as previously mentioned, can decrease distress because it can undo negative emotions by garnering support through social contacts (Bonanno, 2004).

Not only is it important to be able to recognize the pathways to a resilient individual, it is also imperative to know the experiences one may have had to become resilient. In Salvatore Maddi's and Deborah Khoshaba's book *Resilience at work: How to succeed no matter what life throws at you*, the information on resilience they gathered is based on a 12-year study of Illinois Bell Telephone employees as they experienced immense organizational change. Studies revealed early experiences in childhood such as early stress, a sense of purpose, and nurtured confidence can build resilience. The more resilient employees' earlier lives were found to be more stressful than the non-resilient group. This early stress includes serious illness of themselves or others, divorces, unemployment, alcoholism or substance abuse within the family or frequent and disruptive changes in residence. On a more positive note, resilient individuals recalled their parents making them feel special based on a talent, skill, maturity or some other type of unique feature the child had. Through this encouragement, these individuals grew more purposeful in their other areas of life such as school and work. Similarly, resilient individuals were nurtured by adult figures, enabling them to develop a sense of enjoyment out of learning. They realized that they could overcome setbacks or frustrations through the help and encouragement of others (Khoshaba & Maddi, 2005).

Maddi and Khoshaba found conversely that experiences which undermine resilience include little to no family encouragement, no sense of purpose, and a general lack of involvement. These children learned at a young age to avoid life's problems, they see themselves as powerless to change, and fear the instability that change can create (Khoshaba & Maddi, 2005).

Luckily, resilience is not a trait that is set in stone. There will always be those outlying cases that do not fit the schema. There are those who have had disadvantaged childhoods that emerge as resilient and strong individuals, and then there are people who are genetically likely to become resilient and do not (Khoshaba & Maddi, 2005). Resilience involves actions, thoughts and behaviors that can be learned and developed in childhood and adulthood (Comas-Diaz et al., 2002). A finding in the research field found that everyone has an in-born predisposition to become resilient and the ability to learn how to accept change easily and naturally (Siebert, 2005).

In their brochure, the APA and Discovery Health published a list of factors that contribute to resilience. These factors seem attainable and more inclusive to a larger population. They explained that many feel the primary factor is having caring and supportive relationships in all contexts of one's life. These relationships, which can center around love and trust, or the development of a role model, can offer encouragement that helps to augment a person's resilience (Comas-Diaz et al., 2002). Other factors they list include the ability to carry out realistic life plans, having positive self-esteem, good communication and problem-solving skills, and the capacity to manage intense emotions and impulses (Comas-Diaz et al., 2002).

A large part of the APA/Discovery Health campaign was public education specifically around resilience. In a time of crisis, it seemed necessary to teach skills in resilience, and therefore they devoted a sizeable amount of their campaign to helping people develop these skills. They explained that the road to resilience is personal and one person may use different strategies than the next. This is especially true when explaining cultural differences, because some cultures may use resilience or develop resiliency in a different way (Comas-Diaz et al., 2002).

The 10 strategies listed include:

1. Make connections
2. Avoid seeing crises as insurmountable problems
3. Accept that change is a part of living
4. Move toward your goals
5. Take decisive actions
6. Look for opportunities for self discovery
7. Nurture a positive view of yourself
8. Keep things in perspective
9. Maintain a hopeful outlook
10. Take care of yourself (Comas-Diaz et al., 2002).

Resilience also is important for organizations and businesses because these skills can be used to recover from disasters and traumas that may affect the workplace. Organizations with a high percentage of their employees who develop these skills will be able to adapt to challenges, change and adversity more successfully than others. Resiliency skills can be incorporated into organizations through the integration of the skills within disaster training, or by bringing speakers who are familiar with resiliency to teach the employees (Siebert, 2005). It will be the employees who have practiced these skills as well as coping and recovery strategies who will return to pre-incident functioning faster (Allen & Toder, 2004). Not only will employees be able to respond effectively to trauma and major disasters, but they also will apply this to various workplace challenges that may arise (Allen & Toder, 2004). Highly resilient people thrive under pressure, easily manage continuous change, and recover from setbacks stronger than before (Siebert, 2005).

Resiliency Factors at Work

Resiliency factors are common factors in those who show adaptive outcomes to the traumatic event. By understanding the resiliency factors, we can build opportunities to promote resilience (Normal, 2000):

Interpersonally Related Protective Factors

1. *Positive, Caring Relationships:* This includes our social network ranging from family, friends, work and other. This is the single most important factor in promoting resilience.
2. *"High-Enough" Expectations:* Having high but reachable expectations motivates performance and encourages excellence. The person who hears the realistic message, "you can do it!" from significant others internalizes a self-perception of adequacy and is motivated to reach and stretch to their full capacity.

Individual Personality Traits

1. *Self-Efficacy:* Having a solid feeling of self-worth, a positive perception of one's ability to perform required life tasks.
2. *Realistic Appraisal of the Environment:* Better adapted individuals have the ability to more accurately assess the stress they have to deal with, and to realistically appraise their capacity to act and affect the situation.
3. *Social Problem-Solving Skills:* Possessing an array of social problem-solving skills reinforces one's sense of self-esteem, sense of competency and sense of mastery.
4. *Sense of Direction or Mission:* A special talent, passion, faith, or strong interest can spark a sense of meaning or purpose, and strengthen resiliency.

5. *Empathy:* The capacity to understand and respond to another's feelings has been identified as a resiliency trait in many studies.
6. *Humor:* Highly stressed people with greater competence had a greater ability to use humor, were more readily able to find the comic in the tragic, and used humor to reduce tension and restore perspective.
7. *Adaptive Distancing:* The ability to psychologically step back from the distressing environment allows individuals to maintain a healthy separateness from the maladaptive pattern/environment.
8. *Androgynous Sex Role Behavior:* Demonstrating both traditionally masculine and feminine characteristics and acting in a flexible non-sex-typed manner is helpful.

Workplace Strategies When Dealing with Trauma

These strategies can be supported by the company's Employee Assistance Program, but at a minimum the fortification of team-work or group resiliency in the workplace is work that requires a multidisciplinary approach pre- and post-event.

Pre-event preparedness for traumas that may be expected includes:

Operations, Management and Staff Training

- On emergency procedures
- Safety issues
- Lessons learned list
- What to expect as far as personal crisis response
- Maintaining personal well-being pre- and post-event
- The importance of good pre- and post-event team functionality
- Humanitarian Assistance (Deployment of special emergency interdisciplinary resources for employees: water, generators, nonperishable food items provided by the employer to employee and family members). Assess if you need to set up a corporate disaster command center (an ad-hoc call center to provide information to affected employees on employee benefits, leave policies, provisions of corporate sponsored assistance, etc.).

A good example of what a large retail institution provides for its employees includes:

- They are set up to provide information on company benefits.
- HR Leave policies and general supportive information, including Federal and State assistance.

- They also serve as a clearinghouse of information for management to assess the needs of their employee population and determine who needs water, ice, generators and assistance with obtaining housing.
- Employees may be eligible for various loan programs via the company–but they generally do not give out financial aid. They do have a grant program which is a pool of monies donated by co-workers. But this is not emergency aid . . . the process of applying for assistance, which includes advisory board review, takes some time. An application is not a guarantee of assistance.

Post-event resiliency:

- Immediately following an event employees need a chance to pull together so that the cohesion of the group is enabled to stay intact.
- The formulation of buddy-systems is important.
- Employees should be given the opportunity to share home or personal cell phone numbers with one another.
- Depending on the scope of the event, pulling together a set of calls with EAP and management may be useful to establish the level of response in phases.
- Senior management presence following the event is important. The *visibility* of senior leadership is more important than what is said. There is an important symbolic validation conveyed. This is the human touch that employees crave: they need to see visibly that their well-being is a consideration by leadership. Group cohesion should be encouraged by leadership, validation over their courage, bravery, dedication and other positive attributes should be acknowledged.
- A few weeks out: encourage a social event, like a picnic where family members may be invited. If there is no budget for this, have people come together and bring a dish. (Be sure to follow company policy regarding the serving of alcohol at work-related events.) At this event, a senior leader can give a brief welcome. Depending on the group and related policy, you might want to invite a local and beloved member of the clergy to invoke a blessing of the meal and time to be together. EAP may be invited to give a brief talk (15 minutes) about general stress management, self care, care for one another and address family issues if applicable. The EAP professional and senior manager should hang around to mingle and have informal chats with employees, remembering not to be too busi-

ness oriented or clinical. The aspect of normalization and play for adults is helpful during an event. Involve employees in planning the event and be sure to make it fun!

We know that some events are inevitable and may be out of our control but for those we can impact, prevention strategies also need to be part of the planning and integral part of the process.

Prevention Is Possible

As we often hear, an ounce of prevention is worth a pound of cure, so planning efforts designed to prevent occurrences of workplace violence are critical. It is important to have the following be part of that plan (Lee, 2002).

- Educate decision-makers about the price they, and their workers, will pay.
- How trauma affects the workplace and their customers.
- Make the connection between the "why" and "how" of trauma prevention.
- Help the organization develop clear, open communication, especially during times of significant change. The more people feel they are in control the less likely they are affected by traumatic events.
- Help management learn how to deal with difficult subjects.
- Help management develop a clear connection between cause and effect.
- Encourage the organization to invest in employee self-efficiency and resiliency training.
- Teach interpersonal skills to both management and employees.
- Help the employees develop an emotional support system.
- Change management training for all employees is a must.

As companies institute a workplace violence prevention program, there are four questions that will help shape the direction they take:

1. Why is there an increase in workplace violence?
2. How do incidents of violence affect our business economically?
3. Are there warning signs that can aid in the prevention?
4. What are we doing to avoid an incident in our workplace?

CONCLUSION

We know that workplace violence and trauma is on the rise, often due to an increase in drug use, layoffs, poverty and higher stress environments. But not every worker will react in the manner to each event. How resilient the employee is depends on many factors outlined in the discussion. But business will be much better off if it identifies the need, develops a plan with a policy, educates/trains managers and all employees, provides support at all levels at any sign of trouble, is thoughtful and proactive and ensures that expectations are clear and understood. By addressing the problem head-on, businesses will save millions in productivity, litigation and damage control.

REFERENCES

Allen, R., Toder, F. (2005). Developing a resilient workforce through disaster preparedness.www.disaster-resource.com/newsletter.subpages/v74/meet_the_experts.htm. Disaster Resource Guide.

Allen, R., Toder, F. (2004). Disaster Planning as a Tool in Developing a Resilient and Viable Business. HRWest, Vol. 2, No. 4.

Armour, S. (2004). Life after workplace violence. www.usatoday.com. USA Today.

Armour, S. (2004). Managers not prepared for workplace violence. www.usatoday. com. USA Today.

Bonanno, G. (2004). Loss, trauma, and human resilience: Have we underestimated the human capacity to thrive after extremely aversive events? *American Psychologist.* Vol. 59, No. 1.

Bureau of Labor Statistics (1993).

Chappell, D., DiMartino, V. (1999). Asian-Pacific Newsletter on Occupational Health and Safety, Vol. 6, No. 1.

Comas-Diaz, L., Luthar, S. S., Maddi, S. R., O'Neill, H. K., Saakvinte, K. W., Tedeschi, R. G. (2002). The road to resilience. www.helping.apa.org. American Psychological Association.

Daw, J. (2002). Documentary on resilience set to air Sept 11th. www.apa.org/monitor/julaug02/documentary.html. Monitor on Psychology.

Doody, L. (2003). Defusing workplace violence: Learn how to spot and stop a potentially violent situation. *Nursing2003.* Vol. 33. No. 8.

Gray, G. R., Myers, D., Myers, P. (1999). Workplace violence provisions in private sector collective bargaining agreements. *Compensation and Working Conditions.*

Jenkins, L. (1996). Violence in the workplace: Risk factors and prevention strategies. www.cdc.gov/niosh/violcont.html. US Department of Health and Human Services.

Lee, D. (2002). The Hidden Costs of Trauma in the Workplace. http://www.humannatureatwork.com/Workplace-Stress-3.htm. Human Nature@Work.

Luthar, S., Cicchetti, D., Becker, B. (2000). The construct of resilience: A critical evaluation and guidelines for future work. *Child Development*, Vol. 17, No. 3.

Maddi, S., Khoshaba, D. M. (2005). Resilience at Work: How to Succeed No Matter What Life Throws at You.

Mattman, J. (1998). Preventing Violence in the Workplace, Workplace Violence Research Institute.

National Center for Victims of Crime. (1996). Employee Liability for Workplace Violence.

Resiliency Enhancement: Putting the Strengths Perspective into Social Work Practice (2000). Ed. Elaine Norman, Columbia University Press: New York.

Siebert, A. (2005). The Resiliency Advantage: Master Change, Thrive Under Pressure, and Bounce Back from Setbacks.

doi:10.1300/J490v21n03_06

Strategic Specialty Partnerships: Enabling the EAP for Evidence Informed Best Practices in Workplace Crisis Response

Bob VandePol
Richard Gist
Mark Braverman
Lyle Labardee

SUMMARY. Rapid advancement of both research and practice in the field of organizational crisis intervention has brought demands for more substantial breadth and much greater depth in EAP efforts to serve their clients in this critical domain. Once dominant practices (e.g., debriefing groups) have been brought strongly into question while those approaches with solid empirical backing (e.g., trauma focused CBT) remain relatively underrepresented in the intervention armamentarium of most EAPs. Other vital aspects such as organizational crisis planning and longer term recovery management have not been as well developed as might be desirable with respect to human resource impacts, and EAPs need to acquire capability and capacity to assist their clients in these areas as well. This paper reviews how recent advances impact the provision of organizational crisis response and discusses the growing need for specialty partnerships to ensure that information, skills, and resources can be efficiently and effectively deployed to ensure that EAPs are positioned to meet and exceed both client expectations and advancing standards of practice in this rapidly evolving arena. doi:10.1300/J490v21n03_07

[Haworth co-indexing entry note]: "Strategic Specialty Partnerships: Enabling the EAP for Evidence Informed Best Practices in Workplace Crisis Response." VandePol, Bob et al. Co-published simultaneously in *Journal of Workplace Behavioral Health* (The Haworth Press, Inc.) Vol. 21, No. 3/4, 2006, pp. 119-131; and: *Workplace Disaster Preparedness, Response, and Management* (ed: R. Paul Maiden, Rich Paul, and Christina Thompson) The Haworth Press, Inc., 2006, pp. 119-131. Single or multiple copies of this article are available for a fee from The Haworth Document Delivery Service [1-800-HAWORTH, 9:00 a.m. - 5:00 p.m. (EST). E-mail address: docdelivery@haworthpress.com].

KEYWORDS. Crisis response, recovery management, trauma debriefing

INTRODUCTION

Ask a person to tell you a few things about himself or herself and one thing you will likely learn is that person's occupation. Once told a person's occupation, you are likely to ask where that person works. When told the employer, you will be apt to ask, "How do you like working there?" What comes next will likely be a quick summary of that worker's personal statement on job and workplace satisfaction–and the strongest determinant of that will be found in how the employee judges the company's commitment to him or her.

Studies of employee satisfaction suggest that the factors most important in worker commitment and satisfaction are found in the intangible aspects of the employer/employee relationship. A national Gallup poll (2004) found that employees' perceptions of a responsive, concerned employer organization were foremost in shaping job satisfaction and workplace morale. A study commissioned by the Canadian Federation of Independent Business (Pohlman, 1999) reported that job satisfaction centered on intangibles like perceived quality of decision makers, communication between managers and employees, and flexibility toward employees' personal needs. Even core elements such as salary, work hours, and time off fell further down the list.

What shapes those perceptions? Notice that they're not anchored in pay schedules, benefit structures, or personnel policies. These factors fall more into the affective realm–they are based on feelings, perceptions, and appraisals that are defined by emotions and attitudes even more than by actions or outcomes. They demonstrate the old canard that people may dismiss what you say and overlook what you do, but they never forget how you made them *feel*.

Workplace crisis events form enduring perceptions of how a company values and responds to the personal needs of its employees. Organizations that respond quickly, effectively, and compassionately can build an indelible bond with their workers while companies perceived to place employee needs behind business concerns–or, worse yet, companies seen as failing to respond at all–may endure lasting scars that affect quality, productivity, and performance. But how can an employer be fully prepared to respond to the rare and the unexpected without a crystal ball and unlimited resources?

Understanding Crisis Readiness

Larger organizations often hold detailed plans for crisis response and business continuity. Much attention is typically afforded to "mission critical" business considerations such as security of records and data, maintenance of production and distribution infrastructures, and other factors vital to protecting and preserving the "business of the business" from escalating damage and disruption. Most companies seem to acknowledge human impacts in the workforce will be important and must be addressed and company plans generally reflect this. The responsibility to respond to those needs is typically delegated to Human Resources, though often without the same critical attention to risk and hazard analysis, impact projection, and detailed planning afforded the more quantitative aspects of business performance. This can leave the HR manager with huge responsibilities but without the plans and resources immediately at hand to deal with a difficult and unfolding event.

The smaller the organization, the less likely it may be to have a thoroughly developed and researched plan for crisis response and business continuity. Smaller organizations may be even less likely to hold detailed plans for addressing employee impacts and quickly available resources for response. Yet the smaller the employing organization, the more those intangible perceptions of responsiveness determine employee commitment and the more strongly and quickly employee commitment impacts company performance (Pohlman, 1999). No organization can afford *not* to be ready to deal with the employee impacts of a workplace crisis event, and the smaller employer may well face the greatest risk of lasting or even catastrophic impact if unprepared to quickly, effectively, and compassionately react.

Probably the vast majority of company plans center around a solid concept: The use of the organization's Employee Assistance Program (EAP) to provide guidance and assistance in addressing employee crisis needs. There are few things more important in the promotion and maintenance of workplace behavioral health than access to a competent, accessible EAP. EAPs indeed form the nucleus for crisis response, but the rapidly developing field of crisis response has gone far beyond the once simple basic of debriefing sessions and defusing groups–in fact, current empirical evidence now strongly suggests that many of the practices once thought to be "state of the art" can even complicate recovery (see, for example, Gist & Devilly, 2002, for commentary regarding meta-analyses of CISD). Astute businesses are now looking increasingly to ensure that their EAP provider brings a specialty partnership to bear on their workplace crisis needs–not only to help them respond, but also to assist the company in conducting risk and hazard analyses related to human resource impacts, help the company and its EAP develop plans and protocols to ensure timely and responsive reactions from the first moments of a crisis, and work to ensure that all efforts reflect the very latest in evidence based best practices to address the entire range of needs and expectations that will unfold as the event evolves.

Crisis planning and preparedness has become a highly specialized enterprise as risks, on the one hand, have proliferated while research and experience, on the other, have refined approaches and techniques. Where once workplace crisis response focused on limited and more isolated events such as industrial accidents, robberies, or similar events–companies must now be prepared for situations as diverse and far-reaching as terrorist attacks, workplace violence, and large-scale natural disasters. Sometimes the impact will not come from an event that strikes the workplace directly, but may be part of cascading social and economic consequences of events that occurred elsewhere and impact the company's markets, suppliers, financing, or resources. As important as it is to plan for probable and even possible scenarios, few companies are in a position to anticipate all the things they might confront, much less to develop detailed plans for each.

Plan First for the Expected

A substantial portion of workplace crisis responses may actually involve situations that do not involve direct traumatic impacts *per se*. In this volume Greenwood et al. (2006) note that the majority of all requests involve "death impacting the workforce," a category that includes and may even be dominated by death outside the workplace, unrelated to occupational accident or injury. Layoffs and downsizing were another leading category, accounting for more than a quarter of responses in the manufacturing sector and more than 10% of all responses. Robbery and "accidents/injury" together accounted for slightly less than 20%

of responses. Services directed toward prevention of post-traumatic stress disorder (PTSD) and similar techniques would appear misdirected in circumstances where Criterion A exposure has not explicitly occurred (cf. DSM-IV-TR; American Psychiatric Association, 2000).

This is not meant to imply that services in these situations have limited value–indeed, the fact that they represent the majority of client requests indicates their importance to the organizations seeking these services. It should, however, lead us to strongly reconsider the nature of the value these services bring the employer and to reconfigure and redirect our services to most effectively address the client's outcome needs. The shift has been increasingly from delivery of services built around notions of preventing PTSD and similar dysfunctions to approaches centered on supporting resiliency by helping to moderate initial uncertainty and distress, assisting with practical needs, and expressing a compassionate concern for and involvement with employees and work groups as they navigate the demands and impact of any particular event.

The Need for Alternative Approaches

There has been an increasing number of findings reported in the refereed empirical literature regarding inefficacy of debriefing and related approaches to organizational crisis intervention in controlled trials (Van Emmerik et al., 2002) including recently reported data from a large longitudinal sample of military personnel before and after deployment in intact groups, based on strict adherence to the dominant CISD model (Litz, Gray et al., 2004). Some well controlled studies with extended follow up have reported paradoxical outcomes for some subsets of trauma exposed individuals (see, for example, Mayou et al., 2000). Yet most persons receiving the intervention express appreciation (see McNally et al., 2003, for extensive analysis).

The currently favored alternative approach to care has been dubbed *psychological first aid*. It is, by intent, a much more flexible approach to assessing impacts, determining viable points for productive assistance, and generating helping strategies specifically geared toward the express needs and expectations of the organization being served and the employees affected. As such, it is consultative rather than clinical and advocates assistance rather than intervention. Its objectives are practical and palliative rather than therapeutic or therapeutically preventative (see Brymer et al., 2005, for manualized approaches to psychological first aid). While it contains a number of techniques that are in many ways similar, the distinct differences in assumptions, construction, and objectives require a fundamental redesign of the approaches taught to and ingrained in most contemporary EAP providers.

Contemporary crisis consultation approaches, however, require considerably more both before and after any particular crisis event to offer client organizations true "state of the art" assistance (Devilly & Cotton, 2003). Solid crisis planning involves working with clients and EAP responders to assess risks and exposures, develop pre-impact protocols that can be easily accessed and implemented by client HR staff, ensure that effective options for information management and practical assistance can be readily mobilized for any particular event, and provide immediate help with assessing impacts and generating options. If providers from the EAP's own panel or network will be first on scene, it is important to ensure that they've had proper training and preparation to respond according to today's evidence based best practices. If additional response resources will be needed, it is critical that they be ready to merge seamlessly into response, employing the same standards of training and approach. It is also vital to ensure that the client organization receives well structured information regarding the effectiveness of actions taken on its behalf and consultation as needed with predicting and planning for future response needs.

Why Specialty Partnerships?

Today's EAPs bring a widening range of services to employees' disposal, including techniques reaching far beyond traditional counseling roles. Health promotion and wellness resources are often available, along with easily accessible information on dealing with all sorts of life issues and circumstances. Many provide online access for 24/7 availability to employees in the privacy and confidence of their own settings of choice. "Concierge" type services provided through an increasing number of EAPs permit employers to help their workers access anything from childcare to dry cleaning. Crisis response is usually a central element in EAP services that can be best delivered through specialty organizations not unlike some of the EAP services listed above.

Universal approaches such as debriefing and defusing were widely accepted as the standard of care and could be mounted easily by most any provider, needing only limited training (often a single workshop would do). No matter what the circumstance or setting, the same basic pattern could be adapted to meet the demand. Surge capacity for larger incidents seemed the only obstacle requiring preplanning or outsourcing.

The events of September 11th, 2001, changed the nature of workplace crisis response–indeed, some might say that it changed almost everything. It became quickly apparent that ordinary approaches to crisis response were not fully addressing the needs and issues employers and employees perceived to be central. It became increasingly evident that the issue for most was not *trauma* in the way that mental health practitioners ordinarily perceived it but represented instead a broad gamut of intersecting and interacting matters ranging from the practical and the pragmatic to the ethereal and the enigmatic. Moreover, ongoing debates in academic and research circles have spilled into the public arena regarding the prevalence of reactions such as posttraumatic stress disorder (PTSD), the nature and course of post-impact distress, and the efficacy of widely accepted intervention rubrics (Kadet, 2002; Smith, 2005).

But there is also evidence that organizations that reach out to employees at times of workplace disruption see benefits in how their employees fare over time (Boscarino et al., 2005). While these tendencies do not show preventative efficacy for particular interventions, they may indeed indicate overall better affective outcomes where some effort to address employee impact has been visibly attempted. Current research strongly advises that what efforts are to be mounted must be well tailored to the organization, event, work group, and circumstances as they exist and as they evolve. The one thing on which most early intervention authorities seem able to fully agree at this juncture is that we must base our responses first on a direct assessment of these considerations (ISTSS Early Intervention SIG, 2005; Ritchie et al., 2003).

Building productive approaches to evidence informed best practices is no longer as simple as tracking a single resource of information or attending an occasional workshop. There is extensive research to be evaluated, and new techniques are emerging and evolving rapidly. Specialty partnerships ensure that EAPs with primary responsibility to help organizations plan, assess, respond, and react have constant access to the best information available and the most productive practices built on that information, no matter the circumstance or situation. They also help ensure that as new information becomes available and new approaches evolve, the EAPs service to its clients will always represent the best practices available for the matter at hand.

What to Expect from Your Specialty Partner

"Debriefing on demand" was only recently the implied mantra and industry standard. Yet much recent data seriously question whether immediate debriefing response is desirable or even appropriate while empirical evidence increasingly demands that we seek strategies beyond basic debriefing and defusing. Evaluating the situation and circumstance to decide what options and what timing are indeed appropriate is now seen as the essential first step in crisis response. Since few EAPs are likely to have expertise immediately at hand that cuts across the many possible variations in situation and circumstance, it is reasonable to seek the support of an organization that holds a broad range of experience with a wide variety of industries and employers. A partner with a stated and proven commitment to evidence informed best practices is also, of course, critical.

There does, however, appear to be a clear service core that a specialty partner should be prepared to deliver to the EAP and its customers:

1. *Training, information, and preparation in evidence informed best practices.* This extends beyond simple workshops and "cookbook" approaches in any one technique or strategy. EAP providers must constantly assimilate ongoing information from all domains of their practice, not simply from crisis intervention. This creates a huge demand on time and resources. A solid specialty partner should be able to provide access to training materials, information updates, techniques and revisions, and evolving strategies as these emerge to enable the EAP and its personnel to efficiently digest and apply the best practices of the enterprise at any juncture.

2. *Consultation and assistance with client crisis planning.* Crisis planning is a specialty in itself and few clinical providers would expect to be fully adept in its intricacies. But competent planning is the foundation of competent responding, and adapting risk analysis, hazard assessment, and protocol planning for the wide variety of employers in any EAP's customer base is an essential element of providing state of the art crisis response. A solid specialty partner should have the resources to equip and assist its EAP partners to help their clients prepare.

3. *Access to tools, techniques, and instruments.* Sometimes a full specialty response is warranted, but many times a bit of expert assistance and access to some well developed tools can enable the primary responder to address a situation without additional resources. The specialty partner should be a readily accessible resource to ensure that whatever tools the provider needs can be quickly brought to bear. Where training or experience beyond

what the provider holds may be necessary to appropriately or effectively utilize the tool or approach, the specialty partner should be able to provide whatever assistance is needed to ensure that the EAP can be quickly and suitably responsive to the needs of its clients. Quick and easily usable assessment tools for PTSD, for example, are now available for application at three to five weeks post-impact (Brewin et al., 2003) and can be adapted for a wide range of situations; access to such tools and assistance in their dissemination and utilization are important contributions of a competent specialty partner.

4. *Rapid access to trained and capable response staff.* Surge capacity is still a major consideration in larger incidents, and immediate availability of specialty staff for complex or highly sensitive events is a resource that can prove especially valuable. The ability to know and trust the consistency of response strategy and provider performance no matter where or what the incident helps ensure quality performance at the point of service delivery, where the value of the service is formed in the eyes of the client.

5. *Access to evidence based tools and techniques for responding beyond the crisis situation.* Current empirical evidence suggests that development of PTSD, depression, or other serious psychiatric impairment from the types of incidents most frequently seen in occupational exposures will be far less than previously estimated (Bonanno, 2004; Galea et al., 2002 & 2003). Nonetheless, it is also clear that disequilibrium and discomfort are far from uncommon (Silver et al., 2002) and that in those cases where PTSD or depression develop, prompt application of demonstrably efficacious treatments can ameliorate suffering for many.

There are indeed well researched, manualized treatments with demonstrated efficacy for these conditions (NICE, 2005). These are variants of cognitive behavior therapy (CBT) that, while well described, are not widely practiced in many of the settings where they may be needed following occupational trauma. A solid specialty partner should be able to help local practitioners associated with the EAP to prepare themselves to deliver effective follow up treatment and/or to provide access to a network of qualified providers. The capacity to offer assistance through alternative vehicles and approaches (e.g., online intervention) can also be an asset (Litz, Williams et al., 2004).

6. *Evaluation, follow up, and impact analysis.* There is usually much a client needs to know following a major occupational event.

Much of this information will be collected in the observations and syntheses of crisis responders while others will need to be derived from other sources of data and information. Assistance in gathering information, developing data, and assisting clients in planning for future organizational impacts and responses is the critical closing arc of the consultation circle. A solid specialty sponsor can assist the EAP in cementing the value of its crisis assistance by facilitating effective analysis and reporting.

CONCLUSIONS

What employees need most from their organization in times of crisis is informed, compassionate leadership; what organizations need most from their EAP is the professional planning, preparation, response, and reaction that will make that leadership palpable to the client. What the EAP needs from its specialty partner is the training, information, tools, resources, and support needed to ensure that the best practices and approaches consistent with the latest evidence are always at hand for any client situation or need.

The needs are reasonably straightforward. Impacted organizations and people must be able to visualize a new normal and to develop an expectation of recovery. Leading this recovery requires that vision plus execution capability to guide, support, and monitor a series of transitions:

1. *Deprivation of access to basic resources.* The key to this is practicality. Employees at early stages will find themselves almost exclusively focused on gaining safety, shelter, sustenance, and medical care. Application of intrusive clinical models prior to completion of this phase will be met with resistance and results will be harmful or inert.

2. *Moving from isolation to connectivity.* This entails providing opportunities to connect in familiar, natural supportive relationships such as family, friendships, workgroups, neighborhood, and places of worship. When the people and systems that typically surrounded employees reach out to provide support, employees become grounded and focused much quicker than if they must access formal, unfamiliar systems. Involvement of response specialists should not be viewed as a clinical response to the incident, but rather as a means of facilitating and guiding employees toward their natural communities.

3. *Transitioning from chaos to structure.* When overwhelmed by multiple, urgent needs, building a sense of order and structure is beneficial. Simply pulling people together into situations where they can receive pertinent, practical information can provide increased calm. Resumption of normal routines, tasks, and schedules facilitates a sense of control and safety.

4. *Replacing helplessness with efficacy.* Workplace crises produce situations in which people may at first feel helpless. Employees benefit when led toward a focus upon what they can do rather than upon what they cannot. Individual, workgroup, and organizational recovery are facilitated when opportunities are structured for accomplishment of tasks that build momentum towards real and perceived self-efficacy.

5. *Avoiding victimhood.* As recovery progresses to the point where one attempts to make sense of the incident, people and groups behave in fashion consistent with their perceptions of themselves and their situations. Organizations should strive to identify and make visible the achievements accomplished in the process recovery. Doing this reinforces perceptions of one's capacity to act as a positive active agent in one's life rather crystallizing an identity encapsulated by the tragedy.

Plan, prepare, respond, react . . . the contemporary EAP must be prepared to assist clients throughout the process, using the latest in evidence informed best practices to ensure that client needs are anticipated, identified, assessed, and addressed, and to ensure that ongoing impacts of both the incident and the organization's responses are evaluated and reported in ways that facilitate organizational resilience and recovery. Well chosen specialty partnerships provide the contemporary EAP with the assurance that its obligations will be met consistently, reliably, and effectively, no matter the situation or circumstance.

REFERENCES

American Psychiatric Association. (2000). *Diagnostic and Statistical Manual* (4th ed., text revision). Washington, DC.

Bonnano, G. A. (2005). Loss, trauma, and human resilience: Have we underestimated the human capacity to thrive after extremely aversive events? *American Psychologist, 59,* 20-28.

Boscarino, J., Adams, R., & Figley, C. (2005). A prospective cohort study of the effectiveness of employer-sponsored crisis interventions after a major disaster. *International Journal of Emergency Mental Health, 7,* 9-22.

Brewin, C. R., Rose, S., Andrews, B., Green, J., Tata, P., McEvedy, C., Turner, S., & Foa, E. B. (2002). *British Journal of Psychiatry, 181,* 158-162.

Brymer, M., Layne, C., Pynoos, R., Ruzek, J., Steinberg, A., Vernberg, E., & Watson, P. J. (2005). *Psychological first aid: Field Operations Guide.* Washington, DC: National Center for PTSD/National Child Traumatic Stress Network.

Devilly, G. D., & Cotton, P. (2003). Psychological debriefing and the workplace: Defining a concept, controversies, and guidelines for intervention. *Australian Psychologist, 38,* 144-150.

Galea, S., Ahern, J., Resnick, H., Kilpatrick, D., Bucuvalas, M., Gold, J., & Vlahov, D. (2002). Psychological sequelae of the September 11 terrorist attacks in New York City. *New England Journal of Medicine, 346,* 982-987.

Galea, S., Vlahov, D., Resnick, H., Ahern, J., Susser, E., Gold, J., Bucuvalas, M., & Kilpatrick, D. (2003). Trends of probable post-traumatic stress disorder in New York City after the September 11 terrorist attacks. *American Journal of Epidemiology, 158,* 514-524.

Gallup Organization. (2004). Workers most satisfied with coworker relationships, workplace safety. Report accessed at http://www.gallup.com/content/default. aspx?ci=12820&pg=1.

Gist, R., & Devilly, G. J. (2002). Post-trauma debriefing: The road too frequently followed. *The Lancet, 360,* 741-742.

Greenwood, K. L., Kubiak, G., Van der Heide, L., & Phipps, N. (2006). Responding in times of crisis–An exploratory study of employer requests for critical incident services. *Journal of Workplace Behavioral Health, 21*(3/4), 171-189.

International Society for Traumatic Stress Studies, Early Intervention SIG. (2005, November). Discussion held at 21st Annual Meeting, Toronto ON.

Kadet, A. (2002). Good Grief! *Smart Money, 11*(6), 108-114.

Litz, B.T. (2004, November). A randomized controlled trial of Critical Incident Stress Debriefing. In M. Friedman (Chair), *Military psychiatry, then and now.* Plenary session presented at the 20th annual meeting of the International Society for Traumatic Stress Studies, New Orleans, LA.

Litz, B. T., Williams, L., Wang, J., Bryant, R., & Engel, C. C., Jr. (2004). A therapist-assisted internet self-help program for traumatic stress. *Professional Psychology: Research and Practice, 35,* 629-634.

Mayou, R. A., Ehlers, A., & Hobbs, M. (2000). Psychological debriefing for road traffic accident victims: Three-year follow-up of a randomized controlled trial. *British Journal of Psychiatry, 176,* 589-593.

McNally, R. J., Bryant, R. A., & Ehlers, A. (2003). Does early psychological intervention promote recovery from posttraumatic stress? *Psychological Science in the Public Interest, 4*(2).

National Institute for Clinical Excellence. (2005). *The management of PTSD in adults and children* (Guideline No. 26). London, UK: National Health Service.

Pohlman, C. (1999). Study on workplace satisfaction in public, private sectors. Toronto, ON: Canadian Federation of Independent Business.

Ritchie, E. C. (Chair). (2001). *Mental health and mass violence: Evidence-based intervention for victims/survivors of mass violence* (NIH Publication No. 02-5138). Washington, DC: U.S. Government Printing Office.

Silver, R. C., Holman, E. A., McIntosh, D. N., Poulin, M., & Gil-Rivas, V. (2002). Nationwide longitudinal study of psychological responses to September 11. *Journal of the American Medical Association, 288*, 1235-1244.

Smith, S. (2005, September 12). Outsourcing compassion: Debriefing trauma patients. AmericanRadioworks/National Public Radio. Accessible at http://www.npr.org/templates/story/story.php?storyId=4842962.

van Emmerik, A. A., Kamphuis, J. H., Hulsbosch, A. M., & Emmelkamp, P. M. (2002). Single session debriefing after psychological trauma: A metaanalysis. *The Lancet, 320*, 766-771.

doi:10.1300/J490v21n03_07

Compassion Fatigue, Compassion Satisfaction, and Burnout: Reactions Among Employee Assistance Professionals Providing Workplace Crisis Intervention and Disaster Management Services

Jodi M. Jacobson

SUMMARY. Over the past several decades the mental health field has become increasingly concerned about potential negative effects in professionals of providing crisis intervention and traumatic stress services to individuals and groups. The employee assistance (EA) field has not received adequate attention with regard to the study of these negative effects, such as compassion fatigue. This paper highlights results from a national research study of members of the Employee Assistance Professionals Association (EAPA) who were assessed for risk for compassion fatigue and burnout, as well as potential for compassion satisfaction. Additionally, coping methods for dealing with work-related stress resulting from the provision of workplace crisis intervention services were measured. Findings indicate that EA professionals who provide clinical services and/or crisis intervention services in the workplace are at low risk for burnout, moderate risk for compassion fatigue, and have high potential for compassion satisfaction. Implications for the EA field, in

[Haworth co-indexing entry note]: "Compassion Fatigue, Compassion Satisfaction, and Burnout: Reactions Among Employee Assistance Professionals Providing Workplace Crisis Intervention and Disaster Management Services." Jacobson, Jodi M. Co-published simultaneously in *Journal of Workplace Behavioral Health* (The Haworth Press, Inc.) Vol. 21, No. 3/4, 2006, pp. 133-152; and: *Workplace Disaster Preparedness, Response, and Management* (ed: R. Paul Maiden, Rich Paul, and Christina Thompson) The Haworth Press, Inc., 2006, pp. 133-152. Single or multiple copies of this article are available for a fee from The Haworth Document Delivery Service [1-800-HAWORTH, 9:00 a.m. - 5:00 p.m. (EST). E-mail address: docdelivery@haworthpress.com].

terms of training and practice, are discussed. doi:10.1300/J490v21n03_08
*[Article copies available for a fee from The Haworth Document Delivery Service:
1-800-HAWORTH. E-mail address: <docdelivery@haworthpress.com> Website:
<http://www.HaworthPress.com> © 2006 by The Haworth Press, Inc. All rights
reserved.]*

KEYWORDS. Employee assistance, crisis intervention, compassion
fatigue, compassion satisfaction, burnout, coping

INTRODUCTION

Experience demonstrates and research supports the notion that professionals who provide crisis intervention and disaster management services to individuals and groups experience a combination of positive
and negative personal and professional reactions (Figley, 1995; 2002;
Pearlman, & Saakvitne, 1995; Stamm, 1999). These reactions have
been studied in the mental health field, particularly among psychotherapists and first responders (Dunning, & Silva, 1980; Figley, 1983;
Pearlman, & Mac Ian, 1995; Schauben, & Frazier, 1995). The terms
used to describe such reactions include compassion fatigue, secondary
traumatic stress, vicarious traumatization, and burnout. This paper uses
the term *compassion fatigue*, originally conceptualized and defined by
Figley (1995) to describe the cumulative effects of working with traumatized individuals that contribute to secondary traumatic stress.

Compassion fatigue is considered a natural response or reaction to
working with individuals or groups of people who are in crisis (Figley,
1995). Compassion fatigue can develop as a result of the helping professionals' exposure to hearing clients' traumatic material in combination
with the professional's sense of empathy for the client. Theory suggests
that as a therapist's level of empathy increases she or he is at greater risk
for experiencing compassion fatigue. Therefore, the more empathic and
caring the mental health professional, the more 'at-risk' the professional
is for experiencing negative reactions to offering crisis intervention services. Given the idea that compassion fatigue represents a natural reaction to working in the crisis intervention field, it could be considered an
"occupational hazard" (Munroe, 1999). This acknowledgement of compassion fatigue as an occupational hazard has serious implications for
the mental health and EA field.

Exposure to traumatic material through personal experience or hearing about traumatic events from clients, places professionals at risk for experiencing similar symptoms as those reported by primary victims (Beaton, & Murphy, 1995; Dunning, & Silva, 1980; Pearlman, & Saakvitne, 1995; Stamm, 1999). Trauma therapists have been identified as a specific group of helping professionals who are at high risk for experiencing compassion fatigue and secondary traumatic stress as a result of their clinical work with traumatized clients (Figley, 1995, 2002; Munroe, 1999; Pearlman, 1999; Stamm, 2002). Common characteristics of compassion fatigue among helping professionals include cognitive, emotional, physical, spiritual, work-related, interpersonal, and behavioral reactions such as decreased level of concern and empathy for clients, decreased positive feelings for clients, physical and emotional exhaustion, increased levels of job dissatisfaction, and feelings of hopelessness related to the job that can overflow into other areas of the professional's life (Figley, 1995, 2002; Leon et al., 1999; Maslach, 1976; Pines, & Kafry, 1978; Valnet, 1995). The risk for compassion fatigue is believed to increase when professionals experience "shared trauma" or exposure to both primary and secondary traumatic events (White, 2001). For example, many EA professionals who responded to the terrorist attacks on September 11th, 2001, were also personally impacted by the attacks. Theory states that having dual exposure to a traumatic event increases the risk for negative reactions.

Along with negative reactions such as compassion fatigue, there are also positive reactions from working in the traumatic stress field. Stamm (1999) developed the concept that along with feelings of distress brought on by helping trauma victims, there are also feelings of satisfaction. This concept, termed, *compassion satisfaction*, refers to the positive reactions of feeling satisfied with one's ability to offer care and to connect with another person using empathy (Stamm et al., 2001). Few researchers have empirically measured positive reactions of working in the trauma field. Of those who have studied this construct, findings indicated counselors reporting positive growth, increased levels of spirituality and hope, and increased respect for human resiliency (Kassam-Adams, 1995; Schauben, & Frazier, 1995).

While the majority of research has focused on mental health providers, EA professionals, who are constantly confronted with serious mental health and crisis issues, including workplace critical incidents, have not been empirically studied. Critical incidents in the workplace are defined as any event or series of events in a workplace that result in emotional or psychological traumatic stress reactions among people exposed to the incident, either directly or indirectly (Mitchell, 1983). The risk for reactions among EA professionals may be equal to that of other mental health professionals following exposure to workplace critical incidents and individual traumatized clients. It is natural for helping professionals, such as those in the EA field to have reactions to working with people exposed to traumatic events. Vicki Thal, an independent EA professional who responded to the terrorist attacks on the World Trade Center on September 11th, 2001, stated, "We debriefers go through stages similar to those who have experienced the traumatic loss" (Nash, 2001). A strategically integrated EAP is often the first resource management calls for support following a workplace critical incident and therefore the EA professional may be the first mental health professional exposed to working with traumatized persons and work groups. However, researchers have all but ignored this population of 'first-responders' with regard to the empirical study of compassion fatigue and related concepts.

In addition to workplace critical incidents, EA professionals work with traumatized individuals, offering assessment and referral services, and sometimes short-term counseling. The types of problems EAP clients present with today continue to increase in severity. Masi (2000) states, "EAPs are now seeing serious cases that would ordinarily be referred out and handled by mental health services, i.e., violence, sexual abuse, incest, eating disorders, and severe substance abuse." With the continuing changes to the mental health care system in the United States, EAPs are offering more comprehensive assessment and short-term counseling services. EAP counselors are "expected to be able to assist with virtually any problem that presents itself" (Sweeney et al., 2002). A study designed to assess the level of psychological severity among employees experiencing work-related stress and then used their EAP services found that clients using their EAP reported serious mental health symptoms and psychological needs (Arthur, 2002). This increase in severity of problems for individual employees and dependents, added to the continual exposure to workplace critical incidents, places the EA professional at significant risk for secondary traumatic stress and compassion fatigue.

No empirical studies could be located that focused on reactions to working with clients and workplaces in crisis among EA professionals. Considering that the EA professional is usually the primary provider of mental health and psychological support services in the workplace, research on this population is greatly needed.

METHODOLOGY

This study utilized a cross-sectional survey design to answer the following research questions:

1. What is the level of risk for compassion fatigue and burnout among a national sample of EA professionals;
2. What is the potential for compassion satisfaction among a national sample of EA professionals;
3. Which coping methods used by EA professionals are correlated with higher levels of risk for compassion fatigue and burnout, and higher potential for compassion satisfaction?

Sample

During summer 2003, the researcher requested a random sample of 800 members from the Employee Assistance Professional Association's (EAPA) 5580 active U.S. members. A total of 800 surveys were mailed and of those mailed, 81 were returned undeliverable. From the 719 surveys successfully mailed, 325 were returned for a completed response rate of 45.2%. Of the 325 completed surveys, 44.0% (n = 143) were male and 55.7% (n = 181) were female (1 participant did not report gender). Age ranged from 26 to 69 years with a mean age of 50.06 (SD = 8.67). The majority of the sample reported their current living status as married (n = 197; 60.0%), followed by divorced (n = 51; 15.7%). With regard to education, the majority of the sample had completed master's degrees (n = 249; 76.6%) and 12.9% (n = 42) completed a doctorate. The specific area in which their highest educational degree was attained was asked and the most common response was 'social work' (n = 126; 38.8%). The second most common discipline reported was counseling/ family therapy (n = 84; 25.8%), followed by psychology (n = 46; 14.2%). When asked about primary role in the EAP, the majority of participants reported 'Clinician' (n = 155; 47.7%), followed by 'Administrator' (n = 77; 23.7%), and 'Consultant' (n = 43; 13.2%).

The inclusion question for the survey was: "Have you offered clinical and/or crisis intervention services to individual employees or groups of employees in the past as part of an EAP?" The majority of participants, 87.4% (n = 284) responded positively that they had provided clinical or crisis intervention services through an EAP in the past. Participants who reported they had not provided such services were not eligible to complete the remainder of the survey. Results included in this article represent participants who reported providing clinical or crisis intervention services. With regard to clinical work, the average number of clinical hours of work per week for the sample was 21.67 hours (SD = 14.35), including paperwork. The average number of EAP sessions offered to clients was 4.8 (SD = 2.96).

Survey

This study employed an anonymous survey. The survey was eight pages, including the cover letter and a list of national resources available to participants who sought additional supportive counseling services after completing the survey. This study was approved and exempted from further review by the University Institutional Review Board (IRB).

Measures

The Professional Quality of Life Scale: Compassion Satisfaction and Compassion Fatigue Subscales, a 30-item self-test instrument, with three subscales was used to assess compassion fatigue, compassion satisfaction, and burnout (ProQOL; Stamm, 2002). Psychometric properties for the three subscales have shown to be reliable in the past (Figley, & Stamm, 1996) and were reliable in the present study with reliability coefficients ranging from .75 to .88 (Jacobson, 2004).

Coping was measured using the Brief COPE (Carver, 1997). This scale consists of 14 subscales, which were further analyzed using Principal Components Analysis into three subscales for coping (Jacobson, 2004). The three subscales included: Positive Coping (i.e., concentrating efforts on doing something about the stress, getting emotional support and advice from others, taking action to make the situation better, reframing the stressful situation to see things in a better light, and using religion or spiritual beliefs to find comfort); Passive Coping (i.e., expressing or venting negative feelings, learning to live with work-related stress, engaging in activities such as TV watching, reading, etc., to think about the stress less, and using humor); and Negative Coping (i.e., using alcohol and drugs to feel better, denying the situation, criticizing oneself, giving up on trying to cope with work-related stress, and blaming oneself for the stress). Psychometric properties for the three subscales were assessed to have good reliability ranging from .747 to .823 (Jacobson, 2004). Questions for the Brief COPE are answered in response to a specific stressful event. For the purposes of the present study, coping was measured in reaction to work-related stress experienced in the year prior to the survey from offering crisis intervention services to individuals or groups.

Given the variation in educational background in the EA field, it was important to ask a question regarding specific training and education received to provide crisis intervention services. The majority of participants (n = 240; 84.5%) reported, '*Yes*,' they received specialized training or education to provide individual crisis intervention services. Further, 83.5% (n = 237) reported completing formal training to provide group crisis intervention services, such as critical incident stress management services (CISM; Mitchell, 1983). Participants reported offering an average of 2.47 (SD = 4.9) workplace critical incident stress debriefings in the six months prior to the survey. In the year prior to the survey, participants reported offering an average of 5.63 (SD = 12.53) CISDs, and over the course of a career, participants reported offering an average of 28.68 (SD = 32.98) CISDs.

RESULTS

Compassion Fatigue and Related Constructs

Based on results from the ProQOL (Stamm, 2002), the overall sample reported low to moderate risk for compassion fatigue and burnout and moderate to high potential for compassion satisfaction. The ProQOL was used in its naturally occurring continuous form; however, for purposes of describing the data, the ProQOL was scored based on theoretical score cut-points, set by the scale developer (Stamm, 1998). Stamm published average scores based on data from 400 mental health professionals around the world. These scores were used as a comparison with the current sample.

The Potential for Compassion Satisfaction scale ranges from 0 to 50 and the cut-points are as follows (Stamm, 1998):

- Low Potential = 32 or lower
- Middle Potential = 33 to 40
- High Potential = 41 and higher

The Risk for Compassion Fatigue scale ranges from 0 to 30 and the cut-points for are as follows (Stamm, 1998):

- Low Risk = 8 and lower
- Moderate Risk = 9 to 16
- High Risk = 17 and higher

The Risk for Burnout scale ranges from 0 to 50 and the cut-points are as follows (Stamm, 1998):

- Low Risk = 19 and lower
- Moderate Risk = 20 to 27
- High Risk = 28 and higher

The average score for Potential for Compassion Satisfaction was 39.52 ($SD = 6.71$), with a range from 6 to 50. Stamm's (1998) sample scored an average of 37 ($SD = 7.0$), which is slightly lower than the average score for EA professionals. The average score for Risk for Compassion Fatigue was 10.26 ($SD = 5.81$), with a range from 0 to 28. Stamm's sample scored an average of 13 ($SD = 6.0$), which again is slightly higher than scores from the EA professionals. Finally, the average score for Risk for Burnout was 16.78 ($SD = 5.58$), with a range from 5 to 37. Stamm's sample scored an average score of 23 ($SD = 6.9$), which is much higher than scores reported by the EA professionals. The frequencies and percentages for the three scales are presented in Table 1.

Coping Methods

EA professionals who reported experiencing work-related stress in the year prior to the survey as a result of working with traumatized individuals and/or groups were asked to complete the Brief COPE (Carver,

TABLE 1. EA Professionals' Scores for Potential for Compassion Satisfaction Scale, Risk for Compassion Fatigue Scale, and Risk for Burnout Scale

Range	Compassion Satisfaction		Compassion Fatigue		Burnout	
	n	%	*n*	%	*n*	%
High	135	47.5	34	12.0	14	4.9
Moderate	115	40.5	133	46.8	63	22.2
Low	34	12.0	117	41.2	207	72.9

1997). Of the total sample, 147 (*n* = 54.4%) reported '*Yes*' they experienced work-related stress in the past year. Individual items from the Brief COPE suggest that the following coping methods were used most commonly by the sample:

- "I've been accepting the reality of the fact that it has happened" (*n* = 132)
- "I've been taking action to try to make the situation better" (*n* = 130)
- "I've been getting help and advice from other people" (*n* = 125)
- "I've been trying to come up with a strategy about what to do" (*n* = 122)
- "I've been getting comfort and understanding from someone" (*n* = 122)
- "I've been expressing my negative feelings" (*n* = 122)
- "I've been learning to live with it" (*n* = 122)

Individual coping methods were further analyzed using Pearson's correlation to detect potential statistical relationships between the coping subscales (positive, passive, and negative) and the constructs related to compassion fatigue. EA professionals who utilized more positive coping skills reported higher potential for compassion satisfaction (*r* = .263, *p* = .001) and lower risk for burnout (*r* = −.157, *p* = .050). EA professionals who reported using more passive coping skills scored higher on risk for burnout (*r* = .169, *p* = .039). Finally, EA professionals who utilized more negative coping skills scored higher on risk for compassion fatigue (*r* = .426, *p* < .0005), higher on risk for burnout (*r* = .469, *p* < .0005), and lower on potential for compassion satisfaction (*r* = −.362, *p* < .0005). Table 2 shows the correlations for coping styles with compassion fatigue, compassion satisfaction, and burnout.

While not the focus of this study, EA professionals were asked to write the most effective coping method used to deal with work-related stress resulting from offering crisis intervention services in the workplace. The most effective coping method reported by participants was: talking to others about the stress (i.e., peers, colleagues, family members), followed by physical exercise, and then prayer and spirituality. Talking to others and religion/spirituality were both coded on the 'Positive' coping subscale. Physical exercise was not included on the Brief COPE.

In addition to personal and professional coping methods, EA professionals reported whether or not their EAP offered supportive services to help them cope with work-related stress. Unfortunately, only 54 (26.6%) of EA professionals in the total sample reported that their EAP did anything to help them cope with work-related stress. Specific services offered to EA professionals to help deal with work-related stress are listed in Table 3.

Multivariate Analysis of Covariance (MANCOVA) was used to assess potential differences between EA professionals who reported experiencing work-related stress resulting from working with traumatized individuals and/or groups and whether or not their EAP offered any services to help cope with work-related stress. The main effect of work-re-

TABLE 2. Correlations: Coping Style with Compassion Fatigue, Compassion Satisfaction, and Burnout

Coping Style	Compassion Fatigue	Compassion Satisfaction	Burnout
Positive Coping	−.050	.263**	−.157
Passive Coping	.085	.032	.169*
Negative Coping	.426**	−.362**	.469**

*$p < .05$
**$p < .01$

TABLE 3. Services Offered by EAPs to Help EA Professionals Cope with Work-Related Stress

Type of Services	Number of Respondents	Percentage
EAP services (offered by another EAP)	23	42.6%
Individual Counseling	11	20.4%
Multiple Services	9	16.7%
Debriefing the Debriefers	5	9.3%
Consultation	4	7.4%
Stress Management Services	1	1.9%
Fitness Center	1	1.9%
Total	54	100.0%

lated stress was significant, $F(3, 256) = 8.535$, $p < .0005$. The main effect of EAP services to help cope with work-related stress was approaching significance, $F(3, 256) = 2.329$, $p = .075$. The interaction between the two variables was not significant ($p = .891$). In conclusion, EA professionals who reported experiencing work-related stress in the past year as a result of working with traumatized individuals and/or groups scored significantly higher then non-stressed professionals on risk for compassion fatigue ($F = 10.389$, $p = .001$) and risk for burnout ($F = 24.375$, $p < .0005$). EA professionals who reported that their EAPs offered services to help them cope with work-related stress scored significantly lower on risk for burnout as compared to professionals whose EAP did not offer supportive services ($F = 4.0101$, $p = .046$). See Tables 4 and 5 for mean scores and related statistics for the MANCOVA.

TABLE 4. Compassion Fatigue, Compassion Satisfaction, and Burnout by Work-Related Stress and EAP Services

Work-Stress Variables	Compassion Fatigue	Compassion Satisfaction	Burnout
	M (SD)	M (SD)	M (SD)
Work-Related Stress (*n* = 263)			
Yes	11.87 (5.76)	39.61 (6.12)	17.53 (5.43)
No	8.37 (5.39)	39.59 (7.21)	15.58 (5.46)
EAP Services (*n* = 263)			
Yes	10.39 (5.67)	39.70 (6.72)	16.26 (5.20)
No	10.04 (6.22)	39.40 (6.48)	17.37 (6.05)

TABLE 5. Set of Dependent Variables by Work-Related Stress and EAP Services

Independent Variable	Wilkes □	F	df	Error df	p	Eta Squared
Work-Related Stress	909	8.535	3	256	< .0005	.091
EAP Services	973	2.329	3	256	.075	.027
Work-Related Stress x EAP Services	998	.208	3	256	.891	.002

Strengths

There are several strengths related to the present study. To begin, this study represents the first empirical study to assess compassion fatigue, compassion satisfaction, and burnout among the EA population. The use of standardized measures for compassion fatigue, compassion satisfaction, burnout, coping, and stressful life events helps to compare findings from this study to other studies in related fields, such as psychology, social work, and mental health. Finally, the use of a large random sample of EAPA members is useful in trying to generalize findings to the larger EA population. Study participants were geographically representative, with 45 of the 50 United States represented in the sample.

Limitations

As with any research study there are always limitations which need to be discussed. The present study had several limitations; the first relating to sample size and response rate. While using a large random sample from EAPA was a strength of this study, it could also be considered a limitation. Not all EA professionals belong to EAPA. However, EAPA represents the largest professional organization for EA professionals and therefore was the best choice for sampling. The response rate of 45.2% is acceptable for mailed surveys, but far from optimal. Given the exploratory nature of the study, the response rate represents a good starting point, but the need to collect additional research within this population is understood. Due to the anonymous nature of the survey, the researcher was not able to track EA professionals who did not respond to the survey. Finally, the use of self-report measures for reactions and coping is subject to response bias. However, the anonymous nature may have helped improve reliability. Given the limitations for this study, results should be interpreted cautiously.

CONCLUSIONS

Summary and Implications for the EA Field

This study represents the first empirical research study to specifically focus on the reactions among EA professionals to working with traumatized individuals and groups. This research contributes to a limited number of research studies that have begun to assess the reactions of mental health professionals working in the trauma field.

With regard to responding to workplace critical incidents, the current sample reported responding to over 10,000 workplace critical incidents and offering an average of 38 critical incident stress debriefings over the course of their EAP careers. These statistics support the notion that EA professionals are consistently called to help respond to significant numbers of workplace critical incidents, thereby increasing their exposure to traumatic material, either through primary or secondary exposure, or a combination of both, called shared trauma (White, 2001). Further, the statistics support the important role EA professionals assume and will continue to have in the preparation and response to workplace critical incidents and disaster management.

Compassion Fatigue and Related Constructs

The levels of risk for compassion fatigue in the present sample of EAPA members were comparable to other studies of mental health professionals (Ghahramanlou, & Brodbeck, 2000; Meldrum, King, & Spooner, 1999; Ortlepp, & Friedman, 2002). The high level of potential for compassion satisfaction is also not unique to the EA field. Research supports those professionals working with traumatized individuals who generally report both positive and negative outcomes from their work (Schauben, & Frazier, 1995; Wee, & Myers, 2003). It may be encouraging to see that the majority of the sample reported a high level of potential for compassion satisfaction; however, it is concerning that 12% of the current sample reported high levels of risk for compassion fatigue. While other mental health professionals experience similar rates, if not higher levels of fatigue, EA professionals are not usually providing clinical services 100% of the time for their job. Therefore the types of incidents and traumatic material EA professionals are exposed to may be more severe than other groups of mental health professionals. This idea has not yet been studied. Theory also suggests that compassion satisfaction may have a buffering effect or offer the professional protection against burnout and compassion fatigue. This theoretical link has not been empirically tested to date, but is a good question for future research.

Coping

The results on coping are supported in the literature. There is a growing body of research on coping that suggests greater utilization of positive coping styles are related to lower levels of secondary traumatic stress and compassion fatigue (Hollingsworth, 1993; Schauben, & Frazier, 1995) and lower levels of burnout (Brown, & O'Brien, 1998; Carson et al., 1999; Pines, 1983). Research concludes that social support, a concept coded on the Positive coping subscale is related to mitigation of negative effects from trauma work (Fullerton et al., 2000; Kassam-Adams, 1999). Further, Hollingsworth concluded that positive coping skills such as peer support, clinical supervision, and consultation, along with effective boundary setting, and working toward achieving a balance of work and life are associated with reduced levels of compassion fatigue. In contrary, negative coping skills, such as professional isolation, may contribute to higher risk levels of compassion fatigue (Stamm, 1999; Terry, 1999). Creamer and Liddle (2004) concluded that among mental health professionals who responded to the terrorist attacks on September 11th, 2001, those who used maladaptive or negative coping skills reported higher levels of secondary traumatic stress. The EA field is no different. While one of the primary responsibilities of the EAP is to encourage health and wellness in the workplace, there is no clear correlation that knowing how to take care of oneself and actually caring for oneself are related. However, research supports that using positive coping skills, similar to the ones reported being used by EA professionals in the present study, are effective in reducing the risk for compassion fatigue.

Preventing Negative Outcomes

There are serious ethical implications for EA professionals, supervisors, administrators, and educators to consider related to the prevention, identification, and intervention of compassion fatigue among trauma professionals, both inside and outside of the workplace. Traumatized professionals, who may be suffering from symptoms of compassion fatigue, can be ineffective or even detrimental in their clinical work with traumatized clients due to an inability to effectively attend to the client's traumatic material. For example, impaired professionals may discourage clients from exploring important issues related to their traumatic experiences (Munroe, 1999). Without early recognition and intervention, symptoms of compassion fatigue may compromise the work of EA professionals.

What is unique to mental health and EA professionals is that while a significant portion of their job is focused on educating clients about self-care and positive coping, it is not clear if EA counselors effectively utilize their own knowledge of coping in dealing with personal stressful situations. The idea that EA professionals inherently know what defines positive and negative coping does not necessarily translate that they will make good decisions regarding their own well-being. The fact that several EA professionals in the current sample reported using drugs and alcohol to deal with reactions from workplace traumatic stress tell us that despite their knowledge about positive coping, professionals don't always use effective coping skills when exposed to traumatic stress. The use of ineffective coping skills can not only can impact the EA professional, but also the clients and companies they are hired to help.

Also of concern is the fact that EAP companies are generally not doing much to support EA professionals as they cope with work-related stress resulting from offering crisis intervention services. There are several programs suggested in the literature that could be adopted into EA practice. For example, Potter et al. (2003) developed a program called "debriefing the debriefers." This program is designed to help alleviate negative stress resulting from working with traumatized clients or groups and offering CISM services, which can contribute to compassion fatigue and burnout. The program follows the Mitchell (1983) model for critical incident stress debriefing (CISD), but is condensed, consisting of three phases: the review, the response, and the remind phase. Debriefing services for debriefers are traditionally offered soon after the CISD or other crisis intervention response has concluded and an experienced member of the CISM team usually leads the debriefings. Lewis (2002) also recommends using debriefing services as an intervention to foster good self-care habits among debriefers. Of the respondents who reported services being offered, only 9.3% stated that their EAP offered a 'debriefing the debriefer' program. This writer feels that it is essential for EAPs to recognize the natural reactions of doing trauma work and begin to support staff more effectively, while also encouraging personal stress management.

One example of a supportive program offered at the national level is the Colleague Assistance Program (CAP), developed through EAPA following the terrorist attacks of September 11th, 2001. This program, designed to offer a way for EA professionals to provide outreach and support to other EA professionals was revitalized most recently after the devastation caused by Hurricane Katrina. At the time of writing this article, 30 EAPA members have volunteered their personal time to call and e-mail other EAPA members who may have been negatively affected by the recent hurricanes. While empirical research on the effects of participation in these types of outreach and support programs has not been assessed, feedback from EAPA members who have used the services is overwhelmingly positive and encouraging.

What Can EA Professionals Do?

While research on the topic of what is most effective for preventing and minimizing the negative effects of providing crisis intervention work is still in its infancy, the following are some suggestions for professionals and administrators. First, EA professionals can continue having conversations about the natural reactions to working in the crisis intervention field. The first step to resolving a potential risk is to acknowledge that the risk may exist. Acknowledging that EA professionals are human beings and have human reactions to crisis work is a first step in supporting colleagues and others in this field.

From a management and supervisory perspective, it is essential that supervisors monitor EA professionals, especially new practitioners with regard to crisis intervention. Many professional therapists report that their graduate degrees did not adequately prepare them for trauma work, particularly working with victims of abuse (Alpert, & Paulson, 1990; Danieli, 1994; Pope, & Feldman-Summers, 1992). These same professionals often seek additional education and training through continuing education and on-the-job training. The EAP field is no different; many EAPA members in the current study reported receiving no formalized education or training to provide crisis intervention services before actually working in a crisis situation with an individual or group. Through professional development and continuing education, we must provide methods for EA professionals to receive the appropriate training, supervision, and support to work effectively in a challenging field.

Inbar and Ganor (2003) suggest several ways to help professionals cope with continuous exposure to traumatic events. The first intervention they suggest is at the individual level, which includes supportive activities to help professionals "regain basic skills, such as effective time management and restructuring their daily routine" (Inbar, & Ganor). Second, they recommend intervention at a professional level to help professionals develop "caring distancing techniques," such as using humor and supervision in an appropriate and therapeutic manner. The third form of intervention is a cognitive-behavioral intervention, which is designed to help professionals identify signs and symptoms of secondary traumatic stress and address them effectively. Finally, Inbar and Ganor recommend intervention at the social-organizational level, focusing on "designing an organizational culture that prevents or moderates the creation of burnout condition, and encourages effective coping."

According to the EAP Crisis Intervention Continuum, a comprehensive model for workplace disaster prevention and response (Jacobson et al., 2005; Paul, & Blum, 2005), post-incident response to workplace critical incidents includes self-care. Specifically, the model encourages the incorporation of personal self-care among the part of the EA professional and the use of support systems both inside and outside of the EAP, as appropriate. Overall, if organizations can begin to acknowledge that professionals are affected by the work they do in the traumatic stress field, they can begin to foster a work environment where professionals can provide support to each other, rather than blame. Further, as professionals become more comfortable and open to discussing their reactions to working in this field, we can also begin to support and help each other, discussing and debating the most effective coping methods and programs for self-care.

REFERENCES

Alpert, J. L., & Paulson, A. (1990). Graduate-level education and training in child sexual abuse. *Professional Psychology: Research and Practice, 21*, 366-371.

Arthur, A. R. (2002). Mental health problems and British workers: A survey of mental health problems in employees who received counseling from Employee Assistance Programmes. *Stress and Health: Journal of the International Society for the Investigation of Stress, 182*(2), 69-74.

Beaton, R. D., & Murphy, S. A. (1995). Working with people in crisis: Research implications. In C. R. Figley (Ed.), *Compassion fatigue: Coping with secondary traumatic stress disorder in those who treat the traumatized* (pp. 51-81). New York, NY: Brunner/Mazel.

Brown, C., & O'Brien, D. M. (1998). Understanding stress and burnout in shelter workers. *Professional Psychology: Research and Practice, 29*, 383-385.

Carson, J., Maal, S., Roche, S., Fagin, L., DeVilliers, N., O'Malley, P., Brown, D., Leary, J., & Holloway, F. (1999). Burnout in mental health nurses: Much ado about nothing? *Stress Medicine, 15*, 127-134.

Carver, C. S. (1997). You want to measure coping but your protocol's too long: Consider the Brief COPE. *International Journal of Behavioral Medicine, 4*, 92-100.

Creamer, T. L., & Liddle, B. J. (in press). Secondary trauma among disaster mental health workers responding to the September 11th attacks. *Professional Psychology: Research and Practice.*

Danieli, Y. (1994). Countertransference, trauma, and training. In J. P. Wilson and J. D. Lindy (Eds.), *Countertransference in the treatment of PTSD* (pp. 368-388). London: Guilford.

Dunning, C., & Silva, M. (1980). Disaster induced trauma in rescue workers. *Victimology: An International Journal, 5*(2-4), 287-297.

Figley, C. R. (1983). Catastrophes: An overview of family reactions. In C. R. Figley and H. I. McCubbin (Eds.), *Stress and the family: Coping with catastrophe (vol. 2)*. New York: Brunner/Mazel.

Figley, C. R. (1995). Compassion fatigue as secondary traumatic stress disorder: An overview. In C. R. Figley (Ed.), *Compassion fatigue: Coping with secondary traumatic stress disorder in those who treat the traumatized* (pp. 1-19). New York: Brunner/Mazel.

Figley, C. R. (2002). *Treating compassion fatigue.* New York: Brunner-Routledge.

Figley, C. R., & Stamm, B. H. (1996). Psychometric review of Compassion Fatigue Self Test. In B. H. Stamm (Ed.), *Measurement of stress, trauma, and adaptation* (pp. 127-130). Lutherville, MD: Sidran Press.

Fullerton, C. S., Ursano, R. J., Vance, K., & Wang, L. (2000). Debriefing following trauma. *Psychiatric Quarterly, 71*(3), 259-275.

Ghahramanlou, M., & Brodbeck, C. (2000). Predictors of secondary trauma in sexual assault trauma counselors. *International Journal of Emergency Mental Health, 2*(4), 229-240.

Hollingsworth, M. A. (1993). *Responses of female therapists to treating adult female survivors of incest.* Unpublished doctoral dissertation, Western Michigan University, MI.

Inbar, J., & Ganor, M. (2003). Trauma and compassion fatigue: Helping the helpers. *Journal of Jewish Communal Services, Winter-Spring,* 109-111.

Jacobson, J. M. (2004). *Compassion fatigue among employee assistance program counselors* (Doctoral dissertation, University of Maryland, 2004). Dissertation Abstracts International, 65, 1540.

Jacobson, J. M., Paul, J., & Blum, D. (2005). The EAP workplace critical incident continuum. *The Journal of Employee Assistance, 32*(2), 28-30.

Kassam-Adams, N. (1999). The risks of treating sexual trauma: Stress and secondary trauma in psychotherapists. In B. H. Staff (Ed.), *Secondary traumatic stress: Self-care issues for clinicians, researchers, and educators* (2nd ed., pp. 37-50). Towson, Maryland: SIDRAN Institute.

Leon, A. M., Altholz, J. A., & Dziegielewski, S. F. (1999). Compassion fatigue: Considerations for working with the elderly. *Journal of Gerontological Social Work, 32*(1), 43-62.

Lewis, G. (2002). Post-crisis stress debriefing: More harm than good? *Behavioral Health Management, July/August,* 22-25.

Masi, D. A. (2000, June). *EAPs in a managed care environment.* Presentation for SAMHSA's Workplace Resources Center–Online Briefings. Retrieved November 26, 2005, from http://workplace.samhsa.gov/OnlineBriefings/ebriefs/damasi.html

Maslach, C. (1976). Burned-out. *Human Behavior, 9*(5), 16-22.

Meldrum, L., King, R., & Spooner, D. (1999, March). *Secondary traumatic stress among Australian mental health care managers.* Paper presented at the meeting of the APA-NIOSH Joint Conference, on Work, Stress and Health 1999: Organization of Work in a Global Economy, Baltimore, MD.

Mitchell, J. T. (1983). When disaster strikes. The critical incident stress debriefing process. *Journal of Emergency Services, 8,* 36-39.

Munroe, J. F. (1999). Ethical issues associated with secondary trauma in therapists. In B. H. Stamm (Ed.), *Secondary traumatic stress: Self-care issues for clinicians, researchers and educators* (pp. 211-229). MD: Sidran Press.

Nash, J. (2001). Trek to ground zero. *EAP Digest,* 18-20.

Ortlepp, K., & Friedman, M. (2002). Prevalence and correlates of secondary traumatic stress in workplace lay trauma counselors. *Journal of Traumatic Stress, 15*(3), 113-222.

Paul, J., & Blum, D. (2005). Workplace disaster preparedness and response: The employee assistance program continuum of services. *International Journal of Emergency Mental Health, 7*(3), 169-178.

Pearlman, L. A. (1999). Self-care for trauma therapists: Ameliorating vicarious traumatization. In B. H. Stamm (Ed.), *Secondary traumatic stress: Self-care issues for clinicians, researchers, and educators* (2nd ed., pp. 51-64). Lutherville, MD: Sidran Press.

Pearlman, L. A., & Mac Ian, P. S. (1995). Vicarious traumatization: An empirical study of the effects of trauma work on trauma therapists. *Professional Psychology: Research and Practice, 26*(6), 558-565.

Pearlmann, L. A., & Saakvitne, K. W. (1995). *Trauma and the therapist: Countertransference and vicarious traumatization in psychotherapy with incest survivors.* New York: W.W. Norton & Company.

Pines, A. M. (1983). Burnout. In L. Goldberger and S. Breznitz (Eds.), *Handbook of stress: Theoretical and clinical aspects* (2nd ed.). New York, NY: Free Press.

Pines, A. M., & Kafry, D. (1978). Occupational tedium in the social services. *Social Work, 23,* 499-507.

Potter, D., Stevens, J. A., & LaBerteauz, P. (2003). *Practical concepts and training exercises for crisis intervention teams.* MD: Chevron Publishing Corporation.

Saakvitne, K. W. (2002). Shared trauma: The therapist's increased vulnerability. *Psychoanalytic Quarterly, 12,* 443-449.

Schauben, L. J., & Frazier, P. A. (1995). Vicarious trauma: The effects on female counselors of working with sexual violence survivors. *Psychology of Women Quarterly, 19*(1), 49-64.

Stamm, B. H. (1998). *Traumatic stress secondary traumatic stress web site.* Retrieved from http://www.isu.edu/~bhstamm/.

Stamm, B. H. (Ed.). (1999). *Secondary traumatic stress: Self-care issues for clinicians, researchers, and educators* (2nd ed.). Washington, DC: Sidran Press.

Stamm, B. H. (2002). Measuring compassion satisfaction as well as fatigue: Developmental history of the compassion fatigue and satisfaction test. In C. R. Figley (Ed.), *Treating compassion fatigue* (pp. 107-122). New York, NY: Brunner/Mazel.

Stamm, B. H., Higson-Smith, C., & Hudnall, A. C. (2001, December). *Measuring the helper's power to heal and to be hurt, helped, by training.* Presented at the 17th Annual Meeting of the International Society for Traumatic Stress Studies. New Orleans, LA.

Sweeney, A. P., Hohenshil, T. H., & Fortune, J. C. (2002). Job satisfaction among employee assistance professionals: A national study. *Journal of Employment Counseling, 39,* 50-60.

Terry, M. J. (1999). Kelengakutelleghpat: An arctic community-based approach to trauma. In B. H. Stamm (Ed.), *Secondary traumatic stress: Self-care issues for clinicians, researchers, and educators* (pp. 149-178). Lutherville, MD: Sidran.

Valnet, P. (1995). Survival strategies: A framework for understanding secondary traumatic stress and coping in helpers. In C. R. Figley (Ed.), *Coping with secondary traumatic stress disorder in those who treat the traumatized* (pp. 21-50). New York, NY: Brunner/Mazel.

Wee, D. F., & Myers, D. (2002). Stress responses of mental health workers following disaster: The Oklahoma City bombing. In C. R. Figley (Ed.), *Treating compassion fatigue* (pp. 57-84). New York, NY: Brunner-Routledge.

White, G. D. (2001). Near ground zero: Compassion fatigue in the aftermath of September 11. *Traumatology, 7(4),* 151-154.

doi:10.1300/J490v21n03_08

Workplace Crisis Intervention:
A Systematic Review of Effect Sizes

George S. Everly, Jr.
Martin F. Sherman
Amy Stapleton
Daniel J. Barnett
Girish S. Hiremath
Jonathan M. Links

SUMMARY. The workplace, where adults spend about one-third of their lives, would seem an ideal place from which to promote health and respond to crisis. This paper employs a systematic statistical review of experimental and quasi-experimental research on workplace-based crisis intervention programs. Nine studies were identified that met inclusion criteria for further analysis. Results suggest that the workplace can be a useful platform from which to provide crisis intervention programs. doi:10.1300/J490v21n03_09 *[Article copies available for a fee from The Haworth Document Delivery Service: 1-800-HAWORTH. E-mail address: <docdelivery@haworthpress.com> Website: <http://www.HaworthPress.com> © 2006 by The Haworth Press, Inc. All rights reserved.]*

KEYWORDS. Crisis intervention, employee assistance programs, disaster mental health, critical incident stress management

---

[Haworth co-indexing entry note]: "Workplace Crisis Intervention: A Systematic Review of Effect Sizes." Everly, George S. et al. Co-published simultaneously in *Journal of Workplace Behavioral Health* (The Haworth Press, Inc.) Vol. 21, No. 3/4, 2006, pp. 153-170; and: *Workplace Disaster Preparedness, Response, and Management* (ed: R. Paul Maiden, Rich Paul, and Christina Thompson) The Haworth Press, Inc., 2006, pp. 153-170. Single or multiple copies of this article are available for a fee from The Haworth Document Delivery Service [1-800-HAWORTH, 9:00 a.m. - 5:00 p.m. (EST). E-mail address: docdelivery@haworthpress.com].

INTRODUCTION

It is generally accepted as fact that exposure to traumatic events increases the risk of post-traumatic morbidity (American Psychiatric Association, 1994). While this is especially true with regard to large-scale disasters (Noji, 1991; Norris, 1992; North et al., 1999), accidents and violence at the workplace have the potential to engender similar traumatic reactions. Early experience within the wartime military suggests that some form of crisis intervention, rather than more intensive therapy, might serve to reduce the adverse impact of exposure to traumatic events and assist individuals in regaining functionality (Salmon, 1919; Artiss, 1963). The military has historically benefited from the utilization of the fundamental crisis intervention principles of proximity, immediacy, and expectancy (Artiss, 1963; Solomon & Benbenishty, 1986; Deahl et al., 2000). Proximity refers to intervention at, or within close physical proximity to, the trauma or disaster venue. Immediacy refers to intervention within close temporal proximity to the traumatic event. Expectancy refers to intervention based upon the assumption that adverse reactions to trauma are often normal and that education and support, rather than traditional psychotherapy, can often be useful in reducing distress. The civilian variation of crisis intervention was first cogently described by Caplan (1964). Extrapolating from his exposition, one finds that crisis intervention consists of basic steps:

1. stabilization of psychological functioning through meeting basic physical needs, then addressing the most basic of psychological needs,
2. mitigation of psychological dysfunction/distress so as to assist in the return of acute adaptive psychological/behavioral functioning, and/or
3. facilitation of access to the next level of care.

The practice of crisis intervention has become a well accepted and commonly applied endeavor within the mental health professions (viz Roberts, 2005; Danielli & Dingman, 2005). Within employee assistance programs, it is a commonly provided service, if not a key element within many such programs. However, the practice is not without its critics (Rose et al., 2002). In a review of randomized controlled trials of single session counseling with medical patients (referred to as "debriefing"), the authors call for a cessation of "compulsory debriefings pending further evidence." They further note, however, "We are unable to comment on the use of group debriefing, nor the use of debriefing after mass traumas." In specific contrast, however, a subsequent expanded analysis of medical crisis intervention conducted by Stapleton et al. (in press) revealed a beneficial effect associated with such processes.

It would not be an unreasonable intuitive leap to question whether crisis intervention, based in varying degrees upon the same principles as those used in the military and as suggested by Caplan (1964), would be of value when applied through the workplace. It would seem that the workplace, where adults spend roughly one-third of their lives, would be an ideal platform for the delivery of crisis intervention and health promotion programs (Everly & Feldman, 1985). It is the purpose of this article to systematically review selected published research regarding crisis intervention through the workplace among non-military, non-emergency responder populations.

METHODOLOGY:
A STATISTICAL REVIEW OF THE LITERATURE

Rationale

There exist two fundamental methodological approaches to the review of research: (1) narrative reviews, and (2) statistical reviews (Cooper, 1979). Traditional reviews have rested largely upon the narrative process. As Cooper (1979) notes, ". . . summary statements about research areas are usually based on impressions gleaned by the reviewer from a reading of related studies." Cooper (1979) points out that narrative reviews may be seriously flawed and may not serve to progress the relevant science as much as might be assumed initially. As an alternative, Glass (1976) states that the statistically based review "connotes a rigorous alternative to the causal narrative discussions of research studies which typify our attempts to make sense of the rapidly expanding research literature." Statistical reviews would appear to represent a more effective means of advancing science compared to narrative reviews, alone. Finally, as noted by Cooper (1979), "Repeated observation allows for greater confidence in uncovered relations, when observations show consistent or similar results."

In a previous article Flannery and Everly (2004) offered a narrative review of multi-component crisis intervention. As a refinement to the previously publication, we now offer a natural corollary of that prior review. This paper presents a statistical review of research relevant to the field of crisis intervention as applied specifically at, or through, the workplace. Emergency services, military, and disaster response personnel were specifically omitted from this review. As it may be argued that the occupational culture and milieu of the military and emergency response professions is unique when compared to non-military and non-emergency professions, a systematic review of crisis intervention within those occupations would have most meaning when conducted independently.

Search

A literature search was conducted using computer-based search engines including PsychInfo (Psychological Abstracts), Medline, Academic Search Elite, and SciSearch (Social Science Citation Index) up to and including June 2005. The following keywords were utilized in the search: crisis intervention and workplace, work trauma, workplace intervention, and workplace debriefing.

Inclusion Criteria

Studies evaluating adverse mental health outcome(s) (i.e., anxiety, post-traumatic stress, alcohol use, use of sick days/leave, etc.) following some form of crisis intervention to members of a non-military, non-emergency responder work group following a traumatic incident were included. It was required that included studies were published in English. The specific intervention examined may have been in any modality (i.e., individual versus group) using various components (i.e., education, emotional support and catharsis, follow-up services, etc.). In addition, the study must have evaluated the impact of any crisis intervention on adverse mental health behaviors (i.e., anxiety, post-traumatic stress, alcohol use, use of sick days/leave, etc.). Randomized, controlled trials as well as quasi-experimental designs without significant methodological confounds were included.

Analysis

The primary analysis employed with this study was effect size analysis (Hevey & McGee, 1998). It consisted of generating effects sizes for relevant outcome within the constituent workplace based crisis intervention investigations. Unlike the traditional "p-value" which serves as the sine qua non for most inferentially based research data, "Effect size statistics provide an indicator of the magnitude and direction of the effect under investigation. . . . It offers a quantitative estimate of the difference between two groups" (Hevey & McGee, 1998). In this study, Cohen's d (Cohen, 1977), or a reasonable estimation, was chosen as the indicator of effect size. The Cohen's d may be thought of as an expression of the relationship between a measure of central tendency (the means of the dependent variables for contrasted groups when using parametric data) divided by some measure of variation (often the pooled standard deviation, or the standard deviation of the one of the contrasted groups). Cohen's d is the most commonly used metric of effect size. When parametric data were not available, the Cohen's d was approximated through the use of standard conversion formulae (Rosenthal & Rosnow, 1991). The results for each study in the present investigation were transformed into a Cohen's d statistical expression of effect size.

The combinatorial statistical procedure of meta-analysis was then used in the present investigation to evaluate the overall effectiveness of crisis intervention as applied specifically at, or through, the workplace. Meta-analysis allows for the statistical integration of the results of independent investigations so as to summarize and statistically express the overall magnitude of effectiveness of the intervention under investigation. Meta-analysis consists of combining, in some predetermined manner, the expressions of effect size. In order to generate the meta-analytic Cohen's d, selected effects sizes were combined in an unweighted manner and the mean subsequently calculated. While it is common to use a weighting formula in meta-analysis (weighting by sample size or by methodological rigor, etc.), it was determined that clinical sensitivity and meaningfulness might be sacrificed should we use a weighting formulation. Keeping in mind that the tools of effect size and meta-analysis are just that, i.e., tools, not ends unto themselves, we present the combinatorial data as an initial guide to interpretation. Greater clinical sensitivity may be achieved through an analysis of the effect sizes of homogeneous and clinically relevant dependent variables.

RESULTS

Using the aforementioned selection criteria, nine published, empirical investigations assessing the effectiveness of crisis intervention in the workplace were used. These studies were reported from 1995 to 2005, and a majority of studies were reported from the United States.

Traumatic incidents reviewed included terrorist attacks (1), robberies (2), assaults (5), and natural disasters (1).

Table 1 contains a summary of unweighted meta-analytic findings as well as the presentation of the effect sizes of homogeneous and clinically relevant dependent variables.

TABLE 1. Summary of Primary Meta-Analytic Findings by Selected Outcome Variables Expressed in the Unweighted Cohen's d Statistic

---

OVERALL EFFECTIVENESS: 1.53

EFFECT SIZE WITH DATA ON ASSAULTS REMOVED: .60

DIFFERENTIATED CLINICAL OUTCOME VARIABLES:
Post-traumatic distress:
1.66; 1.77 (Campfield & Hills, 2001)
.31; .25 (Richards, 2001)
.73 (Chemtob, Tomas, Law, & Cremniter, 1997)
.56 (Boscarino, Adams, & Figley, 2005)
−.71 (Nhiwatiwa, 2003)
Mean effect size: .65

Assaults:
5.84 (Flannery et al., 1995)
13.10 (Flannery et al., 1998)
2.36 (Flannery, Penk, & Corrigan, 1999)
.41, .42, −0.01 (Flannery, Anderson, Marks, & Uzoma, 2000)
Mean effect size: 3.68

Alcohol use:
.74, .92 (Boscarino, Adams, & Figley, 2005)
Mean effect size: .83

Depression:
.81 (Boscarino, Adams, & Figley, 2005)

Anxiety:
.98 (Boscarino, Adams, & Figley, 2005)

General health and global impairment:
.14 (Richards, 2001)
−.30 (Nhiwatiwa, 2003)
.66 (Boscarino, Adams, & Figley, 2005)
Mean effect size: .166

Listed below are brief summaries of each of the nine constituent studies identified in the search and their effects sizes. It should be noted that effect sizes of .3 to .5 are usually indicative of a moderate magnitude of effect, whereas effect sizes of .7 and greater are generally indicative of large magnitudes of effect. An effect size of .5 indicates a difference of one-half standard deviation between the comparison groups.

1. Campfield and Hills (2001) conducted a randomized controlled trial of crisis intervention subsequent to robbery at the workplace. In this investigation, 77 employees were randomly assigned to an immediate intervention condition (< 10 hours, n = 36), or a delayed intervention condition (> 48 hours, n = 41). The specific crisis intervention was described as Critical Incident Stress Debriefing (CISD). Post-traumatic morbidity was assessed using the Post-traumatic Stress Diagnostic Scale (PDS) at CISD, 2 days post CISD, 4 days post CISD, and 2 weeks post robbery. Campfield and Hills (2001) noted, "For both number of symptoms and severity of symptoms, there was a significant main effect of group: symptoms, $F(1,75) = 52.92$, $p < .001$, eta2 = .41; severity. $F(1,75) = 59.48$, $p < .001$, eta2 = .44. There was also a significant main effect of time interval: symptoms, $F(3,225) = 133.46$, $p < .001$, eta2 = .64; severity, $F(3,225 = 267.28$, $p < .001$, eta2 = .78 (pp. 333-334). These findings were transformed into the following effect sizes:
   (1) For the main effect of group on symptoms, Cohen's d = 1.66,
   (2) For the main effect of group on severity, d = 1.77,
   (3) For the effect of time on symptoms, d = 2.66, and
   (4) For the effect of time on severity, d = 3.76.
2. Richards (2001) conducted prospective field trials wherein he compared two crisis intervention approaches, Critical Incident Stress Debriefing (CISD) and Critical Incident Stress Management (CISM), following armed robberies. The CISD approach involved small group discussions following the robberies. The CISM approach reflected a multi-component crisis intervention approach. The 2 approaches were applied in a serial manner reflecting the evolution of the human resources program with the employing organization. Post traumatic morbidity was assessed using the Impact of Events Scale (IES), Post-traumatic Stress Scale (PSS), & General Health Questionnaire (GHQ-28) applied at 3 days, 1 month, 6 months, and 12 months post robbery for both groups. In the sample of 217 (CISD alone, n = 75; CISM, n = 142),

analysis of between groups psychometrics at follow up (f/up = mean of 3, 6, 12 month scores) yielded the following effect sizes:

(1)   IES effect size, Cohen's d = .31,
(2)   PSS effect size d = .25,
(3)   GHQ effect size d = .14.

The effect size changes within the CISD alone condition from 3 days to f/up were calculated to be:

(1)   IES d = 1.71,
(2)   PSS d = 1.26,
(3)   GHQ d = 1.10.

The effect size changes within the CISM condition from 3 days to f/up were calculated to be:

(1)   IES d = 1.82,
(2)   PSS d = 1.20,
(3)   GHQ d = 1.02.

3. Following a catastrophic natural disaster, Chemtob et al. (1997) conducted an evaluation of a brief psychosocial intervention (group debriefing) applied 6 months post disaster. Two groups were employed in a time-lagged pre and post test intervention assessment paradigm wherein the post test of group 1 (n = 25) was concurrent with the pre test of group 2 (n = 18). Post-traumatic morbidity was assessed using the Impact of Events Scale (IES). Three months separated the pre and post testing for both groups. Analysis of variance for repeated measures (within group factor) was employed for both groups. The between group factor evaluated differences between groups. The authors state, "The within group treatment effect was highly significant (F = 21.13, df = 1,40, p < .001), whereas the between-group difference was not significant (F = 2.62, df = 1,40 p > 0.11)" (p. 416). "Despite the passage of time, the pre-treatment distress scores for group 2 were significantly higher than the post treatment scores of group 2 (t = 4.27, df = 41, p < 0.0001). The continued distress of group 2 before treatment suggests that the change in the Impact of Event Scale scores of group 1 was not merely due to the passage of time." These findings were transformed into the following effect sizes:

(1)   The within group treatment effect was Cohen's d = .73,
(2)   The between group effect was d = .49,
(3)   Comparing group 2 pre (24.8) to group 1 post (12.3) yields a d of 1.29.

4. Assaults upon healthcare personnel represent a major source of stress for those thusly employed (Flannery, 1998). Nhiwatiwa (2003) investigated the effects of an educational program designed to mitigate such distress. "This study aimed to explore the effectiveness of a brief educational intervention (reading a booklet on effects of trauma and coping) in reducing distress in nurses working in medium security settings who are physically assaulted by patients." Forty nurses who had been assaulted by patients were randomly assigned to one of two groups: a self-directed education and assessment condition (reading on one's own time a booklet on trauma and coping) and an assessment only condition. Contacts were initiated within one month of assault and then 3 months later. Assessments were performed using the Impact of Events Scale (IES) and the General Health Questionnaire-28 (GHQ). "The results of a Mann-Whitney test on the IES change variable indicated that assaulted nurses given educational booklet had significantly higher post-intervention distress than the control group ($Z = -2.18$, two-tailed, $P = 0.03$). There was no significant difference in change from baseline for the GHQ-28 ($Z = -0.99$, two-tailed, $P = 0.34$) between the two groups" (p. 565). Between groups effect sizes were $-.71$ for the IES and $-.30$ for the GHQ.

5. The Assaulted Staff Action Program (ASAP) is an integrated multi-component crisis intervention system developed by Dr. Raymond Flannery (Flannery et al., 1995). It is a variation of the strategic, multi-component Critical Incident Stress Management crisis intervention system (CISM, Everly & Mitchell, 1999) originally designed to mitigate distress and facilitate follow up care amongst first response professionals. The ASAP intervention program was established in a 400-bed state psychiatric hospital in support of the healthcare staff therein. In this investigation, the authors examined the effects of the ASAP program upon assaults upon staff personnel. Data on assaults on staff members were collected for a two-year period and compared to baseline data collected previously at the same hospital. Subsequent to the ASAP initiative, assaults declined from base rate of 30 to a base rate of 11, $t(8) = 16.47$, $p < .005$, $d = 5.84$.

6. In a subsequent investigation (Flannery et al., 1998), the ASAP multi-component crisis intervention system was "implemented in a staggered start-up in three state mental hospitals. . . . The staggered start-up permitted the use of a multiple-baseline design in this phased-in approach . . . each hospital served as its own control

group." Assault rates for 3 months prior to ASAP were compared to assault rates in the first four quarters post intervention implementation. The mean number of assaults for three hospitals was reported as follows: pre-ASAP 31 (sd = 2.18) 1st Quarter 3.56 (1.74) 4th Quarter 2.44 (.58).

The authors state, "A repeated-measures analysis of variance showed a statistically significant difference in the number of assaults between the quarters before and after implementation (F = 80.85, df = 4,40, p < .001)." These findings were transformed into the following effect sizes:

(1) Using pre-ASAP (31) versus 1st Quarter (3.56) dividing by pre ASAP standard deviation (sd) yields a Cohen's d of 12.59.

(2) Using pre-ASAP (31) versus 4th quarter (2.44) dividing by pre ASAP standard deviation yields a Cohen's d of 13.10.

7. Flannery et al. (1999) extended the ASAP intervention to a 16-bed acute care suburban community mental health center with 32 direct care staff. Patient assault data were collected for a four-month period prior to initiation of the ASAP and served as the control condition in this single-case experimental design wherein the facility served as its own control. Subsequent to the initiation of the ASAP, assault data were collected for 18 months. The quarterly rate of assaults declined from 11.25 per quarter pre-ASAP to less than one post-ASAP (t = 12.93, p < .05). The authors note, "This decline is statistically significant, and well below the expected occurrence of 68 assaults for this 18 month period (t = 12.93; df = 30; p < .001)." The associated Cohen's d was 2.36.

8. Flannery, Anderson, Marks, and Uzoma (2000) conducted a replicatory investigation of the ASAP initiative previously cited. The article reported on the findings of three independent ASAP investigations. In the first study, the ASAP integrated crisis intervention system was applied to a 125-bed urban mental health care facility. A single case experimental design was employed wherein the facility served as its own control. The outcome variable, as in other ASAP investigations was that of assaults upon healthcare staff by patients. A statistically meaningful decline in assaults was observed for the 12-month period subsequent to the implementation of ASAP, when compared to the 12-month period prior to the ASAP intervention using t-test (t = 1.94, df = 22; p < .035) and simple regression (F = 4.18, df = 1,22, p < .05). The authors noted that one anomalous month was omitted from data analysis. The ef-

fect size was calculated to be .41. In the second study, the ASAP program was applied to 31 community residences with a total of 225 beds. The outcome variable of assaults upon staff members was recorded for 12 months prior to ASAP initiation (15) and then for 12 months post implementation (7). The t-test revealed a t-value of 1.96 (df = 22), while the simple regression was reported as F = 1.77 (df = 1, 22). The effect size was calculated to be .42. Finally, in the third study, the ASAP program was applied to a rural community mental health center. The facility was a 16-bed acute mental health care facility. The outcome variable of assaults upon staff members was recorded for 12 months prior to ASAP initiation (32) and then for 12 months post implementation (34). The t-test revealed a t-value of −0.07 (df = 22), while the simple regression was reported F = 0.004 (df = 1, 22). The change was not statistically significant, but the resultant effect size was calculated to −0.01.

9. Boscarino et al. (2005) conducted a methodologically robust investigation of workplace-based crisis intervention. This study represents a prospective, random sample of 1,681 New York adults interviewed by telephone at 1 year and 2 years after September 11th in order to assess the effectiveness of workplace-based crisis interventions. "We classified respondents who attended these worksite sessions as the brief crisis intervention group (*n* = 180) and all others as the non-intervention group (*n* = 1,501)." Results indicate that crisis interventions in the form of critical incident stress management had a beneficial impact across a variety of outcomes when assessed using the Brief Symptom Inventory-18 (BSI) and various standardized psychiatric interview guides. More specifically, the workplace-based crisis interventions were associated with:
   (1) reduced risks for binge drinking (d = .74),
   (2) alcohol dependence (d = .92),
   (3) PTS symptoms (d = .56),
   (4) major depression (d = .81),
   (5) anxiety (d = .98), and
   (6) global impairment (d = .66), compared with individuals who did not receive these interventions.

An analysis of the specific content of the crisis interventions revealed the following mechanisms:

- Education about symptoms
- Talking about experiences
- Relaxation
- Stress management/coping
- Cognitive reframing
- Social support

Social support was inversely associated with:
- PTS ($d = .38$)
- Depression ($d = .19$)
- Global impairment ($d = .34$)

Finally, the plateau effect for crisis intervention was reached at 2-3 sessions.

The authors conclude, "Based on our analyses, it appears that worksite crisis interventions provided by many NYC employers following the events of September 11th, 2001, had a beneficial impact on the mental status of employees across a spectrum of outcomes. As was seen, these outcomes included a significant reduced risk for binge drinking, alcohol dependence, PTSD symptoms, major depression, somatization, anxiety, and global impairment, compared with comparable individuals who did not receive this treatment. In addition, it appeared that 2-3 brief sessions achieved the maximum benefit for most of the outcomes we examined." They further note, "Based on our current findings, we suggest that crisis intervention services should be considered as a first line of emergency management for those potentially affected by large-scale community disasters."

CONCLUSIONS

Nine published studies evaluating some form of crisis intervention in the workplace were synthesized and analyzed. Eight studies' results indicated a positive effect of the crisis intervention on adverse mental health behaviors. Positive effects of crisis intervention were noted on measures of binge drinking, alcohol dependence, PTSD, post-traumatic distress, anxiety, depression, assault rates, and global impairment. Resultant effect sizes were robust (mean effect sizes: 1.66 overall; .60 when assault data were removed). One study investigating a self-directed educational intervention after physical assaults, however, indicated significantly higher post-intervention distress compared to individuals who did not receive the intervention (Nhiwatiwa, 2003).

In contrast to the generally negative findings for single session crisis intervention with medical and surgical patients reported by Rose et al. (2002), the results of the current statistical review are generally supportive of the value of crisis intervention when applied at or through the workplace. The interventions reviewed consisted largely, not of single session interventions, but of multiple session interventions, and in some instances, the potential to use a wide array of integrated tactical interventions in a coordinated manner.

Implications for Program Development

In stark contradistinction to the findings of Rose et al. (2002), the studies contained herein tended not to employ single session, standalone crisis interventions. Of the nine studies investigated herein only two chose such an intervention procedure: Campfield and Hills (2001) and Nhiwatiwa (2003). In the case of Nhiwatiwa (2003), the intervention was actually self-directed readings, thus falling short of what many might consider an actual intervention. Interestingly, the study by Nhiwatiwa (2003) contributed the greatest negative effect to the overall analysis. Thus from a program development perspective, rather than a univariate approach to crisis intervention, based upon the present review, a coordinated multi-component crisis intervention initiative would seem to warrant consideration.

The use of a phase-sensitive multi-component intervention approach may be inferred from the earliest of disaster relevant treatises (Raphael, 1986) and has been suggested elsewhere (National Institute of Mental Health, 2002). Current consensus recommendations reflect this notion.

The Employee Assistance Professionals' Association Disaster Response Task Force (2002) has delineated specific recommendations for critical incident response at the workplace. In short, they note the following:

- Employee assistance programs (EAPs) should develop workplace disaster plans.
- Plans should consist of the following:
  - Training in crisis intervention, resiliency training, risk assessment, and policy development
  - Acute response recommendations

- Post incident intervention (e.g., assessment, briefings, debriefings, referral, self-care)
- Follow-up service (supervisory briefings, assessment, training)
- Post incident review and plan reformulation

The National Volunteer Organizations Active in Disaster (NVOAD) represents the largest non-governmental disaster relief consortium in North America. This group, within its Early Psychological Intervention Subcommittee, addressed the issue of early psychological intervention after disasters. Their consensus points document (NVOAD, 2005) was released in May of 2005 and consisted of the following key points:

- Early Psychological Intervention (EPI) is valued
- EPI should consist of a multi-component system to meet the diverse needs of those impacted
- Specialized training in early psychological intervention is necessary
- EPI is one point on a continuum of psychological care. This spectrum ranges from pre-incident preparedness, acute response, to post-incident psychotherapy, when needed
- Cooperation, communication, coordination and collaboration are essential to the delivery of EPI

The finding of this present investigation would seem to support the recommendations of both EAPA and NVOAD as well as the continued utilization of workplace crisis intervention programs.

Public Health Implications

This analysis suggests that workplace-based crisis mental health interventions may have a useful effect on reducing adverse mental health outcomes post-trauma in non-emergency response workers. These findings have potentially significant public health implications, as high rates of psychological, physical, and productivity impacts have been observed among victims of workplace trauma.

A study by Northwestern National Life Insurance Company (1993)–one of the first to analyze public health impacts of workplace violence in a non-emergency response cohort–found that in addition to 79% experiencing negative psychological impacts, 40% experienced work life disruption, 28% were physically injured or sick; only 15% experienced no negative effects from the event.

Data by Miller-Burke et al. (1999) on 141 victims of bank robberies from 42 different bank branches reveal similar trends, with 80% of respondents reporting negative effects on concentration and productivity; 67% reporting experiencing anger and stress; and 24% of employees reporting that their physical health was "worse" or "much worse" after the robbery.

The scope of workplace violence is considerable. The Northwestern National Life Insurance Company study (1993) found that two million Americans had been victims of a physical attack at work during the past year, while another six million Americans workers were threatened, and 16 million were harassed. The economic impacts of workplace violence are profound as well: a 1994 survey by the U.S. Department of Justice (Bachman, 1994) found that workplace crime victimizations cost approximately half a million employees 1,751,100 days of work each year–an average of 3.5 days per crime; this missed work time resulted in over $55 million in lost wages each year, not including days covered by sick and annual leave; six out of 10 workplace incidents identified in this survey occurred in private companies.

These data, coupled with terrorism-related post September 11th realities, suggest that workplace trauma in non-emergency response occupations needs to be studied more comprehensively as a public health issue, to identify and refine best practice models for primary, secondary, and tertiary prevention. This will require enhanced research collaboration between public health and the mental health and corporate spheres.

Limitations

The studies in the current review included only one randomized controlled trial (RCT; Campfield & Hills, 2001) and one survey-based approximation (Boscarino et al., 2005). The remainder of the investigations are variations on a theme of quasi-experimentation, with some being more robust than others. Clearly the "gold standard" in evidence based practice is the randomized controlled trial (RCT), sometimes referred to as an "efficacy trial." However, that is not to say the evidence generated by non-RCT designs should be excluded from systematic reviews. Petticrew (2001) concludes that there is a common misconception held by researchers that "systematic reviews are applicable only to randomized controlled trials and that they are incapable of dealing with other forms of evidence, such as from non-randomized studies or qualitative research." Seligman (1996) has noted "efficacy studies are not necessary, sufficient, or privileged over effectiveness studies," while Cronbach (Cronbach et al., 1980) has argued non-equivalent comparison groups serve as reasonable substitutes for randomized trials.

This analysis utilized both parametric and nonparametric data in the generation of effect sizes. Thus, in the latter condition, the effect sizes should be seen as approximations. In those conditions, the effect sizes were by far the largest and served to dramatically inflate the overall magnitude of effect. Nevertheless, the findings themselves within those investigations were quite striking from a behavioral perspective. Table 1 reports mean effect sizes absent the nonparametric assault data in addition to the effect size for "overall effectiveness."

In sum, it is generally acknowledged that field research is difficult, especially in mass disaster situations (NIMH, 2002). In such cases, it may be necessary to employ studies with the greatest generalizability rather than internal validity. Recalling the comments of Cooper (1979), "Repeated observation allows for greater confidence in uncovered relations, when observations show consistent or similar results." While the studies presented herein do not represent the gold standard RCT and as such are vulnerable to alternative sources of effect, there is clearly a trend of evidence that supports the use of crisis intervention at the workplace as a means of reducing the adverse effects of trauma and disaster.

REFERENCES

American Psychiatric Association. (1994). *Diagnostic and statistical manual of mental disorder* (4th ed.). Washington, DC: American Psychiatric Press.

Artiss, K. (1963). Human behavior under stress: From combat to social psychiatry. *Military Medicine, 128*, 1011-1015.

Bachman, R. (1994). *Violence and theft in the workplace.* National Crime Victimization Survey, Bureau of Justice Statistics, U.S. Department of Justice, Washington, DC.

Boscarino, J., Adams, R. E., & Figley, C. R. (2005). A prospective cohort study of the effectiveness of employer-sponsored crisis interventions after a major disaster. *International Journal of Emergency Mental Health, 7*, 9-22.

Campfield, K. A., & Hills, A. M. (2001). Effect of timing of critical incident stress debriefing (CISD) on post-traumatic symptoms. *Journal of Traumatic Stress, 14*, 327-340.

Caplan, G. (1964). *Principles of preventive psychiatry.* New York: Basic.

Chemtob, C. M., Tomas, S., Law, W., & Cremniter, D. (1997). Postdisaster psychosocial intervention: A field study of the impact of debriefing on psychosocial distress. *American Journal of Psychiatry, 154*, 415-417.

Cohen, J. (1977). *Statistical power analysis for the behavioral sciences.* New York: Academic Press.

Cooper, H. (1979). Statistically combining independent studies: A meta-analysis of sex differences in conformity research. *Journal of Personality and Social Psychology, 37*, 131-146.

Cronbach, L. J., Ambron, S., Dornbusch, S., Hess, R., Hornick, R., Phillips, D., Walker, D., & Weiner, S. (1980). *Toward reform of program evaluation.* San Francisco: Jossey-Bass.

Danielli, Y., & Dingman, R. L. (Eds.). (2005). *On the ground after September 11.* New York: Haworth.

Deahl, M., Srinivasan, M., Jones, N., Thomas, J., Neblett, C., & Jolly, A. (2000). Preventing psychological trauma in soldiers. The role of operational stress training and psychological debriefing. *British Journal of Medical Psychology, 73*, 77-85.

Employee Assistance Professionals' Association (EAPA). (2002). Critical Incident Management for EAPA and EAPs. Report of the Employee Assistance Professionals' Association Disaster Response Task Force.

Everly, G. S., Jr., & Feldman, R. L. (Eds.). (1985). *Occupational health promotion: Health behavior at the workplace.* New York: Wiley.

Everly, G. S., Jr., & Mitchell, J. T. (1999). *Critical Incident Stress Management (CISM). A new era and standard of care in crisis intervention.* Ellicott City, MD: Chevron.

Flannery, R. B., Jr. (1998). *Assaulted Staff Action Program (ASAP).* Ellicott City, MD: Chevron.

Flannery, R. B., Jr., Anderson, E., Marks, L., & Uzoma, L. L. (2000). Assaulted Staff Action Program (ASAP) and declines in rates of assault: Mixed replicated findings. *Psychiatric Quarterly, 71*, 165-175.

Flannery, R. B., Jr., & Everly, G. S., Jr. (2004). Critical incident stress management: An updated review. *Aggression and Violent Behavior, 6*, 319-329.

Flannery, R. B., Jr., Hanson, M. A., Penk, W. E., Flannery, G. J., & Gallagher, C. (1995). The Assaulted Staff Action Program: An approach to coping with the aftermath of violence in the workplace. In L. Murphy, J. Hurrell, S. Sauter, & G. Keita (Eds.), *Job stress interventions* (pp. 199-212). Washington, DC: APA Press.

Flannery, R. B., Jr., Hanson, M. A., Penk, W. E., Goldfinger, S., Pastva, G. J., & Navon, M. A. (1998). Replicated declines in assault rates after implementation of the Assaulted Staff Action Program. *Psychiatric Services, 49*, 241-243.

Flannery, R. B., Penk, W. E., & Corrigan, M. (1999). The Assaulted Staff Action Program (ASAP) and declines in the prevalence of assaults. Community-based replication. *International Journal of Emergency Mental Health, 1*, 19-21.

Glass, G. V. (1976). Primary, secondary, and meta-analysis research. *Educational Researcher, 5*, 3-8.

Hevey, D., & McGee, H. M. (1998). The effect statistic: Useful in health outcomes research? *Journal of Health Psychology, 3*, 163-170.

Miller-Burke J., Attridge, M., & Fass, P. M. (1999). Impact of traumatic events and organizational response: A study of bank robberies. *Journal of Occupational and Environmental Medicine, 41*, 73-83.

National Institute of Mental Health. (2002). *Mental health and mass violence.* Washington, DC: Government Printing Office.

National Volunteer Organizations Active in Disaster (NVOAD). (2005). *Report of the Early Psychological Intervention (EPI) Subcommittee.* May 27, 2005.

Nhiwatiwa, F. G. (2003). The effects of single session education in reducing symptoms of distress following patient assault in nurses working in medium secure settings. *Journal of Psychiatric and Mental Health Nursing, 10,* 561-568.

Noji, E. K. (1991). The nature of disaster: General characteristics and public health effects. In E. K. Noji (Ed.), *The public health consequences of disasters* (pp. 3-20). New York: Oxford University Press.

Norris, F. H. (1992). Epidemiology of trauma: Frequency and impact of different potentially traumatic events on different demographic groups. *Journal of Consulting and Clinical Psychology, 60,* 409-418.

North, C. S., Nixon, S. J., Shariat, S., Mallonee, S., McMillen, J. C., Spitznagel, E. L., & Smith, E. M. (1999). Psychiatric disorders among survivors of the Oklahoma City bombing. *Journal of the American Medical Association, 282,* 755-762.

Northwestern National Life Insurance Company. (1993). *Fear and violence in the workplace.* Minneapolis, MN.

Petticrew, M. (2001). Systematic reviews from astronomy to zoology: Myths and misconceptions. *British Medical Journal, 322,* 98-101.

Raphael, B. (1986). *When disaster strikes.* New York: Basic.

Richards, D. (2001). A field study of critical incident stress debriefing versus critical incident stress management. *Journal of Mental Health, 10,* 351-362.

Roberts, A. R. (Ed.). (2005). *Crisis intervention handbook* (3rd ed.). New York: Oxford.

Rose, S., Bisson, J., & Wessely, S. (2002). Psychological debriefing for preventing post traumatic stress disorder (PTSD). *The Cochrane Library,* Issue 1. Oxford, UK: Update Software.

Rosenthal, R., & Rosnow, R. L. (1991). *Essentials of behavioral research: Methods and data analysis.* New York: McGraw-Hill.

Salmon, T. S. (1919). War neuroses and their lesson. *New York Medical Journal, 108,* 993-994.

Seligman, M. (1996). Science as an ally of practice. *American Psychologist, 51,* 1072-1079.

Solomon, Z., & Benbenishty, R. (1986). The role of proximity, immediacy, and expectancy in frontline treatment of combat stress reaction among Israelis in the Lebanon War. *American Journal of Psychiatry, 143,* 613-617.

doi:10.1300/J490v21n03_09

Responding in Times of Crisis–
An Exploratory Study of Employer Requests
for Critical Incident Response Services

Kristina L. Greenwood
Gosia Kubiak
Laurie Van der Heide
Nolan Phipps

SUMMARY. Increasingly, employers play an active role in assisting their employees in dealing with crisis. This exploratory study conducted analyses using a large national database to examine how companies representing various industry types differed in the frequency of requests for critical incident response services, the types of incidents that evoked the requests, the types of interventions utilized, and the delay time between the request and provision of services. Results demonstrated substantial variability in the types of incidents and frequency of service utilization. However, some consistent patterns were noted. For example, over half of all critical incident response services across industry types were delivered in response to a death impacting the workforce. A different pattern was evident for the Finance/Insurance/Real Estate industry, where robberies were most prevalent and the delay time between the incident and the critical incident response delivery date was shortest. There appeared to be an inverse relationship between the size of the company and the use of critical incident response services. This study has implications for further research regarding the training of practitioners administering critical incident

---

[Haworth co-indexing entry note]: "Responding in Times of Crisis–An Exploratory Study of Employer Requests for Critical Incident Response Services." Greenwood, Kristina L. et al. Co-published simultaneously in *Journal of Workplace Behavioral Health* (The Haworth Press, Inc.) Vol. 21, No. 3/4, 2006, pp. 171-189; and: *Workplace Disaster Preparedness, Response, and Management* (ed: R. Paul Maiden, Rich Paul, and Christina Thompson) The Haworth Press, Inc., 2006, pp. 171-189. Single or multiple copies of this article are available for a fee from The Haworth Document Delivery Service [1-800-HAWORTH, 9:00 a.m. - 5:00 p.m. (EST). E-mail address: docdelivery@haworthpress.com].

171

response services and determining the most effective crisis interventions for the situation and recipient population. doi:10.1300/J490v21n03_10 *[Article copies available for a fee from The Haworth Document Delivery Service: 1-800-HAWORTH. E-mail address: <docdelivery@haworthpress.com> Website: <http://www.HaworthPress.com> © 2006 by The Haworth Press, Inc. All rights reserved.]*

KEYWORDS. Critical incident, workplace stress management, crisis intervention

INTRODUCTION

The impact of a crisis event on an individual's health and well-being and the effectiveness of crisis intervention, including critical incident stress debriefing (CISD) and critical incident stress management (CISM), have been the subject of many publications over the past three decades (Everly et al., 2000; Everly & Lating, 1995; Flannery, 1994; Mitchell, 2003; Mitchell & Everly, 1996). While there has been recent and fairly heated debate over which interventions are effective (Bisson et al., 1997; Carlier et al., 2000; Conlon et al., 1999; Kenardy et al., 1996; Mitchell, 2003) and the most appropriate timing of those interventions (Campfield & Hills, 2001; Everly, 2000; van Emmerik et al., 2002), there still exists general agreement that intervention is warranted (Everly, 2000). Extreme critical incidents such as acts of terrorism, natural disasters, serious injury, or threat to the victim's physical safety, may result in psychological trauma and Posttraumatic Stress Disorder (PTSD; American Psychiatric Association, 1994; Everly & Lating, 1995; Flannery, 1994). Breslau et al. (1998) noted that an estimated 90% of Americans will be exposed to a traumatic stressor during their lifetime. At the same time, the U.S. Department of Health and Human Services concludes that about 9% of people exposed to a crisis event will develop PTSD (2000). Fortunately, a growing positive outcome literature finds that CISM and CISD "reduce staff anxiety, facilitate coping skills, help employees to return to work, lead to cost-savings for the organization and have other positive benefits" (Robinson, 2004).

For the purposes of clarity, the following definitions of key terms will be used in this article. A *crisis* occurs when a stressful life event overwhelms an individual's ability to cope effectively in the face of a perceived challenge or threat (Flannery & Everly, 2000). The event that precipitates the crisis, a *critical incident*, is a stressor event that has the potential to lead to a crisis response in many individuals. *Crisis intervention*, as defined by Everly and Mitchell (1999), refers to the provision of emergency psychological care to those who have experienced or otherwise been impacted by a crisis event. The intervention is meant to assist the victim in returning to an adaptive level of functioning and to prevent or mitigate the potential negative impact of psychological trauma. Flannery and Everly (2000) note that while multiple models of crisis intervention have been developed there exists common agreement on the general principles to be employed by behavioral health workers to "alleviate the acute distress of victims, restore independent functioning, and prevent or mitigate the aftermath of psychological trauma." One of the most widely accepted sets of guidelines for supplying comprehensive crisis intervention is referred to as Critical Incident Stress Management (CISM). CISM (Everly & Mitchell, 1999) includes eight core elements: (1) pre-crisis preparation; (2) large scale demobilization procedures for public safety personnel as well as large group crisis management briefings for civilian victims of crisis; (3) individual acute crisis intervention; (4) brief small group discussions called defusings to assist in acute symptom reduction; (5) longer small group discussions known as Critical Incident Stress Debriefings (CISD; Mitchell & Everly, 1996); (6) family crisis intervention procedures; (7) organizational development interventions; and (8) referrals for additional psychological assessment and treatment where indicated. Organizations including the Federal Aviation Administration (FAA), the Airline Pilots Association (ALPA), the United States Air Force, the United States Secret Service, and the Federal Bureau of Investigation (FBI) are among those that have adopted some variation of this model.

Over the past two decades, employers have increasingly played an active role in assisting their employees in dealing with crisis, independent of whether the crisis occurs inside or outside of the actual workplace. During times of organizational upheaval or personal crisis, employers frequently access the services of mental health workers to help mitigate the long-term consequences of these occurrences. Employers understand the risks to employee well-being that are associated with traumatic events and are willing to implement programs in the workplace that are designed to diminish the negative sequelae of those events, including lost productivity and increased use of sick time (Amundson et al., 2004; Hoffman, 2001). Shouton et al. (2004) note that "the workplace serves as a major organizing factor in the lives of most adults and as a source of social support; it is an essential part of the local community. When disaster strikes that community, the effects on the individual and organization can be widespread and long lasting."

As a result of the "ownership" by employers in providing these services, ValueOptions, as a supplier of behavioral healthcare and Employee Assistance Programs to large employers, has frequently been asked to both advise customers on how to deal with crisis before it arises, as well as to supply services and interventions in times of crisis. While benefit packages purchased by employers vary, most include some arrangement whereby ValueOptions supplies crisis response services. In order to meet this demand, ValueOptions has a partnership with a specialty company, Crisis Care Network (CCN: www.crisiscare.com), to be the sole supplier of on-site crisis services for its employer clients. The partnership also provides us with a single source for a wealth of information about the crisis services requested by and provided to a broad range of employers.

In reviewing the literature, we found two articles that conducted analyses using crisis services data from several employers. Sacks, Clements, and Fay-Hillier (2001) described the impact of the CISM services supplied by a nurse-directed team providing crisis intervention for private sector employers in the northeast who had experienced robbery, downsizing, or sudden employee death. Their article included anecdotes regarding the "typical employee reactions to on-site CISD interventions" and concluded that, with specialized training, nurses were well-suited to supply these types of services. Amundson, Borgen, Jordan and Erlebach (2004) looked at the "positive ness" or "negative ness" of actions taken by several different employers that were downsizing, as rated by the employees. While none of the interventions were actually called CISD or CISM and represented various forms of critical incident responses, most of the actions taken by the employers that were ultimately seen as having been positive involved counselor-led workshops or individual sessions in which the employees had the opportunity to discuss and validate their emotional reactions. This finding held up across all types of businesses.

The following study takes advantage of our unique position by comparing various types of businesses to understand the types of critical incidents that lead to a request for crisis intervention services, the prevalence, utilization rates and actual types of services used, and the time period between the request and the actual provision of services.

METHODOLOGY

This study explored the utilization of on-site critical incident response services provided by Crisis Care Network (CCN) on behalf of

ValueOptions. All analyses were completed using CCN's database, which was utilized to track all on-site critical incident response services. The analyses were limited to full calendar years 2003 and 2004 in order to evaluate the impact of seasonality factors. During this period there were 647 requests representing 4,113 hours of on-site interventions for crisis response services by 101 unique companies, representing a total population of 2,584,153 employees.

Variables used in the analyses included: (1) industry type of the company requesting the service, (2) location of incident, (3) date of critical incident, (4) date of the critical incident response services, (5) type of incident, (6) number of participants in the intervention (number of group sessions, participants per group, and the number of individual sessions), and (7) total number of on-site hours during the critical incident response service.

The industry type of the company that requested critical incident response services was determined by using the Standard Industrial Classification (SIC) System Division Structure from the U.S. Department of Labor, Occupational Safety and Health Administration (www.osha.gov). The most frequently occurring four (4) industry types subsequently included in all analyses were: (1) Manufacturing, (2) Transportation/Communication/Electric/Gas/Sanitary Services, (3) Finance/Insurance/Real Estate, and (4) Services. An additional category (labeled Other Industries) of 51 cases (7.9% of the total sample) combined Construction, Wholesale Trade, Retail Trade, and Public Administration. There were no companies in this sample that were categorized in the SIC Divisions of Agriculture/Forestry/Fishing or Mining.

The top five (5) incident types included in all analyses were: (1) Death Impacting Workforce, (2) Accident/Injury, (3) Layoff/Downsizing, (4) Robbery, and (5) Suicide. In order to minimize variance and problems due to small sample sizes, a separate category (labeled Other Incidents) combined the remaining 75 incidents (11.6% of the total sample) and included Murder, Natural Disaster, and Threat of Violence. While there has been some debate in the industry as to whether or not Layoff/Downsizing represents a "critical incident," we have included it in this analysis because it is often perceived as such by employers and results in such service interventions. In order to evaluate the delay (time lapse) from the critical incident to the delivery of the critical incident response service, the number of days between the date of the incident and the date when the first critical incident response services were administered was calculated as a simple subtraction between dates.

RESULTS

Overall, the majority of crisis response service requests were received from employers in the Transportation/Communications/Electric/Gas/Sanitary Services and Manufacturing industries (see Table 1), and over half (52.2%) of all incidents involved a Death Impacting Workforce (see Table 2).

Table 3 compares the frequency of critical incident response services by both industry and incident type. There were significant differences in the proportion of incident types within each industry ($X^2 = 272.85$, df = 12, p < 0.001). Within the manufacturing industry, 51.5% of all cases were death impacting workforce, followed by layoff/downsizing (25.8%). For transportation/communications/electric/gas/sanitary ser-

TABLE 1. Frequency of Critical Incident Response Services by Industry Type

Industry Type	N	Percentage
Transportation/Communications/Electric/Gas/Sanitary Services	241	37.2%
Manufacturing	231	35.7%
Services	65	10.0%
Finance/Insurance/Real Estate	59	9.1%
Other*	51	7.9%

* Combines types: Construction, Wholesale Trade, Retail Trade, and Public Administration

TABLE 2. Frequency of Critical Incident Response Services by Incident Type

Incident Type	N	Percentage
Death Impacting Workforce	338	52.2%
Accident/Injury	78	12.1%
Layoff/Downsizing	68	10.5%
Other*	75	11.6%
Robbery	47	7.3%
Suicide	41	6.3%

* Combines types: murder, natural disaster, threat of violence

TABLE 3. Prevalence of Critical Incident Response Services by Incident and Industry Type

	Incident Type				
Industry Type	Death Impacting Workforce	Accident/ Injury	Layoff/ Downsizing	Robbery	Suicide
Manufacturing	51.5%	12.1%	25.8%	2.0%	8.6%
Transportation/Communications/ Electric/Gas/Sanitary	70.6%	15.8%	4.5%	3.2%	5.9%
Services	66.7%	16.7%	3.7%	0%	13.0%
Finance/Insurance/Real Estate	26.9%	3.8%	7.7%	61.5%	0%

vices, 70.6% of all cases were death impacting workforce, followed by 15.8% of cases involving an Accident/Injury. Results were somewhat similar for the Services industry, with 66.7% of all cases due to a Death Impacting Workforce, and 16.7% related to Accident/Injuries. However, in comparison to other industries, suicide incidents were most prevalent within the service industry (13.0%). There was evidence of a very different pattern within the finance/insurance/real estate field, since the majority of cases (61.5%) of cases were related to robbery. Further analyses excluded the data for the finance/insurance/real estate industry due to the disproportionate number of robbery cases, although the significant differences were maintained ($X^2 = 52.16$, df $= 8$, p < 0.001).

Additional analyses examined the number of critical incident response cases per 1,000 employees for each industry. Overall, there were 0.25 cases per 1,000 employees across all industry types. The average number of critical incident response cases per 1,000 employees by industry type was analyzed, using the Kruskal-Wallis test of rank due to substantial variance and excluding the other industries category. Significant differences were found ($X^2 = 11.94$, df $= 3$, p $= 0.008$), with the smallest average number of cases per 1,000 in manufacturing (0.55) and the largest average in finance/insurance/real estate (9.88). It is noteworthy that there was an inverse relationship between the total number of employees for each industry and the average number of critical incident response cases per 1,000, since manufacturing had the largest number of employees and finance/insurance/real estate had the least.

Regional Differences in the Location of Incidents

Five regions (New England, Great Lakes, Central, South, and West) were established based on the state in which the incident occurred. The states assigned to each regional category are listed in the Appendix. Overall, the greatest number of incidents occurred in the West (26.7%), followed by the South (21.5%), New England (19.6%), Great Lakes (18.4%), and Central (13.8%) regions.

Analyses of regional prevalence of incidents by type demonstrated significant differences ($X^2 = 59.74$, df $= 16$, p < 0.001). As reported in Table 4, the most frequent incident type for all regions was death impacting workforce (approximately 60% of all cases). For the West and New England regions, the second most prevalent incident type was layoff/downsizing (18.3% and 11.6%, respectively). Accident/injury was the secondary incident type within the South (17.9%) and Central (13.9%) regions, and Robbery (23.8%) was the second most frequent type of incident within the Great Lakes region.

TABLE 4. Prevalence of Critical Incident Response Services by Incident Type and Region

Region	Incident Type				
	Death Impacting Workforce	Accident/ Injury	Layoff/ Downsizing	Robbery	Suicide
West	85	22	28	4	14
	55.6%	14.4%	18.3%	2.6%	9.2%
Central	53	11	9	3	3
	67.1%	13.9%	11.4%	3.8%	3.8%
Great Lakes	53	11	8	25	8
	50.5%	10.5%	7.6%	23.8%	7.6%
South	80	22	10	5	6
	65.0%	17.9%	8.1%	4.1%	4.9%
New England	67	12	13	10	10
	59.8%	10.7%	11.6%	8.9%	8.9%
Total	338	78	68	47	41
	59.1%	13.6%	11.9%	8.2%	7.2%

There were also significant differences in the frequency of critical incident response requests by industry type in each geographical region ($X^2 = 102.68$, df $= 12$, p < 0.001). In the West and Great Lakes regions, the majority of cases were associated with Manufacturing (55.9% and 38.9%, respectively). The transportation/communications/electric/gas/ sanitary services industry was most widely represented in the South (58.2%), Central (48.8%), and New England (38.3%) regions. Comparisons of regional differences did not indicate any significant differences with respect to the types of interventions utilized ($X^2 = 12.99$, df $= 12$, p $= 0.369$). However, there were statistically significant regional differences in the total number of on-site hours delivered during the critical incident response service, using the Kruskal-Wallis Test of Rank ($X^2 = 14.66$, df $= 4$, p $= 0.005$). The average total on-site hours by region were as follows: West (8.82), Central (7.16), New England (6.02), South (5.00), and Great Lakes (4.24).

Seasonal Differences

Overall, the proportion of cases were fairly similar between years, with 265 cases (46.3%) occurring during calendar year 2003 and 307 cases (53.7%) during 2004. Significant differences ($X^2 = 36.29$, df $= 4$, p < 0.001) were identified in the distribution of incidents by type and year, as displayed in Table 5.

Additional analyses demonstrated no significant differences in the distribution of incident types across months ($X^2 = 54.67$, df $= 44$, p $= 0.130$). The highest month(s) (in parentheses) were as follows: death impacting workforce (October), layoff/downsizing (October), accident/

TABLE 5. Prevalence of Critical Incident Response Services by Incident Type and Year

	Year		
Incident Type	**2003**	**2004**	**Change**
Death Impacting Workforce	57.0%	60.9%	+
Accident/Injury	11.7%	15.3%	+
Layoff/Downsizing	17.0%	7.5%	−
Robbery	3.4%	12.4%	++
Suicide	10.9%	3.9%	−

TABLE 6. Prevalence of Critical Incident Response Services by Incident Type and Intervention Type

	Incident Type					
Intervention Type	Death Impacting Workforce	Accident/ Injury	Layoff/ Down- sizing	Robbery	Suicide	**Total**
Neither	16	2	6	3	1	N = 28
	4.7%	2.6%	8.8%	6.4%	2.4%	4.9%
Individual Sessions Only	49	18	30	10	5	N = 112
	14.5%	23.1%	44.1%	21.3%	12.2%	19.6%
Group Sessions Only	56	16	7	5	13	N = 97
	16.6%	20.5%	10.3%	10.6%	31.7%	17.0%
Both	217	42	25	29	22	N = 335
	64.2%	53.8%	36.8%	61.7%	53.7%	58.6%

injury (May), suicide (March), and robbery (March, June). Also, no significant differences were found when comparing quarters of both years combined ($X^2 = 15.37$, df = 12, p = 0.222), although layoff/downsizing and death impacting workforce cases occurred most frequently during the fourth quarter (October to December) (41.2% and 29.9% respectively).

Overall, there were significant differences in the distribution of incident types between quarters during 2003 ($X^2 = 25.15$, df = 12, p = 0.014) but no differences between quarters in 2004 ($X^2 = 5.94$, df = 12, p = 0.919). As presented in Figure 1, a comparison of critical incident response service requests across quarters and years indicated a dramatic increase in the incidence of death impacting workforce cases throughout 2003, with a somewhat more stable pattern during most of 2004 with the exception of a decline in the third quarter. The frequency of layoff/downsizing cases also increased steadily from the beginning to the end of 2003, and then decreased considerably during 2004. In contrast, there was a substantial increase in robbery incidents for all quarters of 2004 as compared to 2003. However, the robbery incidents are primarily influenced by the addition of a single, large company in the finance/insurance/real estate industry starting in January 2004, rather than evidence of a true seasonal trend.

FIGURE 1. Frequency of Critical Incident Response Services by Incident Type Across Quarters and Years

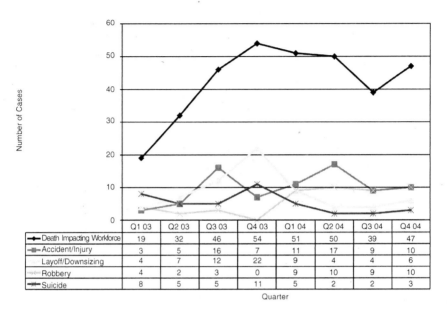

	Q1 03	Q2 03	Q3 03	Q4 03	Q1 04	Q2 04	Q3 04	Q4 04
Death Impacting Workforce	19	32	46	54	51	50	39	47
Accident/Injury	3	5	16	7	11	17	9	10
Layoff/Downsizing	4	7	12	22	9	4	4	6
Robbery	4	2	3	0	9	10	9	10
Suicide	8	5	5	11	5	2	2	3

Quarter

Analyses of seasonal differences by industry type were also conducted. After excluding the large financial services company with data only in 2004 (as noted above), there were no significant differences between years ($X^2 = 6.63$, df $= 3$, p $= 0.085$). Although the frequency of cases increased in the September through November time period for all industries, there were no significant differences between industries in the distribution of cases by month ($X^2 = 26.033$, df $= 33$, p $= 0.788$) or quarter ($X^2 = 4.35$, df $= 9$, p $= 0.887$).

Time Period Between Incident and Critical Incident Response Services

Overall results indicated an average of 2.54 days between the incident and date of service, although it is noteworthy that 24.7% of the cases involved services delivered on the same day as the incident. Two cases were considered outliers and excluded from this set of analyses, since they involved critical incident response services that were provided prior to the incident date. One case received services three days prior to a natural disaster (storm); while another case involved a planned downsizing/layoff where critical incident response services were provided 58 days prior to the event.

Comparisons of delay time by industry type demonstrated substantially different variances between the industries. The greatest variation in delay days was observed within manufacturing, while the least variation occurred within the finance/insurance/real estate industry. Using the Kruskal-Wallis Test of Rank, significant differences ($X^2 = 15.79$, df = 3, p = 0.001) were found in the average delay days among industries types, with the shortest delay for finance/insurance/real estate (1.25 days) and the longest for manufacturing (3.05 days).

Analysis of delay days depending on the incident type also identified significant differences ($X^2 = 24.39$, df = 4, p < 0.001), after excluding the other incidents category. The greatest average delay of critical incident response services occurred for layoff/downsizing (3.30 days), while the shortest delay occurred following a robbery (1.36 days).

The relationship between the total number of on-site hours delivered during the critical incident response service and delay time was examined for all cases and also stratified by incident and industry type. The only significant finding was a mildly positive correlation between the number of on-site hours and delay time for incidents of robbery (Pearson's $R = 0.371$, p = 0.010, N = 47), indicating that longer delays were associated with a greater number of on-site service hours.

Intervention Types and On-Site Service Hours

This set of analyses compared the type of interventions utilized, categorized as individual sessions only, group sessions only, both individual and group sessions, or neither. Results by incident type are summarized in Table 6. Across all incident types, 58.6% of cases utilized both group and individual sessions, 19.6% used individual sessions only, 17.0% used group sessions only, and 4.9% used neither (i.e., services were available but not utilized). There is strong statistical evidence of differences in the method of interventions utilized depending upon the incident type ($X^2 = 47.47$, df = 12, p < 0.001). All incident types, except layoffs/downsizing, used both individual and group sessions for the majority of cases. Only individual sessions were utilized in 44.1% of all layoff/downsizing cases. Suicide cases had the greatest proportion of group only sessions (31.7%).

Comparisons of the intervention types by industry indicated a trend toward statistical significance ($X^2 = 15.36$, df = 9, p = 0.081). Across industry types, 57.7% of all cases were involved in both individual and group sessions, 20.1% of the cases utilized individual sessions only, 16.3% used group sessions only, and 5.9% used neither method of intervention. A combination of individual and group sessions was the most prevalent intervention strategy for each industry type. There were fairly similar rates of groups only as compared to the exclusive use of individual sessions for the transportation/communication/electric/gas/sanitary services and services industries. However, individual sessions were used more frequently than groups alone for manufacturing (24.7% vs. 12.1%) and finance/insurance/real estate (23.7% vs. 15.3%).

Additional analyses compared the total number of critical incident response on-site hours as a measure of the availability of services. There was considerable variability in the range of on-site hours, with 99.5% of all cases utilizing between 30 minutes to 60 hours of services. Using the Kruskal-Wallis Test of Rank, significant differences were found ($X^2 = 50.95$, df $= 4$, p < 0.001) across incident types. On average, the highest total on-site hours were utilized for layoff/downsizing incidents (13.4) and the least number of hours for robbery (2.6). There were also significant differences across industry types in the total number of critical incident response on-site hours utilized ($X^2 = 14.66$, df $= 4$, p $= 0.005$), with the most hours utilized in manufacturing (8.1) and the least in the services industry (3.5).

DISCUSSION

This exploratory study clearly demonstrated that while many employers are offering critical incident response services to their employees, there is substantial variability in the types of incidents that evoke their use and the frequency with which they are utilized. Some key patterns, however, were evident. A consistent finding across various types of industries was that over half of all incidents involved a death impacting workforce. Due to the nature of this particular study and the available data sources, it cannot be determined whether death impacting workforce cases occur more frequently than other types of incidents or are simply more likely to lead to a request for critical incident response services. However, this finding could have relevance for the training of practitioners involved in administering these services regarding the types of incidents they are most likely to encounter. This warrants additional research.

Overall, there was great variability in the number of critical incident response cases between companies within a particular industry classification. This makes it difficult to interpret the results of analyses related to the number of cases per 1,000 employees. However, it appears that there is an inverse relationship between the size of the company and the number of critical incident response requests per 1,000 employees. Future studies using this type of standardized measure could be very useful in comparing and understanding critical incident response utilization patterns across companies of various types and sizes. Such studies need to identify additional variables that might help to explain these differences in crisis care utilization. Anecdotal explanations from account executives working with these clients suggested that differences in company culture with respect to acceptance of behavioral health interventions, as well as communication of information about benefits and available resources within an organization, might help to account for some of the variability of use of critical incident response services found in our study.

As compared to other industries, the finance/insurance/real estate industry has a very different pattern of critical incident services. This is due to the higher frequency of robberies within this industry category. Significant differences were found between the finance/insurance/real estate and manufacturing industries on several dimensions, including the prevalence by incident type, total number and average number of cases per 1,000 employees, and the average delay time (as well as variance in delay time) between the critical incident and the intervention. Although further exploration is necessary, the finding of significant pattern differences lends support to recent recommendations from experts in the profession for matching interventions to the needs of the situation and recipient population. Campfield and Hills (2001) suggested that interventions that are effective in one context may be less so or even counterproductive in another. They hypothesized that factors such as the nature of the traumatic event as well as other factors relating to characteristics of the population probably impact the effectiveness of the interventions.

One of the noteworthy findings from the analysis of seasonal differences was the substantial increase in death impacting workforce cases during all quarters of 2003. However, it is unclear whether this reflected a true increase in the frequency of incidents or a greater tendency to request critical incident response services. Layoff/downsizing and death impacting workforce cases were more prevalent during the fourth quarter. If these results were replicated through additional studies, this could have implications for educational and prevention strategies within the workplace.

The analyses related to the delay time between the incident and critical incident response service delivery date demonstrated the shortest time delay for the finance/insurance/real estate industry, primarily for robbery incidents, and the longest delays within the manufacturing industry with a high incidence of layoff/downsizing incidents. A possible explanation for this finding is that layoff/downsizing incidents are more easily anticipated within the workplace as compared with unanticipated events that involve a death, accident, or robbery. Campfield and Hills (2001) described the debate related to the impact of timing on the effectiveness of the intervention. They pointed out that there is currently no empirical evidence that indicates the optimal debrief time, but noted that "a common recommendation is that the intervention should be provided immediately and in conjunction with medical assistance." Others have recommended intervention at 24 to 48 hours (Kenardy et al., 1996), or 48 to 72 hours after the incident (Busuttil, 1995; Thompson, 1993). Still other authors (Devilly & Cotton, 2003) suggest that waiting and screening for impact a month after the incident may be the most advantageous.

Everly (2000) has also addressed the concept of possible premature crisis intervention. He elucidates four principles for determining the timing of crisis interventions. He stresses that appropriate crisis intervention tactics and the timing of those tactics be based on observable signs and symptoms of distress and/or dysfunction and that they be based on the "psychological readiness, rather than the actual passage of time." This issue clearly warrants further investigation.

One variable that enters into the issue of the timing of the intervention is the request of the client organization. Again, anecdotal reports from Account Executives indicate that organizations in the midst of a crisis may not make appropriate decisions about what they need. Robinson (2004) notes that early intervention may be requested by the impacted organization or by the victims themselves. She suggests that specialty organizations be prepared to give advice to management of organizations as they set up their critical incident response programs. Many critical incident response programs incorporate internal peer support that enables early assistance and information gathering regarding individual needs immediately after an incident. Such information would be invaluable in assisting the organization to determine their critical incident response needs, including the more proactive timing of interventions after an incident.

It was clear from this study that the majority of interventions during the 2003 to 2004 time period utilized both individual and group crisis intervention techniques. Groups alone were utilized somewhat less frequently than were individual sessions alone. The use of more than one type of intervention is in line with more current models that advocate a comprehensive, systematic and multi-tactic approach for crisis intervention (Mitchell, 2003). At the same time, it is critically important to conduct further research regarding which interventions or combinations of interventions are most effective with which populations in what types of situations.

There was substantial variability in the number of on-site hours delivered per incident (ranging from 30 minutes to 60 hours), so it is difficult to interpret these results or use this as a meaningful measure of the "availability" of critical incident response services. Although the percentage of cases that did not utilize offered services was relatively small (4.9%), it is important to understand any barriers from the perspective of the employees and the recipient organization that may have contributed to this circumstance. Overall, these results highlight the need for further research to determine the relative importance of factors that contribute to "best practices," including the impact of the number of service hours, the time period between incident and service, and the type of intervention(s).

The major limitations of this study relate to the constraints of the available data, since the methodology involved a retrospective rather than a prospective design. For example, analyses regarding *actual* critical incidents that occurred within the workplace were not possible, since the database tracked only incidents that involved requests for critical incident response services. It is unknown how many critical events occurred that might have benefited from critical incident response interventions where a request was not initiated. Although a primary strength of this study was the focus on a relatively large national population of companies and employees, it was limited to a database maintained by one critical incident response vendor on behalf of one managed behavioral healthcare/EAP organization. Therefore, the results may not be representative of all critical incident response services. Analyses of potential organizational factors, such as duration of the EAP contract and employer benefit design, were beyond the scope of this study.

The available data sources did not permit separate analyses of Natural Disaster or Threat of Violence cases due to insufficient sample sizes. Future research in these areas is especially relevant for a comprehensive understanding of critical incident response services, given recent events in the U.S. (such as Hurricanes Katrina and Rita) that have had a direct or indirect impact on a substantial number of companies and their employees.

Finally, a very significant limitation of this study was the lack of access to data regarding outcomes or effectiveness of the critical incident response services, at the member or company level. This is an essential topic for further research in order to determine the impact of critical incident response services on future healthcare utilization and costs (both physical and behavioral health) and specific workplace outcomes such as absenteeism, presenteeism, and productivity.

REFERENCES

American Psychiatric Association. (1994). *Diagnostic and statistical manual of mental disorders* (4th ed.). Washington, DC: Author.

Amundson, N.E., Borgen, W.A., Jordan, S. & Erlebach, A.C. (2004). Survivors of downsizing: Helpful and hindering experiences. *The Career Development Quarterly, 52,* 256-271.

Antai-Otong, D. (2001). Critical incident stress debriefing: A health promotion model for workplace violence. *Perspectives in Psychiatric Care, 37,* 125-139.

Bisson, J.I., Jenkins, P., Alexander, J., & Bannister, C. (1997). Randomized controlled trial of psychological debriefings for victims of acute burn trauma. *British Journal of Psychiatry, 171,* 78-81.

Breslau, N., Kessler, R., Chilcoat, H., Schultz, L., Davis, G., & Andreski, P. (1998). Trauma and posttraumatic stress disorder in the community. *Archives of General Psychiatry, 55,* 626-633.

Busuttil, A. (1995). Psychological debriefing. *British Journal of Psychiatry, 166,* 676-681.

Campfield, K.M. & Hills, A.M. (2001). Effect of timing of critical incident stress debriefing (CISD) on posttraumatic symptoms. *Journal of Traumatic Stress, Vol. 14,* 327-340.

Carlier, I.V.E., Voerman, A.E., & Gersons, B.P.R. (2000). The influence of occupational debriefing on post-traumatic stress symptomatology in traumatized police officers. *British Journal of Medical Psychology, 73,* 87-98.

Conlon, L., Fahy, T.J., & Conroy, R. (1999). PTSD in ambulant RTA victims: A randomized controlled trial of debriefing. *Journal of Psychosomatic Research, 46,* 37-44.

Devilly, G.J. & Cotton, P. (2003). Psychological debriefing and the workplace: Defining a concept, controversies and guidelines for intervention. *Australian Psychologist, 38,* 144-150.

Everly, G.S. (2000). Five principles of crisis intervention: Reducing the risk of premature crisis intervention. *International Journal of Emergency Mental Health, 2,* 1-4.

Everly, G.S., Flannery, R.B., & Mitchell, J.T. (2000). Critical incident stress management (CISM): A review of the literature. *Aggression and Violent Behavior, 5,* 23-40.

Everly, G.S. & Lating, J.T. (Eds.) (1995). *Psychotraumatology: Key papers and core concepts in post-traumatic stress.* New York: Plenum.

Everly, G.S. & Mitchell, J.T. (1999). *Critical incident stress management: A new era and standard of care in crisis intervention.* Ellicott City, MD: Chevron Publishing Corporation.

Flannery, R.B. (1994). *Post-traumatic Stress Disorder: The victims guide to healing and recovery.* New York: Crossroads Press.

Flannery, R.B. & Everly, G.S. (2000). Crisis intervention: A review. *International Journal of Emergency Mental Health, 2,* 119-125.

Hoffman, C. (2001). Responding to workplace trauma. *Trauma Response, 7*(1), 14-15.

Kenardy, J.A., Webster, R.A., Lewin, T.J., Carr, B.J., Hazell, P.L., & Carter, G.L. (1996). Stress debriefing and patterns of recovery following a natural disaster. *Journal of Traumatic Stress, 9,* 37-49.

Loomis, D., Marshall, S.W., & Ta, M.L. (2005). Employer policies toward guns and the risk of homicide in the workplace. *American Journal of Public Health, 95,* 830-832.

Mitchell, J.T. (2003). Crisis intervention & CISM: A research summary. Available at: www.icisf.org/articles/cism_research_summary.pdf.

Mitchell, J.T. & Everly, G.S. (1996). *Critical incident stress debriefing: An operations manual for the prevention of traumatic stress among emergency services and disaster workers (2nd ed. Rev.).* Ellicott City, MD: Chevron Publishing Corporation.

Robinson, R. (2004). Counterbalancing misrepresentation of critical incident stress debriefing and critical incident stress management. *Australian Psychologist, 39,* 29-34.

Sacks, S.B., Clements, P.T., & Fay-Hillier, T. (2001). Care after chaos: Use of critical incident stress debriefing after traumatic workplace events. *Perspectives in Psychiatric Care, 37,* 133-136.

Shouton, R., Callahan, M.V., & Bryant, S. (2004). Community response to disaster: The role of the workplace. *Harvard Review of Psychiatry, 12,* 229-237.

Thompson, R. (1993). Posttraumatic stress and posttraumatic loss debriefing: Brief strategic intervention for survivors of sudden loss. *The School Counsellor, 41,* 16-22.

U.S. Dept. of Health and Human Services. (2000). Mental health: A report of the Surgeon General. Rockville, MD: Author.

van Emmerik, A.A.P., Kamphuis, J.H., Hulsbosch, A.M., & Emmelkamp, P.M.G. (2002). Single session debriefing after psychological trauma: A meta-analysis. *Lancet, 360,* 766-771.

doi:10.1300/J490v21n03_10

APPENDIX
Distribution of States/Provinces by Region

Region	State/Province
West	Alaska
	Arizona
	California
	Canada
	Colorado
	Montana
	New Mexico
	Nevada
	Oregon
	Utah
	Washington
Central	Arkansas
	Kansas
	Kentucky
	Louisiana
	Missouri
	Nebraska
	Oklahoma
	Tennessee
	Texas
Great Lakes	Idaho
	Iowa
	Illinois
	Michigan
	Minnesota
	Ohio
	Wisconsin
South	Delaware
	Florida
	Georgia
	Maryland
	North Carolina
	South Carolina
	Virginia
	Washington, DC
	West Virginia
New England	Connecticut
	Massachusetts
	New Hampshire
	New Jersey
	New York
	Pennsylvania
	Rhode Island

Index

Page numbers followed by f or t refer to figures or tables respectively.

BOOK ORDER FORM!

Order a copy of this book with this form or online at:
http://www.HaworthPress.com/store/product.asp?sku= 5943

Workplace Disaster Preparedness, Response, and Management

—— in softbound at $28.00 ISBN-13: 978-0-7890-3451-9 / ISBN-10: 0-7890-3451-4.
—— in hardbound at $48.00 ISBN-13: 978-0-7890-3450-2 / ISBN-10: 0-7890-3450-6.

COST OF BOOKS _____

POSTAGE & HANDLING _____
US: $4.00 for first book & $1.50
for each additional book
Outside US: $5.00 for first book
& $2.00 for each additional book.

SUBTOTAL _____

In Canada: add 6% GST. _____

STATE TAX _____
CA, IL, IN, MN, NJ, NY, OH, PA & SD residents
please add appropriate local sales tax.

FINAL TOTAL _____

If paying in Canadian funds, convert
using the current exchange rate,
UNESCO coupons welcome.

❏ BILL ME LATER:
Bill-me option is good on US/Canada/
Mexico orders only; not good to jobbers,
wholesalers, or subscription agencies.

❏ Signature _____

❏ Payment Enclosed: $_____

❏ PLEASE CHARGE TO MY CREDIT CARD:
❏ Visa ❏ MasterCard ❏ AmEx ❏ Discover
❏ Diner's Club ❏ Eurocard ❏ JCB

Account #_____

Exp Date_____

Signature_____
(Prices in US dollars and subject to change without notice.)

PLEASE PRINT ALL INFORMATION OR ATTACH YOUR BUSINESS CARD

Name _____

Address _____

City _____ State/Province _____ Zip/Postal Code _____

Country _____

Tel _____ Fax _____

E-Mail _____

May we use your e-mail address for confirmations and other types of information? ❏ Yes ❏ No We appreciate receiving
your e-mail address. Haworth would like to e-mail special discount offers to you, as a preferred customer.
We will never share, rent, or exchange your e-mail address. We regard such actions as an invasion of your privacy.

Order from your **local bookstore** or directly from
The Haworth Press, Inc. 10 Alice Street, Binghamton, New York 13904-1580 • USA
Call our toll-free number (1-800-429-6784) / Outside US/Canada: (607) 722-5857
Fax: 1-800-895-0582 / Outside US/Canada: (607) 771-0012
E-mail your order to us: orders@HaworthPress.com

For orders outside US and Canada, you may wish to order through your local
sales representative, distributor, or bookseller.
For information, see http://HaworthPress.com/distributors

(Discounts are available for individual orders in US and Canada only, not booksellers/distributors.)

Please photocopy this form for your personal use.
www.HaworthPress.com

BOF06